Bulb Forcing

for

Beginners and the Seriously Smitten

Bulb Forcing

for

Beginners and the Seriously Smitten

by

Art Wolk

AAB Book Publishing LLC
Voorhees, New Jersey
Books that enrich, entertain, and enlighten

AAB

Published by AAB Book Publishing LLC, P.O. Box 749 Voorhees, NJ 08043
First edition
First printed January 2012.

Visit our website at www.artwolk.com

Cataloging-in-Publication Data
Wolk, Art
        Bulb Forcing for Beginners and the Seriously Smitten
        Art Wolk. – 1st ed.
                p. cm.
        Includes bibliographic references and footnotes.
        ISBN: 0-97297-30-5-2 ISBN-13: 978-0-97297-30-5-2
1. Forcing (Plants) Handbooks, manuals, etc. 2. Bulbs (Plants) Handbooks, manuals, etc. 3. Flower shows Anecdotes 4. Gardening—Anecdotes.
1. Title.
SB425 .W65 2012
635.944 WOL

                                Library of Congress Control Number: 2011913672
                                OCLC number: 747099638

10 9 8 7 6 5 4 3 2 1

All photos by Art Wolk (except where otherwise indicated)
Front jacket design by Wendell Minor
Editors: Pete Johnson and Art Wolk
Copy editors: Barbara J. Crawford and Art Wolk
Interior illustration by Laurie Baxendell, Baxendell's Graphic
Interior design by Art Wolk
Jacket photo of Art Wolk by Krassan and Kovnat Photography, Cherry Hill, NJ
Printing by Sheridan Books, Ann Arbor, Michigan, 48103

Front jacket photo: *Tulipa* 'Leen Van Der Mark', back jacket photo: *Narcissus* 'Las Vegas',
spine photo: *Crocus chrysanthus* 'Gipsy Girl', front flap photo: *Ipheion uniflorum* 'Rolf Fiedler'

Dedicated to Arlene and Beth

Attention colleges and universities, corporations, and writing and publishing organizations: Quantity discounts are available on bulk purchases of this book for educational training purposes, fund raising, or gift giving. Special books, booklets, or book excerpts can also be created to fit your specific needs. For information contact Marketing Department, AAB Book Publishing Company, LLC, P.O. Box 749, Voorhees, NJ 08043. aabpublishing@aol.com.

How to contact the author:
Art Wolk is available for programs and speeches and can be contacted at the address below and through the email address, artwolk@aol.com.

Readers of this book are also encouraged to contact the author with comments and ideas for future editions.

Art Wolk, AAB Book Publishing LLC
P.O. Box 749
Voorhees, NJ 08043
Phone: (856)-751-8286
artwolk@aol.com
Website: www.artwolk.com

Table of Contents

FOREWORD

Brent Heath and Art in front of the 13-division daffodil display at the Philadelphia Flower Show. (Photo by Arlene Wolk)

Thank goodness Art finally wrote this book!

We've forced a tremendous number of bulbs through the years, but we do it only for fun – without attempting to aim flowering for a particular date or event.

Art's been very successful at forcing a great variety of bulbs for home display and to win loads of blue ribbons at the famed Philadelphia Flower Show. AND, he's done all of it inside his home or, later, in a tiny greenhouse – not in a high-tech environment with temperature- and humidity-controlled rooms, warming cells, or the fancy greenhouses that professional forcers use.

We first became aware of him in 1998, when he decided to take on the task of forcing all twelve divisions of daffodils for a display at the Philly Show.

But, wait, that's not quite right.

In the fall of 1998, he bought all the daffodils he thought he needed, then, in late November, he discovered that the number of divisions had been increased to thirteen. He called us desperate for *Narcissus bulbocodium* hybrids, but we were flat out.

Neither of us thought about it after his call, but then, Brent learned the whole story when he was a judge at the 1999 Philadelphia Flower Show. And, sure enough, Art pulled it off. Brent had never seen such a perfectly forced potted display of all thirteen daffodil divisions.

And, that's when Brent and Art first met.

Since then, our paths have crisscrossed around North America, including at the New England Flower Show and the Toronto Garden Writers Symposium, where Art won a prestigious writing award.

But, back to bulb forcing: it's one thing to put a bulb in the soil and watch it bloom when Mother Nature decides to let it bloom. It's quite another thing to put bulbs in a pot and get them to bloom one, two, or even three months ahead of their typical week of outdoor springtime splendor. And, going one step further, it's even more difficult to force bulbs so they'll be at their peak when judges stare at them on a predetermined date, or when you're forcing a truckload of bulbs for a given two-day *Better Homes and Gardens* photo shoot.

Art has mastered this seeming sleight-of-hand and proven his capability year after year. Indeed, he's used his expertise to twice win the Grand Sweepstakes Award at the Philadelphia Flower Show, where every blue ribbon tells the world you've beaten the best. So, Art's 125 blue ribbons, amassed from 1993-2000, showed everyone that he was the bulb forcer to beat.

Although Art has grown almost every kind of garden plant, his first love and forte is forcing bulbs. His blossoms are almost always at their peak at the exact moment they're needed. This, by itself, is a testament to his ability. In his hunger for blue ribbons and bulb-forcing know-how, he's looked at every important variable and discovered how the home gardener can control them.

Simply put, home gardeners couldn't get information on bulb forcing from a better source. And, what's especially wonderful is that his humorous writing will pull you through what would otherwise be a boring recitation of step-by-step instructions. Without realizing it, you'll quickly become a knowledgeable bulb forcer.

Whether you want to produce a stunning pot of tulips or daffodils for either your home or a flower show, he'll reveal how to get the greatest number of blooms possible from even the smallest pot.

We're thrilled to be able to suggest this book to everyone who wants detailed, proven ways to force bulbs successfully. Even so, we have just one warning about *Bulb Forcing for Beginners and the Seriously Smitten*: be sure to loosen your belt before the first chapter, because you'll have guaranteed belly laughs along the way.

Brent and Becky Heath

ACKNOWLEDGEMENTS

Without the support of my wife Arlene and daughter Beth, this book would have been merely an idea. They've been my cheerleaders and advisors throughout my horticultural and literary career and gave indispensable feedback for every photo in this book.

I also want to thank my friends Fran and Bob Chvala and my Uncle Jerry for their advice while this book was being written.

And, there are many others whose help I must acknowledge. They include:
- Brent and Becky Heath for their generosity and encouragement,
- Betty Mackey, who has been my best advisor as I steered my way to publication,
- Liz Ball, my mentor, who has been very supportive of all my horticultural endeavors,
- Ellen Spector-Platt, who gave me a million ideas for marketing my books, and
- Sylvia and Louis Budman, Gil Cohen, and Ruth and Brian Nielson for their consistent confidence in my literary capabilities.

My editors, Pete Johnson and Barbara J. Crawford were invaluable. Both had boundless enthusiasm for this project.

Wendell Minor, who's simply the world's best cover artist, again assembled a first-class book jacket. And, Laurie Baxendell, a highly-skilled artist, provided wonderfully creative cartoons that melded perfectly into this book.

Without my adventures and even more misadventures at the Philadelphia Flower Show, I might never have written my first magazine article or this book. It's a show staged by the Pennsylvania Horticultural Society (PHS) that has been a vital force in the Philadelphia area and, increasingly, around the world. It was guided by two visionary leaders, Ernesta Ballard and Jane Pepper. And, now, the current President, Drew Becher, is pushing the creative envelope that will ensure the continued success of the PHS and the flower show.

My success at the Philly Show would not have been so quickly realized without the generous advice of Walt Fisher, Lee Raden, and Ray Rogers.

There are also numerous friends who gave unstinting assistance at the Philadelphia Flower Show leading up to and during the two insane years when I won the Grand Sweepstakes Award. More than anyone else, I must thank Joan Hemphill who helped during both the good and desperate times. Others include Vicki Berberian, Monica Dubel, Judy Gates, Meg and Rich Good, Bill and Mary Harkell, Alan Kornblau, Marie Lamancusa, Ellie Lloyd, Harriet Monshaw, Barbara Ogle, Pete Parker, Frank Rivera, Joan Smith, Todd Sokol, and Claudia Sumler.

I must also include –
- Dave Scharfstein, who generously provided assistance in the construction of one of my cold frames, and
- Lorrie Baggett-Heuser, who provided Library of Congress information to make this book easier to find for readers around the world.

INTRODUCTION

Dark trees, dark clouds, deep mud, and deep, dark mood swings. It's a gloomy gloaming that makes you wonder whether spring weather will ever arrive.

Desperate for escape from the dreary winter, you sprint

The view from my greenhouse in January. A great day for bulb forcing!

to your computer to find a weather website. All atwitter, you enter your town's name or zip code, then, with widened eyes and wider hopes, you await the results. The first screen appears, and you look for answers to your burning questions: is there a 40% chance for a blinding yellow crocus? Is a warm front headed north, along with scented daffodils? Will the forecast foretell a reason to crumble soil, scan the sky for migrating birds, or look for enough greens to produce a saliva-inducing, chlorophyll-filled salad?

Finally, the ten-day forecast appears. Quickly you scan the screen only to learn that every day will have "cloudy skies with a 100% chance of melancholia."

Should you book a room on the top floor of a tall hotel? Should you look for the highest bridge in your county? Would it be best to unhook your seatbelt and slam your careering car into a deserted brick building? Or, abandoning these schemes, perhaps a call to a crisis-intervention hotline is in order?

My emphatic and empathetic answer is *no*.

Your eyes, nostrils, and fingers can allay your dark world, because by learning the simple techniques of bulb forcing, you'll be able to produce mid-winter flowers inside your seemingly subterranean abode.

Forcing bulbs is a mode of mood elevation that's so easy, you'll "get it" before you get to the end of this book.

And, please don't close this book because you think you don't have a Green Thumb. I know you've swallowed all the bilge about the color of your first digit, but it's idiocy dreamed up by elitist gardeners who want you to think gardening is harder than running at the speed of light.

The fact is, gardening is easy.

So let me say from the outset, that there is NO Green Thumb . . . except perhaps in a dermatologist's office or a mortuary. It might help to have a green thumb if you're growing bored, but not if you're growing plants, and especially not if you're growing bulbs. When it comes to growing bulbs, it's all about the grey matter between your ears. And, you neither have to be smart enough to write the Great American Novel, nor clever enough to create a new, economically-viable energy source that replaces oil.

A much better view on a cold, winter day. I planted 'Yellow Purissima' and 'Flaming Purissima' tulip bulbs in the same pot, and they bloomed simultaneously.

If you can fill a flower pot with moist soil and healthy bulbs, you have more than enough neurons to make bulbs bloom. So, don't listen to negative thoughts telling you, "I can't do this. Art Wolk thinks it's easy because he has secrets he'll never divulge."

To the contrary, you're holding a book that discloses my

The self-arranging arrangement pot: Since each flowering bulb is grown separately in potting mix, the arrangement lasts 2-3 times longer than cut-flower arrangements. And, it gets better as time goes by…without your assistance. (See Chapter 23.)

closely-guarded bulb-forcing secrets. Specifically, the secrets I've learned or developed after more than thirty years of experimentation.

And, for beginners there's something else: occasionally, you can go back and revisit your childhood by experiencing something so new, awe inspiring, and jaw-droppingly wonderful, that you simply glow with excitement.* Your first pot of forced bulbs is such an experience.

I envy you.

Five Promises

A woman once told me that garden writing, "is the most plagiarized published material in the world."

You'd probably think I was shocked by her accusation.

_____

* Einstein may not have been a gardener, but he once said something that all gardeners can identify with: "[We] never cease to stand like curious children before the great mystery into which we were born."

But, no, my reaction was a nod and a smile. Why? Because informational garden publications use much the same words over and over to describe common horticultural activities. Examples would include:

- Add organic matter to clay soil.
- Prune azaleas after they bloom.
- Don't over-water African violets.
- Use moist soil to germinate seeds.
- Wait until your soil is friable before tilling in the spring.
  And, on and on it goes…

You'd have to go far into the past to find the first garden writer who published instructions like these – perhaps before the first Gutenberg bible for some horticultural commandments. So, it comes as no surprise that there have been thousands of books written about bulbs, many with much the same essential information.

So why read my book? There are five reasons:

First: I will not give you instructions for forcing a type of bulb unless I've forced it successfully myself.

I admit in advance that I *do* compare my methods with other growers. I *do* include information found in

Crocus 'Blue Pearl'. It's stunning and easy to force. (See Chapter 14.)

research reports. And, I *do* include information about cultivars (**culti**vated **var**ieties) that I haven't forced. *But in every case, I've forced that type of bulb successfully.*

Second: This book is neither a botanical research text nor a cobbled together coffee-table book high on color and low on information.

I point this out for two reasons:

First: To calm your fears that unless you've taken advanced botany or horticulture courses, you won't understand my advice. To the contrary: *as long as you can read and are motivated to produce wintertime flowers, you'll understand every chapter.* And a further clarification: this book is for **both** *"I couldn't care less about flower show blue ribbons"* gardeners as well as *"I prefer flower show blue ribbons over blue diamonds"* gardeners.

Second: Although, like coffee-table books, you might find the photos in this book gorgeous, they *are actually here for a purpose, namely, to help you learn how to force bulbs, not to help you fall asleep on your couch.*

Third: I'll share a forcing technique I've invented that I've never seen published by anyone else.

It's a technique that allowed me to win bundles of blue ribbons and silver cups at the world-famous Philadelphia Flower Show (which, since 2010, has been known as the *Philadelphia International Flower Show*).*

Promise #4: Flowers shown are flowers grown.

Indeed, my fellow competitors, many of whom are flat-out *amazing* bulb forcers, have never used this technique. Nor have any professional bulb growers with whom I've spoken. And, I haven't seen it in Internet publications, *meaning there's how-to-force-bulb information in this book that you've never read before.*

Fourth: Every "Art Wolk" photo of forced bulbs will only include flowers grown by me, not grown using digital procreation.

Let's face it: photography has undergone cataclysmic changes in the past ten years. Now, any gardeners who know how to use a photo editing program like Adobe Photoshop can alter photos to make themselves look like horticultural geniuses. What's happened, as my friend and world-class photographer Liz Ball would say, is that, "you don't know what's real anymore." So, I pledge that if you see my photos of forced flowers, I added zero flowers to the picture. In all honesty, (which in my case is occasionally the case), I could find no useful purpose in showing you photos of impossible forced-flower pots. All it would lead to is frustration and a sense of failure on your part. The opposite is true: I've done everything possible to show what's possible for you to achieve – regardless of previous experience.

Fifth: I tried to make the entire text in this book not only informational, but also entertaining.

"Huh?" you say. "Art, do you realize you've just put a wrinkle in the universe's space-time continuum?"

Well, maybe I have, but I have company. Other garden writers entertained their readers even when they

* The Philadelphia Flower Show is the only indoor flower show listed in the well-regarded book by Patricia Schultz: *1,000 Places to See Before You Die* (New York: Workman Publishing, 2003) 700-1.

Food for thought: these gastronomic bulbs prove how simple it is to force bulbs. There's nothing special about the potting mix this onion needed to begin growing. Every bulb in this basket has a gorgeous, flowering relative that's easy to force into bloom.

described ordinary garden chores. They didn't just think about themselves and how they gardened, they thought about you and tried to give you a non-coma-inducing experience when you read their published words.

They are my heroes and heroines and, among others, include Henry Mitchell, Katherine White, and Cassandra Danz (a.k.a. Mrs. Greenthumbs, who wasn't above throwing around a bit of sexual innuendo in her books).

Obviously, I can't claim to be the first, the hundredth, thousandth, or – as Forrest Gump would say – the "gozillionth" garden writer to make this attempt. But what I *can* tell you is that I busted my brain to do it.

So, sit back, and – hopefully – have an entertaining experience when you read this book.

Then, after you're finished, place it on a shelf, because there's useful information inside that you can revisit whenever it's needed.

1

THE 40TH PARALLEL

OR

IT'S NOT ALWAYS A BEAUTIFUL DAY
IN THEIR NEIGHBORHOOD

The 40th parallel? As in 40 degrees north of the equator?"

"But why," you might ask, "are you starting a book about bulb forcing with an artificial, geographic line, a human invention of all things?"

The answer is simple: almost everything you need to know about bulb forcing is within a mere 600 miles of the northern hemisphere's 40th parallel.

As it turns out, the 40th parallel in Europe, the Middle East, and Asia is the spine of the geographic distribution of almost all the spring-blooming bulbs you long for each winter when you're scraping ice off your windshield, spreading salt on your sidewalk, or enduring frigid rain dripping down the back of your neck.

Figure 1.1 *(left) and* **Figure 1.2** *(above) A cool day in the hills of northern Israel. It's not the best place for a picnic, but it's a perfect location for wild* Tulipa systola. *(Photos copyright © by Ori Fragman-Sapir.)*

It's here, in the mountain ranges all the way from the Serra da Estrela in Portugal to the Kangnam in North Korea, where your favorite bulbs cavort and thrive.

Which is an interesting fact, but why should you care where bulbs grow in the wild?

Because there's just one basic rule for growing plants in and around your house and it's this: give the plant the same (or similar) conditions as the place from which it came, and it will grow. It took me a long time to get this, so I'm sharing the news with you to save time. Do you get it? Because that's really all there is to get.

Honestly.

To be a great gardener, get off your derrière and find out where your plant is from, what the soil is like, how much sun it receives, how much humidity it likes, how much water it gets, then do your damnedest to give the plant the same conditions. And, if you do this, a wonderful thing happens: *it doesn't die!*

If you understand this one concept, you'll succeed much more than I did when I started gardening (and, unfortunately, even when I was well past the start), because I killed hundreds of plants before I "got it."

If you look at topographical maps of Europe and the Middle East and follow the 40th parallel line (see figures 1.3 and 1.5), you'll notice a common feature I've already

Figure 1.3 *Topographical map of Europe. Note how mountainous it is around the 40th parallel. This is where many spring-blooming bulbs frolic with gleeful abandon. (Map courtesy of CIA World Factbook)*

Figure 1.4 *Note how incredibly UNESSENTIAL "good drainage" is.*

gardens.

Here, there are cold, wet winters and hot, dry summers. And, most important, the soil is full of air, meaning these bulbs ABHOR sopping wet, air-deprived roots. When it rains in these areas, the soil barely gets wet, the roots barely get wet, and the air in the soil stays put. It's not the kind of garden you'd want to construct, but it's the environment in which these bulbs flourish.

What can we learn from this environment? Obviously, it's that these bulbs love air around their roots. In fact, if they could speak, they would scream, *"Give us soil with abundant air or we'll not only not bloom, we'll drop dead!"*

But, before we go further, I must tell you about the most deceptive delusion that's traveled around the horticultural world faster than kudzu or mile-a-minute vine: it's the so-called importance of "soil drainage" or "well-drained soil."

Indeed, many expert gardeners and garden writers will tell you the most important factor in growing spring-blooming bulbs is "good drainage."

mentioned: it's mountainous, meaning these beautiful plants grow in places where you'd have difficulty plunging a shovel more than three inches into the ground. Although this would be an awful place to grow 'Silver Queen' corn, it's a delightful place for tulips, daffodils, hyacinths and the rest of their spring-blooming brethren.

If you take a springtime trek into the rocky hillsides of northern Israel, you'll find the wild, red tulip known as *Tulipa systola* (see figures 1.1 and 1.2). It blooms amid stones and rocks jutting out from the soil. In fact, there's not a lot of noticeable soil at all. And, these conditions are repeated over and over in the mountain ranges near the 40th parallel. They are, indeed, nature's ultimate rock

Figure 1.5 *Topographical map of Middle East. Note, again, how mountainous it is near the 40th parallel – especially in Turkey and neighboring countries. This is where tulips stage fertility rites every spring. (Map courtesy of CIA World Factbook)*

These are all misused phrases that should be expunged from every bulb book and lecture, because **drainage makes absolutely no difference to bulbs**. It's *AIR CONTENT* that matters, not drainage.

If you've heard or read about the "drainage commandment" and believed it, you've been hoodwinked. After all, if the speed with which water moves through soil is important, why is it possible to grow these plants hydroponically (see Chapter 21)? In fact, the hydroponic water is basically going *nowhere*, as in *not draining in the least*. As you may have guessed, hydroponic solutions have high air content. And, more important to the subject at hand, bulb jars (see figure 1.4) are set up so the bottom of the bulb isn't immersed in water. Instead, the roots go through air

before finding water.

Now that you know about the importance of air instead of drainage, you'll have a mental "hiccup" whenever you read a garden book that states the importance of "good drainage." I apologize, since this will take away from the joyous, scintillating, can't-put-the-book-down experience of reading a garden "how-to" text (like this one). But, at least you can chuckle and skip the rest of the sentence, paragraph, page, or chapter.

By the way, many of my fellow-garden writers will, no doubt, be offended by my clarification. As a result, you can expect to read that I've been tortured on a rack, forced to walk the plank, and guillotined. I only say this to warn you not to search the Internet for my photo, because it will permanently stain your computer screen red. How can an Internet

"No, no, it's AIR, not DRAINAGE. You've got to understand. I'm innocent, innocent do you hear?"

photo possibly stain your computer screen? Obviously, it's because my blood has "good drainage."

****

Now that you know the kind of soil in which bulbs like to grow, it's time we moved ahead to find out how you can grow them in a pot without hauling a moving van full of rocks into your living quarters.

That's the subject of Chapter 2, so let's head there next.

2

SOMEWHAT MOUNTAINOUS SOIL

Now that you know where most spring-blooming bulbs live, I'll raise a few issues that may be at the forefront of your frontal lobes:

1. You're going to grow bulbs in pots, not in the rocky soil of Asian or European mountains.
2. You're going to include something besides bulbs in your pots.
3. You have to decide what the "something" is.
4. The "something" has to include air.

Having raised this quartet of quandaries, let me smooth the furrows in your brow by saying that most expert bulb forcers use what's called a "professional growing mix" (see figure 2.1). But before I get to the ingredients of such a mix, please retrieve your just-completed application to a collegiate school of horticulture, because you *do not* have to be a professional horticulturist to use professional mix.

Here, I have to admit that when I first heard this term, I thought I had to be either a professional horticulturist to procure this mix or buy it from a professional. (Please note that in none of my books have I ever claimed to have a high IQ. My horticultural expertise is derived solely from mistake, after mistake, after mistake.)

Actually, there are undoubtedly more amateurs using professional mix than professionals, but no self-respecting amateur gardener would ever buy a growing mix called "amateur mix."

But I digress.

Here's what most "professional" soil mixes usually contain:

1. Sixty to seventy percent sphagnum peat moss.
2. Ten to thirty percent perlite.
3. Zero to twenty percent vermiculite.

Figure 2.1 *Fafard 1-PV is an excellent potting mix for bulb forcing that, when bagged, is also a stunning subject for photography.*

Figure 2.2 *Perlite is made from small pieces of porous volcanic rock.*

4. A dash of fertilizer.

5. A wetting agent.

6. Lime or other chemicals to give the mix a balanced pH (i.e., acid/base neutrality).

7. Absolutely no outdoor garden/farm soil, which is why this "soil" mix is usually called a "soil*less* mix."

Figure 2.3 *Dry sphagnum peat moss. How dry is it? Without a wetting agent you could pour a bathtub full of water onto it, and it would still be dry.*

Now that you're scratching your head, let me tell you about the most important of the first five ingredients: it's perlite, because it virtually refuses to absorb water.

This is the white, light, airy material in the potting mix (see figure 2.2). Given the information mentioned in the past few pages, you now know why perlite is used. ("Yes, Art," you're thinking, "since you've beaten me over the head about this, it's air. The perlite is there to guarantee a supply of air to bulb roots.") So now, you're genuinely closer to becoming a bulb-forcing expert.

Since you're crackling with anticipation and can barely contain yourself, I'll mention the purpose of the other ingredients.

Sphagnum peat moss* is exactly what you'd think: it's a type of moss called sphagnum. It comes from bogs all over the world and is harvested, dried, and milled

---

* Some garden books will tell you that sphagnum peat moss is being depleted and will become as extinct as wooly mammoths. But the opposite is true: in Canada, peat "farms" harvest sphagnum each year on the same fields (see www.bergerpeatmoss.com, last accessed on 6/20/2011).

(ground) before it becomes part of a potting mix.

Vermiculite is "exploded" mica, which can hold water, but also keeps a potting mix airy. (But, this is probably the *least* important ingredient in the mix.)

Fertilizer is included for the same reason that food is included in the space shuttle: just like the relationship between food and humans, without plant food, plants can get sick and die. But be warned: there's very little fertilizer in these mixes. After less than a month, it's usually depleted.

And the "wetting agent"? No, it's not an FBI agent who's never been toilet trained. To the contrary, it's a chemical that helps "wet" water make non-wet sphagnum peat moss wet.

Clear as mud?

Give me one more try.

Try pouring water through plain, dry sphagnum peat

Figure 2.4 *Expanded mica, otherwise known as vermiculite.*

moss and you'll understand the need for a wetting agent. The water does absolutely nothing except pass through the sphagnum, leaving it as dry as Death Valley. (This is extremely hard to believe, so go ahead and give it a shot…of water.)

On the other hand, if your mix contains a wetting agent, it will act like garden soil, meaning it stays wet when you wet it.

For many years, my mix of choice was plain Pro-Mix BX, which was a "sterile mix," meaning it was made without any soil or added microorganisms. But as of 2008 it wasn't at local garden centers or online garden websites. Instead, there are now non-sterile choices: Pro-Mix BX with Mycorise-pro (a mix inoculated with a beneficial fungus) or Pro-Mix BX Biofungicide (a mix inoculated with a bacterium – *Bacillus subtilis* – that helps plants fight root disease).

I used the Mycorise Pro-Mix with…well…mixed results. But I plan to do further testing.

Interestingly, I heard a rumor that the Fafard Company jumped in when Pro-Mix jumped out, meaning they created a mix that's supposed to be very close to the old Pro-Mix BX. It's called Fafard 1-PV, and, whether the rumor is true or not, I found it to be every bit as good as the old Pro-Mix BX.

So, now, for most bulb forcing, Fafard 1-PV is my mix of choice.

The only other growing medium I use is Sunshine Mix #4, which is an extremely high-perlite (and, naturally, high-air-content) mix. I can recommend it for growing lilies, anemones, and any other spring-blooming bulbs that aren't planted in more than one layer (see Chapter 9, pages 70-72).

You'll probably obtain excellent results with my favorite professional mixes. Or, perhaps you have your own formulation. My advice is simple: if what you use works, keep using it.

****

I think by now you have an idea of the kind of potting mix in which your bulbs will thrive. But, what are these things you'll be planting in your containers?

Although they're all called bulbs, there are actually five different kinds. So, let's move on to Chapter 3 for a full-frontal peek at each of them.

3
WHAT ARE THEY?*

There's a bevy of beautiful bulbs out there waiting to be adopted from your local garden center, nursery, or mail-order bulb orphanage. But please put down your credit card a moment, because it's important that I give you – and, please, don't run away screaming – a tiny botany lesson. You see, there are actually five "things" called bulbs, but only one is a "true" bulb. They're the most recognizable, so let's begin with them.

What they have in common are thickened leaf scales, concentrically arranged, and connected to each other by a disk of hardened stem tissue called a basal plate (see figure 3.3). It's from this plate that roots burst forth and vigorously go on a journey toward the center of the Earth.

And now, here's the whole point: what's also in the middle of the thickened subterranean stem tissue is a…FLOWER! It's already there, even before you plant it, even when you let bulbs roll through your hands at your garden center, and even when you order them from a

Figure 3.2 *'Baby Moon' daffodil bulbs. This is about as close to twins as two bulbs can get. When offsets are this developed, they can be carefully separated.*

True Bulbs

These are the bulbs virtually all of us know and are addicted to. First there are daffodils and tulips in all their shades and shapes. There are also bulbs like hyacinths and oriental lilies that can knock you over with their overpowering, odoriferous flowers. And, there are many, many other bulbs, like *Iris reticulata*, amaryllis, and snowdrops.

Figure 3.1 *(left) A cornucopia of bulbs you can force into glorious bloom each winter.*

---

*If you couldn't care less about what they are, what they aren't, what they used to be, or what they will be, go straight to Chapter 4 before you retch or attack this book with a meat cleaver.

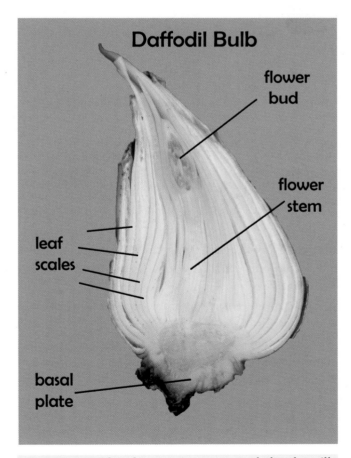

Daffodil Bulb

flower bud

flower stem

leaf scales

basal plate

Figure 3.3 *This shows every anatomical detail you'll need to know about the inside of true bulbs…which is probably a great deal more than you ever **wanted** to know about the inside of true bulbs.*

Figure 3.4 *The great diversity in tulip shape and color seen at the Philadelphia International Flower Show.*

Figure 3.5 *A Freesia corm, which looks very much like a Gladiolus corm, which looks very much like a Crocus corm, which looks very much like a...well, you get the idea. You won't fall in love with the bulbs, but you **will** fall in love with their flowers.*

bulb company in August. What's especially wonderful is that with some of these bulbs *there's more than one flower inside.*

What this means is, you must work extremely hard to screw this up. Meaning, you don't have to work hard to get it right. No Thumb of Any Color needed. You don't even have to trump Einstein and figure out a unified theory of the universe. In other words, growing this stuff is E-A-S-Y.

Corms

Now that we've gotten past true bulbs, does it mean that the other four types are false, fictitious, or felonious?

Not by any means, they're just anatomically different, but bulbs nonetheless. All corms have a swollen underground stem packed with nutrients. Like true bulbs they have a thin papery covering of dried leaves as well as a root-generating basal plate, but unlike true bulbs, there are no thickened, concentric leaf scales.

All these anatomical terms are enough to make a gardener change hobbies (or, more accurately, change reading material). So let me simplify things and tell you what EVERY SINGLE TYPE OF BULB (including those described both above and below) has in common: they all store food underground and must have a piece of stem tissue. No stem tissue means no stem, no leaves, and definitely no flowers.

Corms often look like flattened balls ranging in size from flattened ping-pong balls (crocuses) to flattened tennis balls (*Gladiolus*). They feel sturdier than many other garden bulbs, and are built to last.

You should also be aware that they reproduce below ground like rabbits above ground.

Case in point: the first bulbs I ever grew in a summer garden were gladioli. When I dug them up in the fall for winter storage (they're not hardy in New Jersey), I found about eight tiny bulbs (cormels) stuck to the bottom of each bulb. I removed them, replanted them the next two

Figure 3.6 *Backlit* Freesia *'Corona'. Yes, it really is this gorgeous. And, let me be the first to tell you that the cold-temperature requirements of freesias aren't nearly as extreme as many bulb experts have led you to believe. (See Chapter 7.)*

summers, and they bloomed the third year. So, plant a dozen of these one year and three summers later you have almost one hundred blooming bulbs. Now, that's what I call really bad prophylaxis, but really productive repro-

duction (even though this means of procreation has nothing to do with sex and everything to do with self-adoration, because cormels are clones).

The most common and easiest corm to force is *Crocus.** There are many others, but my best of the rest nod goes to freesias, a bulb with lovely flowers and a spicy scent (see figure 3.6).

Figure 3.7
The not-very-obvious upper side of an Anemone coronaria *bulb.*

Tubers

Don't even try to tell me you can't give me an example of a tuber. One of the most common is on your breakfast, lunch, and dinner plate, at your fast food and gourmet restaurants, and stacked in pyramidal piles at your supermarket.

Have you guessed yet? Of course, I refer to the potato (or potato*e* in Quaylean parlance). Yes, those ordinary things you buy and eat almost every day are tubers.

You won't force potatoes into bloom indoors - unless you're in serious need of a very serious talk with an extremely serious therapist. After all, you'd need to remove your dining room set to have enough room to do so. But they're anatomically similar to other tubers that *are* worth forcing, like *Arisaema* and *Anemone*, that will bloom without displacing furniture or family members.

Like true bulbs and corms, tubers have thickened stems that store food. But unlike the other two, they have neither a basal plate – the roots sprout from everywhere on the bulb's outer surface – nor are they covered with dried leaves. Instead, they have skin that can be almost as tough as leather.

One last point about these bulbs: they're about as gorgeous as cow dung, and some are shaped just like it.

Not only are the bulbs not beautiful, one in particular is quite confusing. Here, I refer to *Anemone*, a plant with gorgeous flowers (especially the poppy-flowered *Anemone coronaria*), but one of the oddest looking bulbs on our planet. They basically look like small globs of mud, stuck together and hardened in a kiln (see figure 3.7). Whenever gardeners first see them, their universal response is, "Which end of the bulb goes up?" And, the

Figure 3.8 Anemone coronaria *'Mr. Fokker'. A two-dimensional photo doesn't do justice to the three-dimensional elegance and beauty of these flowers. If I were limited to growing just one type of bulb each winter, it would be this one.*

---

*As you probably know, crocuses are one of the first outdoor bulbs to bloom. And, that's what makes them easy to force: the earlier the bulb blooms outdoors, the easier it is to force indoors.

only way to tell is to look closely for the bowl-shaped appendages, and plant the bulb so that the top of the bowl points upward.

If you still can't distinguish top from bottom, all is not lost. Just plant the damned thing sideways. The roots will still head down toward Hades and the flowers up toward your awaiting eyeballs.

Tuberous Roots

This seems more than a bit redundant. After all, don't the already-described tubers have roots, and, if they do, aren't the roots called tuberous roots? Okay, you're right, but there's another category of bulb called tuberous roots that has nothing to do with roots on a tuber. Got it? Or, am I as clear as manure tea?

Enough semantic banter, let me step back and start again.

Indeed, the fourth type of bulb is named tuberous roots, and for good reason: this is the only group of bulbs in which the food storage is in root tissue, not thickened stems or swollen leaf scales. In fact, tuberous roots begin to form swollen roots soon after their seeds germinate. But, like all bulbs, they have stem tissue. In their case, it grows from buds at the end of the swollen roots.

If you don't understand what I'm babbling about, have a look at the *Ranunculus* roots in figure 3.9. These tuberous roots have more than a passing resemblance to the all-time worst hair-do (or perhaps hair-*don't*) adorned by Greek mythology's Medusa (see figure 3.10). The all-important stem tissue is what the roots are attached to, and is commonly called the *crown*.

The queen of backyard tuberous roots is the *Dahlia*. These are the flowers that can grow so large and showy, they could take the place of all the neon signs on Broadway. But dahlias occasionally demand the steady hand of a pediatric surgeon. Although their swollen roots get almost as large as a sweet potato, the connection between it and the crown, which has the all-important stem tissue, can be more fragile than thin windows in a gale. If you break the connection between the two, and then plant what's leftover, you'll be the proud parent of nothing. That's right, *nothing*. Underground the incomplete bulb is busy rotting or being devoured by all the non-human vegetarians that live in or visit your precinct. As I've mentioned with every other type of bulb: no stem

Figure 3.9 *Ranunculus bulbs. Want to remember what tuberous roots look like? Just picture Medusa's hair (see figure 3.10) after every snake eats a rat, and you'll never forget.*

Figure 3.10 *Medusa (by Caravaggio) with her ill-advised tuberous root-like, serpentine hairstyle. Glance quickly! Mythology tells us she was so monstrous that onlookers were turned to stone.*

tissue means no plant and no flowers.

There are fine garden and container plants in this group. Examples include winter aconite, which seemingly can push its way through an iceberg to bloom; then there's the already-mentioned *Ranunculus*, a wonderful bulb to force, with flowers that resemble old fashioned

Figure 3.11 Ranunculus *'Sunset'. As unbelievable as it seems, these flower stems don't topple despite zero extraneous support.*

roses plunked on thin, but strong, 8" stems (see figure 3.11); and finally there are the tall basketball players of the botanical world called foxtail lilies (*Eremurus*), which can top out at nine feet – meaning they can touch a basketball net without using Nike equipment and a trampoline.

Rhizomes

And now, I feel a bit like the character toward the end of Orson Welles's radio broadcast of *War of the Worlds*, who somberly intoned the words, "Isn't there anyone…? Isn't there anyone…? Any…one?"

I must be realistic about this, and understand that getting any gardener like me to the fifth section of a

Figure 3.12 Canna *bulb. It looks exactly the way you'd expect a rhizome to look: it moves laterally under the soil and sends up shoots every 6"-12".*

chapter on bulb anatomy is like getting my wife to kill a cricket without screaming at the top of her lungs.

Still, for the seriously smitten gardeners who've made it this far, I will describe the last type of bulb, namely rhizomes. These bulbs have thickened subterranean stems that grow horizontally. They're like underground submarines that occasionally send buds to the surface for air, light, and to show off their foliage and flowers (see figure 3.12).

My favorite is the calla lily (*Zantedeschia* species and hybrids, see figures 3.13 and 3.14), whose bulb doesn't have the typical horizontal shape.

Canna bulbs look exactly the way you'd expect for a rhizome. And, this is one of the best bulbs for the summer

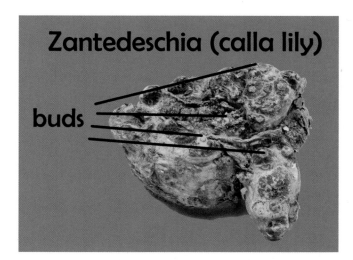

Figure 3.13 Zantedeschia *(calla) rhizome. It has more than a passing resemblance to a particular digestive byproduct…or perhaps a mud pie dried in an oven. It isn't comely, but, oh my, look at the flowers it produces (see figures 3.14 and 20.17-20.21).*

Figure 3.14 *A Zantedeschia aethiopica (calla lily) blossom with its bisexual spadix. The male flowers are directly above the female flowers. It's a somewhat Puritanical arrangement that isn't creative, but it gets the job done.*

I'll say no more of them. You've been warned.

****

I think...no, I'm *sure*... you've had your fill of preliminary information about bulbs. After all, you bought or were given this book to learn about getting bulbs to produce gorgeous flowers in the winter.

And, in the next few chapters you'll find out how to do exactly that. In fact, before you know it, you'll go from being a novice to an enlightened bulb forcer.

So, let's move ahead to Chapter 4.

flower garden because it's free-flowering, meaning it continues producing flowers all summer. Its only detraction is that individual flowers are at their peak for a short time, and the withered flowers linger. Still, for the attentive gardeners who are willing to regularly remove dead flowers, cannas can contribute greatly to their flower borders. And there are so many colors available, many of which are stunning (see figure 3.15).

Still another example of rhizomatous bulbs is lily of the valley (*Convallaria majalis*), a lovely plant for the garden as long as you don't try to change its location once it becomes entrenched.

And, here I must relate a story about a former coworker of mine named John. Many years ago, he decided to use a sloped bank in his yard as a rock garden. But he had one horrible obstacle: lily of the valley covered the entire bank. He and his father spent an entire week removing them, and then required a long rest before replacing the thick-rooted, former resident with different plants.

John decided to consult me first, so he asked which plants he should purchase. Of course, I kiddingly suggested he might start with lily of the valley, at which point he threw a heavy book at my head.

Figure 3.15 *Cannas in full bloom inside a Longwood Gardens conservatory (Kennett Square, Pennsylvania).*

4

BULB FORCING/COAXING/PERSUADING/
ENTICING/CHARMING

Bulb forcing" is such a terrible term. It sounds like an outright assault – as if we're jamming botanical specimens into a pipe with a too-narrow opening. Of all the terms used in the above title, I think "bulb enticing" is the most accurate, since the end-product is so seductive and sensuous. So, please bear with me if I occasionally stray from the usual phraseology.

Beginning before the Beginning

Let me stress something that's important, regardless of the type of bulbs you force:

If you're "aiming" potted bulbs for a special occasion or a flower show, always allow more time than you think you'll need. As you gain experience, you'll learn how long it takes to force a particular bulb in your growing conditions.

If it normally takes six weeks for you to force an amaryllis into bloom, plant it seven weeks before the target date. It's easier on your plant – and your mental health – to hold back a plant than it is to push it ahead (see Chapter 25).

But, let's forget what we call this activity and find out what the activity is. For most spring-bloomers, bulb forcing means enticing bulbs to bloom indoors, well ahead of their outdoor sisters and brothers.

There are heaps of gorgeous, incredibly easy-to-force bulbs that can blossom with little more than a pot, potting mix, light, and water (see Chapter 6). And, there are millions of happy bulb forcers who limit themselves to these bulbs.

But I think you'll eventually want to force typical spring-blooming bulbs like tulips, daffodils, crocuses, and hyacinths. Almost all of them require an 8-13 week

period of temperatures averaging 40°-50°F, with 48°F being ideal. It's important to fix your eyes on the "8-13 week period," above. If, in the northern hemisphere, we accept the fact that outdoor soil temperatures dip below 50°F in November, then eight weeks in the future would occur some time in January, and twelve weeks would occur in February. These are not months known for riots of colorful flowers in your backyard.

This means that the required chilling, also called

Figure 4.1 *The cold frame is just one of many ways to chill (vernalize) spring-blooming bulbs before indoor forcing. See Chapter 10 for other, truly easy ways to chill bulbs.*

Figure 4.2 *'Ancilla' is a quick, easy-to-force tulip that instantly dispels the winter blues. Typical of all Kaufmanniana tulips, it has short stems and striking blossoms. Like other tulips, they require chilling before the final stage of forcing. Believe it or not, 'Ancilla' would have virtually no flower stems at all without a sufficient period of cold temperatures.*

have dwarflike, stalkless blooms at soil level. Can you guess why?

Of course, you can.

You've already become a semi-expert, because you know that the bulbs didn't get a sufficient chilling period (vernalization) to allow the flower stems or stalks to elongate. Do you get it? And, do you see how easy this is? Now, you're almost ready to produce cheerful pots of daffodils and many other types of spring-blooming flowers, simply because you "get it."

****

Before I set you loose to blithely entice bulbs into bloom, I should tell you about some of my particularly idiotic errors, so you can avoid them.

It's best that I begin with my first pot, so let me tell you about...

vernalization, is finished by the time your backyard loam is frozen hard enough to require a jackhammer to do what a shovel does the rest of the year. It also means that in January and February bulbs are sitting in the ground, doing absolutely nothing necessary for them to flower. They're just waiting for warmer soil temperatures before they burst into bloom.

If you accept this fact, then you're on your way to understanding why, in mid-winter, you can give potted, vernalized bulbs spring-like temperatures indoors to produce blossoms on your windowsill.

And, oh my, having a pot of tulips on your side of the window when icicles are on the other is like telling winter you don't care an icy iota about what it does. Those tulips are guaranteed to produce pure wintertime glee.

The chilling/vernalization at 40°-50°F is necessary for two reasons. First, it's vital for **root growth**, and second, it breaks flower-stem dormancy that allows **stems to elongate**.

We've all been in stores with potted hyacinths that

Figure 4.3 *(right)* Narcissus *'W. P. Milner', with its ridged nose (corona), twisted petals, and downward-facing blossoms, is one of my favorite diminutive daffodils. Note that its flowers are at a uniform height above the foliage. Without sufficient chilling, the blooms would be hidden inside the foliage.*

5

WHEN THE FORCE WAS FIRST WITH ME

OR

DAFFODILS IN THE TROPICS

So, how did I get into this habit-forming hobby? On a chance glance, that's how.

Back in 1975, my wife's parents lived in southern Florida, and we were going to visit them during Easter Week. That seems innocuous, except that we were about to do one of those insane things only done by people under thirty: travel twelve-hundred miles in twenty-four hours by car.

Before Arlene and I began our journey, we stopped to buy fruit. And, while in the checkout line, I noticed a pot of about-to-bloom daffodils in tight bud. I barely saw them with a slight glance to my right. To this day I wonder how my life would have meandered if my eyes hadn't wandered.

Alas, it was too late. The siren's song of the narcissi called out to me, and I was willingly seduced.

Most gardeners, quite logically, force their first pot of bulbs on a windowsill or under fluorescent lights. I was about to force them wedged between suitcases in the back of a Chevrolet moving due south at 60 m.p.h.

I doubt if anyone else on Earth has ever forced their first pot of daffodils in such circumstances. I also doubt that

anyone else has been idiotic enough to even attempt it.

We began our journey amid a late March cold snap. There were northwest winds and temperatures below freezing. Naturally, we put the car heater on, and unnaturally, within a few hours, the first daffodil bud opened. Aside from the screaming-yellow color, it sent its perfume into the tiny bit of unused space inside our car.

I realized immediately that warmth and flowering were intimately related, so I turned the heat off. This, of course, resulted in a less-than-intimate response from Arlene, who asked me if I was crazy.

"Crazy?" I said, "What do you mean?"

"The heat, that's what!" Arlene said.

"Yeah, but what about the daffodils we're bringing to your mom."

"What about them?"

"Don't you want her to see the flowers when we get to Florida?" I asked.

"Well, I suppose. But why can't we use heat?"

"It'll make every flower bloom too soon," I said.

"Guess what, Art, we're going to have to compromise or the daffodils can go out the window."

"OK, we'll put some heat on."

So I turned it on, but as soon as she looked away, I

"Art...turn off that heater again
and you'll lose a hand!"

Figure 5.1 *(left) Narcissus 'Golden Echo' is a striking daffodil that you can easily force on your windowsill.*

Figure 5.2 Narcissus *'Carlton' is a showy, easy-to-grow daffodil that's ideal for first-time bulb forcers.*

turned it off.

Thus began the ritual performed by every successfully-married couple: the War of the Thermostat.

I soon learned that heat wasn't the only problem: sunlight streaming into the car also stimulated flowering. So as the daffodils continued on their southern journey, I repeatedly shifted them away from sunlight. This went on for twelve hours, until sunset. By that time, five blossoms had opened.

After driving all night, we stopped for breakfast in northern Florida. I knew sunlight would drive the temperatures in the car above 90°F, so I took the daffodils with us inside restaurant. By then, eight blossoms had opened.

Once indoors, the owner of the restaurant thought we had pulled off a miracle. He hadn't seen daffodils since

moving south from New York fifteen years before. During our meal, the owner couldn't take his eyes off them, which is why I kept the daffs within twelve inches of my fork at all times.

The last three-hundred miles of the trip was basically a repeat of the first nine hundred, except that Arlene and I were fighting over the air conditioning, not the heat. To stop the bulbs from blooming, I got the temperature inside the car down to 50°F, which resulted in frigid looks and chilling threats from my wife.

The daffodil's interminable trip finally ended in Hallandale, Florida, where they were the first item whisked from the car and presented to Arlene's amazed mother.

Although this seems like a ridiculous way to force a first pot of bulbs, I learned important lessons that would help me produce photogenic pots and win Philadelphia Flower Show blue ribbons. I found, even inside a car, that the most important variables in forcing spring-blooming bulbs were **light, temperature, and time**. There are other variables that can affect blossoming, but after potting bulbs and giving them a chill, these three will always be the most vital in getting a pot of bulbs to reach perfection.

Still, even though my trek was a learning experience, I suggest that you force your first pot on a windowsill or growing bench. Skip the 1200-mile tropical trip with daffodils, or your significant other might make sure your first forced pot will be your bulb-forcing finale.

****

Thinking back on that experience, I realize that it was an ideal first pot to force, since I didn't have to go through any preliminary bulb chilling or rooting. And, that degree of non-difficulty might be a great place for you to start...and for some indoor gardeners a perfectly satisfactory place to *end*.

Which is why I've written the next chapter especially for you. You see, **there are many bulbs that don't need any special treatment before they're forced**, so let's begin with them.

6
EASY BULBS FOR ADAPT-TO-MY-HOUSE-OR-DIE GARDENERS

Now that I've put wrinkles in your brow and mine by describing the five types of bulbs (see Chapter 3), here's the nub: when it comes to bulb forcing, there are just two kinds of bulbs, those that need a chill before blooming and those that don't.

It's that simple, really.

If you live somewhere on Earth that has an honest-to-God winter (meaning snow, ice, and thoughts of moving to Polynesia) and you put bulbs like tulips and daffodils in the ground in autumn, virtually all of them require a chill before they'll blossom. I'll soon tell you exactly what to do to get these cold-temperature-loving bulbs to

---

Clean Pots = Happy Bulbs

I've done virtually all my bulb forcing in clay pots – mostly old clay pots. Before planting, I clean each pot in soapy water and then let it spend fifteen minutes soaking in 10% bleach (1 part Clorox to 9 parts water). This solution kills many of the harmful bacteria and fungi that find bulbs delectable. Following this semi-sterilization, I put the pots in plain water for at least ten minutes, then rinse them with a hose. This rinsing is vital, because bleach is non-discriminatory: it not only kills microbes, but can also butcher your bulbs. (See Appendix 2, figure 12 [labeled as A2.12] for the amazing results before and after cleaning)

---

bloom indoors. But for now, we'll focus on bulbs that don't need chilly temps to blossom. They're especially suited for adapt-to-my-house-or-die gardeners. Meaning, all you have to do is stick bulbs in a pot containing moist growing mix, put the pot on a windowsill, and enjoy the ensuing flower show.

My favorite example of these easy-to-force bulbs is the amaryllis (*Hippeastrum*). Here, you have a true bulb

the size of a softball that's packed with flowers. And, it requires no chilling because it's native to tropical South America, where it grows happiest in the sun.

The directions for growing an amaryllis are forthcoming, but first you need a flower-pot lesson.

To grow bulbs in pots you should know that there are three different types. They are 1) **standard pots** that have a top-of-the-pot diameter approximately equal to the pot's height, 2) **azalea pots** (which, despite the name, can be used to grow virtually any plant) that have a height

Figure 6.1 *Pot anatomy 101.*

that's three-quarters the diameter, and 3) **bulb pots** (also called bulb pans) that are half as tall as they are wide. As you can tell, what I'm really referring to, respectively, are tall, squat, and seriously squat pots.

It seems inconsequential, but some horticultural books throw these terms around as if you emerged from you mother's womb knowing them. I've defined them here, because a few of you probably didn't.

You can grow almost any bulb in all three of these pots, but for aesthetic reasons I usually grow diminutive bulbs (e.g., *Crocus* and *Iris reticulata*) in bulb pots, medium-height bulbs (e.g., daffodils and tulips) in azalea pots, and tall bulbs (e.g., *Arisaema serratum* and *A. yamatense* – see Chapter 18) in standard pots.

Clay vs. Plastic Pots and... Why Plain Plastic is Plain Poisonous!

You cook bulbs almost every day. There are potatoes, sweet potatoes, onions, garlic, and many more.

But few of us eat bulb roots. On the other hand, many of us destroy roots unknowingly by forcing bulbs in plastic pots. These are thin, dark containers that, when placed on a sunny windowsill, get so hot they literally cook roots. One day you have gorgeous, white roots galloping their way through potting mix, the next you have brown, dead roots not able to budge another nanometer.

The difference in temperature is startling (see figures 6.2a-6.2d). On a sunny windowsill, the high temperature in a 4" clay pot is 74°-78°F, while in green plastic pots, it's close to 100°F! Is it any wonder that bulb roots growing in such containers die?

This is the kind of failure that mystifies gardeners and causes many to give up bulb forcing altogether. After all, you use healthy bulbs, then water, fertilize, and use proper forcing temperatures, yet fail completely without any idea why. If you're using plastic pots and this happens, carefully tap the soil ball out of the pot. When you see

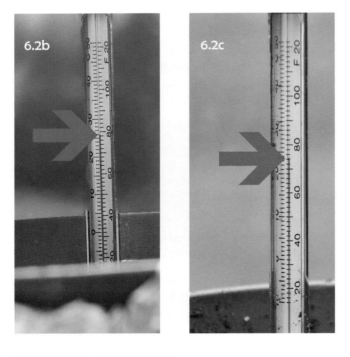

Figures 6.2a-d *A sunny window with three different containers. Clay and aluminum foil-covered plastic have a maximum temperature of 74°-78°F, but plain plastic can hit 96°-100°F. The latter is just dandy if you want to eat cooked bulbs and roots. It's not so dandy if you want bulbs to produce blossoms.*

Figure 6.3 *White-tipped* Anemone *roots grown in a clay pot, happily going about their business.*

Figure 6.4 *Brown-tipped* Anemone *roots roasted in a plastic pot, unhappily going nowhere, doing nothing.*

cooked brown roots…or perhaps no roots at all…you'll understand why plastic pots can be such a bad choice (see figures 6.3 and 6.4).

Please think about this for a moment.

Way back in Chapter 1, I said that if you want to successfully grow a plant, find out how it grows in its native land. Of course, all typical spring-blooming bulbs grow in soil that gets quite cold in the winter, perhaps even frozen as hard as concrete. If there happens to be a warm day in January or February, the outdoor soil temperature changes very little. It takes many weeks before the soil around bulb roots begins to warm – regardless of wide swings in outdoor temperatures.

To the contrary, if you try to force these same bulbs in plastic pots, all it takes is one sunny day of photons blasting into your pot for the roots to go from vigorous, healthy white to rigor-mortis brown. Meaning, to many gardeners, that they've become roots in rigorous need of prayers, incense, and bended knee – which, I'm sorry to say, might help your conscience, but not your bulbs' brown, dead roots.

Keep in mind one fact: *clay pots help prevent wide temperature variations in the soil, plain plastic pots do not.*

If, despite this fact and all my apocalyptic warnings, you still want to force bulbs in plastic pots on a sunny windowsill, there are a few tricks you can use to keep white roots white.

First, you can surround the outside of the pot with aluminum foil, with the shiny side facing outward. Be sure to cover the entire outer surface of the pot. This will reflect light and heat away from the pot.

Another choice, although not as effective, is to use an extra plastic pot on the outside to create an insulating layer of air. You can either use an outer pot that's one size larger than the pot that contains your bulbs, or you can

Figure 6.5 *If you can't plant bulbs when they arrive, take them out of their boxes and either spread them out on trays or put them in mesh bags or stockings. Circulating air will limit the spread of disease.*

use the same pot size, but put something at least a half-inch high – perhaps a crumpled piece of aluminum foil – in the bottom of the outer pot. This raises the inside pot and keeps it away from the sides of the hot outer pot. The goal in both cases is to create an air space between the outer and inner pot. It will keep the inner pot from baking bulb roots. (Remember: baking may be fine for flour, but not flower-bulb roots.)

The one exception to my dread of plastic pots is when pots are forced under lights, which means that light and (depending on the light source) heat come from straight overhead.

Figure 6.6 *Excellent results achieved by Sherry Santifer from just one amaryllis bulb* (Hippeastrum *'Barbados'). The second bloom stem is about three days behind the first. I prefer this kind of sequence at home, but flower show judges want every flower fully developed, in peak condition, and at the same stage.*

Amaryllis

If there's a single bulb in the world that would qualify for the name Circus Maximus, it's the amaryllis (*Hippeastrum*). Everything is huge: the bulb, the blossoms, and the leaves.

Here are instructions for growing it (see figure 6.7):

1. Get a standard pot about 2" wider than the diameter of the bulb (usually an 8"-wide pot).
2. Fill the pot about one-third with moistened professional mix and shape the mix into a cone (see figure 6.7b).
3. Put the bulb in the center of the pot and spread out the roots over the cone.
4. Add mix to about one inch below the top of the pot. At this point, the top of the bulb will be about 2"-3" above the soil.
5. Put the pot on a sunny windowsill in a room that's at least 60°-75°F.
6. Once flower buds begin to emerge, turn the pot one-quarter turn (90°) per day so the stem stays vertical and blossoming is uniform.* Enjoy the show about six weeks later.

Simple stuff. Honest-to-goodness easy. And, oh boy, will you ever impress the non-gardeners that come to visit. There will be a pot with long strapping leaves and a flower stalk with four HUGE, bell-shaped flowers. And, sometimes more than one stalk blooms at the same time, meaning eight HUGE blossoms at once.

I've forced dozens of amaryllis for the Philadelphia Flower Show, and some won blue ribbons. So, I can share a few secrets that will help the seriously smitten among you to produce a gorgeous pot for home or show.

This is extremely easy, but first a tiny bit of botany: if you have a large bulb, it probably has three sets of four flowers inside. That's 3 X 4, meaning 12 flowers per bulb, which is spine-tingling arithmetic.

Now, if you can get two of the three stalks to bloom at the same time, you'll have a wonderful pot. But if you get all three to bloom simultaneously, you'll have a sensational pot.†

Here's the secret: ***HEAT***. That's right, heat. You must cook the bulb. Well, not literally. After all, it's flowers we're after, not lunch or brown roots. But if you pot your amaryllis bulb, then put it on a heating/seed germination mat set at 80°-85°F, it makes the bulb send up all its bloom stems at virtually the same time. It's that simple.‡

---

* Virtually every pot of blooming bulbs in the photographs of this book was turned one-quarter turn per day during active growth, regardless of their indoor forcing location.

† And, for flower-show exhibitors, this would definitely be a blue-ribbon pot.

‡ This seems counter to my previous warnings, but *Hippeastrum* is a *tropical* bulb, not a typical spring-blooming bulb. Even so, please don't let the soil temperature get anywhere near 100°F.

6.7a

6.7b

6.7d

6.7e

6.7c

Figures 6.7a-e *The amaryllis 'Orange Sovereign', from bulb planting to flowers. The two bloom stems in figure 6.7d emerged together, which is why they produced the uniform display shown in figure 6.7e.*

Figure 6.8 *Grouped amaryllis is ideal for photography.*

I know that most of you don't have germination mats, so I can suggest another technique: put the amaryllis pot in the smallest room in your house, and use an electric heater to pump the heat up to 85°F before you leave for the day. I also suggest you do this AFTER your significant other is long gone. And, for safety's sake, be sure to check twice that you've turned the heater off before you leave.

Admittedly this "cook the amaryllis" method isn't a guaranteed thing, since what's going on inside the bulb varies from batch to batch and year to year, but it's the best way I know to get as many flowers as possible to bloom at once.

If your wintertime home is heated to seventy degrees, the four blossoms on each stem will last about a week. I usually place the pot in a cool location overnight – as low as forty degrees – to make the show last longer. At colder temperatures, the flowers can be damaged even if they stay above freezing. Keep in mind: these are tropical plants, and like many tropicals their leaves and flowers chatter when they get in the neighborhood of 33°- 39°F – a "neighborhood" that's wonderful for the Winter Olympics, not wintertime amaryllis.

While your amaryllis is in bloom, you'll undoubtedly run for your camera (although if you're my age, it's far safer to walk for your camera). Once you take photos, don't expect to be bowled over by the results. It's more likely that you'll be bowled under. In your three-dimensional world, you can walk around your amaryllis and see all four blossoms; alas, your camera cannot. So, the most your camera will "see" are two or three blooms at a time. The best way to produce amaryllis photos that truly

"pop" is to have lots of pots blooming at the same time. With so many flowers, it's possible to arrange your pots so you can fill the photographic frame with color (see figure 6.8).

Once your flowers are spent, it's time to recharge the bulb for the following year. After blooming, this bulb is as exhausted as you might be after running a marathon. So, you've got to maximize photosynthesis to fatten these depleted bulbs. That's how flower buds are produced for the following winter.

First, cut off the bloom stem. Then, when spring temperatures are warm enough (reliably above 50°F at night), take your potted amaryllis outside. Fertilize it throughout the growing season, and give it as much sun as possible. I know this is counter to what many bulb books say, but sun is exactly what these bulbs get in their native area in South America; NOT dappled sun, NOT semi-shade, but SUN.

Come fall, it's time to give your amaryllis bulbs a rest…a thorough rest. It puts these bulbs into a dormant

Figure 6.9 *Want to save your amaryllis for next winter? Let it spend the summer in the sunniest place available, and fertilize it throughout the growing season. In the fall, cut the leaves off, let the pot go dry, and ignore it for at least two months. Then start the process again for a second winter of gorgeous flowers.*

state that helps trigger flower stem extension when you're ready to force them. Giving these bulbs a rest is so easy: simply treat them the way you'd like to treat your most hated co-worker or relative. Well, perhaps not literally, since it would mean murder or mayhem. Just tip them over (your bulbs, not your victims), put them on the floor, and turn your back on them for two months. Don't water, don't fertilize, and don't pay any attention to them.

Then, come late fall or early winter, you'll be able to step on the gas so they'll zoom into bloom. I usually loosen the roots and repot my amaryllis bulbs using new potting mix wherever there's space.

Before we leave the world of amaryllis, I thought I'd tell you about a rather atypical entry at the Philadelphia Flower Show (see figure 6.10). But, what in the world is this? Is it, perhaps, flowers from a basketball-sized amaryllis bulb?

Well, no, it's not.

What it is, quite simply, is an example of incredible patience and horticultural expertise. Virtually all true bulbs produce small offspring called offsets at the base of the bulb. Most bulb producers in Holland, as well as gardeners around the world, eventually separate these offsets to get additional flower bulbs.

And, then there's Ray Rogers.

Here's the story: Rogers is, of course, one of the most creative and competitive exhibitors at the Philadelphia Flower Show. In spite of our overheated competition for blue ribbons, we've remained friends over the past twenty years.

Toward the end of one Show in the 1990s, he told me he had a "surprise" for the following year. He gave me no further information.

I was curious, but didn't press him for details. Besides, it would have been a futile endeavor. His lips were sewn shut. And, to be honest, within a week I forgot about his "surprise."

Then, the following March, he showed up with a pot of amaryllis that made my – as well as everyone else's – eyes pop. He had kept all the offsets of the "mother" bulb attached, producing a clump of bulbs that produced a clump of flowers that had never been seen before. And, here, I'm not just referring to the Philadelphia Flower Show. If, before the 1990s, you've ever seen any amaryllis pot like this, please let me know. I'll be quite surprised if I hear from a single one of you.

The funny thing about Ray's secrecy was, well, his secrecy. If I had somehow found out what his "surprise" was going to be the following March, did he really think I could have grown such a clump in one year, when it had probably taken him at least five?*

Figure 6.10 *An incredible pot of* Hippeastrum *(amaryllis) 'Pamela' grown by Ray Rogers. It's one bulb plus offsets of offsets of offsets of offsets. You can produce this kind of display from a single clump of bulbs, but expect it to take at least five years.*

Figure 6.11 *(over)* Hippeastrum *'Fairytale' doesn't understand the word "quit." This bulb produced four bloom stems with up to 6 flowers per stem. It's an ideal amaryllis for the first-time or long-time grower.*

* When I recently reminded Rogers of his secrecy and the impossibility of producing such an amaryllis clump in one year, he chuckled and told me that some exhibitors tried to do exactly that. I can only assume that these growers prayed often, performed horticultural fertility rites, and crossed their fingers and toes...all to no avail.

But then, I suppose I've been just as secretive at times. Such is the overheated competition the Philadelphia Flower Show engenders, which is precisely why winning a blue ribbon at this show is so euphoric. Win one here and you've beaten the best.

One last footnote about Rogers' 'Pamela': when he brought it into the Show, he left the other competitors with single bulb entries in the dust. It really was akin to a tiny little league team going against a World Series Championship team.

I was quite content that I didn't have an amaryllis entry that year. Those who did, had mouths agape for nine days…which is precisely what all exhibitors, in their heart of hearts, want from their fellow competitors.

Paper Whites
(alias "Scentus noninterruptus")

Paper whites are actually daffodils (*Narcissus*).* Unlike the vast majority of daffodils, you don't have to produce chilly conditions for them to root and begin flower stem elongation (see pages 72-73). It's easy to understand why: they're from the Mediterranean Coast where wicked win-

ters are almost non-existent.*

Now the bad news: if you've never grown or sniffed paper whites, you're either going to hate them or love them, nothing in between. The typical paper white found at your garden center or supermarket each fall will have flowers with so much scent, you'll be able to smell them from one end of your house to the other…and perhaps from one end of your town to the other.

But, you won't know whether you'll love or hate them until you give them a try.

Case in point: I once convinced a next-door neighbor to purchase a bulb-forcing collection. He was ecstatic all winter as tulips, crocuses, and irises bloomed. Then came the paper whites.

The morning after the first floret opened, I spied his pot of paper whites outside the front door on a cold day in February. The first nanosecond that my neighbor's wife saw me, she peppered me with questions about why such malodorous flowers would be forced into bloom by anyone.

Figure 6.13 *A single layer of paper whites. Yes, the bulbs can touch each other! Although the top growth is curved, it straightens as it grows (see figures 6.16 and 6.17).*

Figure 6.12 *A stack of healthy paper whites (*Narcissus tazetta*) at OO (olfactory overload) minus 20 days.*

* All narcissi are daffodils, and all daffodils are narcissi.

* Remember the movie *Enchanted April?* I'm sure anyone living through a frigid winter would be just as enchanted with the warmth of the Italian Riviera. Whether they're also enchanted with the scent of the Riviera's paper whites is a toss-up.

I chuckled quietly, then told her that I liked the scent. She stopped dead in her tracks and was speechless.

Ever since that day, she's never asked me for one iota of gardening advice. And, it wouldn't have mattered if I had a PhD in horticulture and three thousand books published. My information was forevermore tainted and banished from her household.

Figure 6.15 *Green leaves appear within 7-10 days.*

Figure 6.14 *Paper whites planted in professional mix. If forced in a sunny window at 60°-68°F, there's usually no need to support the leaves and flower stems.*

1. Fill about one-half of a bulb pot (the seriously squat pot from page 37) with pre-moistened, but not soaking wet, potting mix, and level the soil.
2. Put as many bulbs as possible onto the soil.
3. Fill the rest of the pot with pre-moistened potting mix to within 1" of the top.
4. Place the pot on a sunny windowsill in a room where the temperature doesn't exceed 70°F. Why? Because if paper whites are forced at temperatures above 70°F they get very tall and ungainly. At cooler forcing temperatures, the stems and leaves

Having warned you about the scent of paper whites, I should also say that these are absolutely the easiest bulbs to force in the universe. That's right, the universe. I know there must be other life somewhere out there, but the odds of there being anything that looks like a bulb that also forces into bloom easier than paper whites is equal, by my extremely unscientific estimate, to be 1 with a trillion trillion zeroes to 1.

In other words, they're practically effortless. If you're not convinced, I should tell you that I've occasionally seen a few paper white bulbs ready to bloom *before* I potted them. So, although you won't feel like a world-famous horticulturist by getting paper whites to bloom, you will be, unless you attack them with a blowtorch, virtually guaranteed to succeed.

To force paper whites, follow this simple procedure:

Figure 6.16 *Paper whites zoom into growth quickly. This is about 12-14 days after planting.*

stay at a manageable height.

5. Turn the pot one-quarter turn per day, which helps produce a pot with bulbs that bloom uniformly.* If you don't turn the pot, the bulbs closest to the sunny window will bloom well ahead of those on the other side.

6. As the bulbs grow, add five 12" bamboo or green florist sticks equidistant inside the pot, against the outer wall (see pages 232-235). Be sure to push them firmly into the soil. Attach green string or twine around the sticks, so the foliage and bloom stems will be supported.

7. When the bulbs start to bloom, you'll either love the aroma or want to take your paper whites to the local dump. If you love the aroma, keep the pot next to the window and continue turning the pot one-quarter turn each day.

8. When half the florets have opened, you can move the pot to a desired location in the house for everyone to enjoy. Just don't be surprised if your pot disappears within 24 hours…or less.

9. To prolong blossom life, put them in a cool place each evening. They can take temperatures down to 33°F.

---

* I'm sorry to be redundant, but I want to make sure that every reader sees this at least twice.

10. When your paper whites are finished blooming, throw them away whether you like the scent or not. The reasons? 1) Because paper whites are not winter hardy, they'll turn to mush in most temperate zone gardens, and 2) you can't force them two years in a row, since forcing this type of bulb weakens it.*

Figure 6.17 *Narcissus tazetta 'Israel' three weeks after planting. These bulbs were forced at 60°-64°F, so no external support was necessary. The scent is toned down compared to the paper white 'Ziva'.*

---

* But if you like paper whites and live in a location where the soil doesn't freeze any deeper than two inches, then go ahead and plant them outdoors after the foliage turns yellow (see Chapter 27).

Figure 6.18 *'Pickled Paper Whites' from the research of Dr. William Miller at Cornell University. His study shows that tipsy 'Ziva' paper whites won't tip over. You pick the desired height. From left to right, 0%, 2%, 4%, 6%, 8%, and 10% ethyl alcohol-treated paper whites. (See the web address listed below.)*

If these steps seem easy, it's because they are. A few words of warning, then a bit of advice:

You're going to hear a few gardeners tell you that you *must* force paper whites in pebbles. I certainly won't dispute that you *can* force them in pebbles. As I've already said, I've found paper whites practically in bloom before they're planted, so they're one of the least fussy bulbs on Earth. The problem with pebbles is that it's hard to use stakes with them, meaning you'll have leaves and flower stems flopping like flaccid flags* on windless days.

In the end, the growing medium you use is your choice. Almost anything will work, except hot coals.

But, speaking of "anything will work," Professor William Miller of Cornell University enlisted the aid of student Erin Finan to conduct experiments using diluted ethanol (as in booze) when she watered 'Ziva' paper whites. They found that it's   only detrimental effect was that the stems and leaves were one-third to one-half shorter, meaning there was no need for support of any kind.† I've yet to test this technique, but I applaud their creativity. And, for those of you who think Cornell is staid and stolid, have a look at www.hort.cornell.edu/miller/bulb/Pickling_your_Paperwhites.pdf (last accessed in 11/2007). In their article, they say, "As with humans, paper whites can also suffer alcohol overdoses! We suggest 6% as a normal and safe range."

Don't even try to tell me the Horticulture Department at Cornell University doesn't have a sense of humor!

Finally, my advice is that if you hate the odor of typical paper whites, don't give up. Bulb hybridizers have toned down their scent, so you might want to try the cultivars (i.e., **cult**ivated **vari**eties) 'Nazareth', 'Grand Primo' or 'Israel' (see figure 6.17). You'll probably find them in the catalogs or websites of at least one of the mail-order bulb companies listed on pages 242-243.

****

You could spend the rest of your bulb-forcing life growing only paper whites and amaryllis, but that would be like spending a week in Hawaii without leaving the hotel swimming pool.

There's simply so much more that's guaranteed to give you goose bumps and make you tingle.

The next group of bulbs isn't quite as foolproof as the adapt-to-my-house-or-die bulbs described in this chapter. And yet, they need minimal additional care, which for most of you will mean simply raising your window just a smidge.

So let's head to Chapter 7 where you'll expand your bulb-forcing palette to include every color in a Hawaiian rainbow.

Figure 6.19 *A handsome display of 'Ariel' paper whites grown by The Shipley School's horticulture teacher, Leila Peck. It's reputed to have a milder scent than most paper whites. I'll believe it when I grow it! I'll report on my results in future editions of this book.*

---

*Although "flags" may not be the best noun to use in this case.
† This, by itself, is quite surprising since inebriation in humans almost always results in a need for support.

7

REALLY COOL BULBS

The world is full of paradoxes.

Some are of human origin and "most ingenious," as pointed out by Gilbert and Sullivan in their operetta *The Pirates of Penzance*.*

But there's also a botanical paradox that I find intriguing, namely, the tremendous range of plants that thrive at temperatures close to freezing, but die when they reach freezing. This is a bit like a snake-lover waltzing with a thirty-two-foot anaconda: so sinuous, so seductive, so deadly.

Yet, such plants exist. They rejoice at temperatures from 33°-60°F, but are in critical, grave, or in-the-grave condition below thirty-two degrees.

A host of them reside along the Mediterranean Coast, as well as in southern Africa, New Zealand, and other temperate zones. And, of course, some of them are bulbs.

I've already told you about one such bulb: Mediterranean-derived paper white narcissi.

But, there are three other cool-temperature-loving bulbs you should try forcing. One is worth two tries, meaning, if you fail the first time, please try again. If you succeed, I can promise a lifelong love affair with...

Freesias

This corm is one of my favorite "cool" bulbs. It probably would be yours as well, if not for misleading information

Figure 7.1 *Backlit* Freesia *'Priscilla'. This is my favorite cultivar. Just imagine a pot with 125 of these blossoms, add a heavenly scent, and you'll be seduced into growing them.*

Figure 7.2 *(left) Unlike humans, the closer you get to* Ranunculus *flowers, the more beautiful they are.*

* The paradox in *The Pirates of Penzance* involves someone apprenticed to pirates until he reaches his twenty-first birthday. However, he was born on February 29th, meaning he wouldn't leave the pirates until they were ready to – as nineteenth-century English sailors would say – "commit his body to the deep, to be turned into corruption."

Figure 7.3 *Thirty-seven* Freesia *corms in a 12" pot. Each bulb produces up to a dozen flowers. It's a floral extravaganza!*

that's taken as gospel. Try searching the Internet or books that give instructions for growing freesias, and you'll probably learn that nighttime temperatures for this bulb *must* be 45°-50°F.

This information must have been originally circulated by someone bent on eliminating freesias from your list of bulbs to force.

Although this bulb comes from southern Africa and cavorts at 55°-60°F, it *can* grow at temperatures inside your home. So, forget the above temperature range, which

Figure 7.4 Freesia *foliage twenty-two days after bulb planting.*

Figure 7.5 *Oh, joy of joys! After three weeks there's nothing but foliage (see figure 7.4). Then, after another two weeks, the first bloom stem emerges.*

Figure 7.6 *Freesias or snakes? These are the most light-sensitive flower stems in my bulbous universe. They'll move as much as 12" in one day...meaning you'll temporarily change hobbies, from gardener to snake charmer.*

would make your teeth chatter and prompt your non-gardening family members to lace your lunch with strychnine.

I've found that if you can make sure growing temperatures stay below sixty-five in a sunny or artificially-lighted room or basement, you'll be in for a treat. Here, we have a plant with delightful sword-shaped, dark-green foliage – like diminutive gladioli leaves – gorgeous tube-shaped flowers, and a spicy aroma.

After temperature control, the next most important ingredient is an ingredient to exclude.

I realize that's about as clear as coal dust, so let me explain. You see, of all the plants I've ever grown, freesias are the most sensitive to fluoride. Yes, the chemical in your water that makes your teeth stronger is quite toxic to freesias. Fortunately, there are ways to exclude it, which I discuss in Chapter 24, pages 207-209.

The next factor that can make forcing flop is, well, floppiness. By that, I mean flopping flower stems. I could tell you which chemicals some growers use to make flower stems shorter and more erect,* but since I have

Figure 7.7 Freesia *'Priscilla' is just getting started. At 60°-65°F, it will blossom for at least three weeks.*

zero experience with these agents, I'll tell you what you can do without chemicals to get the same results.[†]

The most important variables for short, strong flower stems are temperature and light. If you can grow freesias at temperatures as low as 55°F in sunlight, the entire plant will be more compact. Warm temperatures and

---

* So, in one way, these chemicals work like a botanical Viagra, in another way, like ice water.
† For seriously-smitten bulb forcers who are curious about these chemicals, see *Holland Bulb Forcer's Guide* in the Bibliography.

---

weaker light levels have the opposite effect.

If you can't provide these cool conditions – usually because the rest of your family puts their comfort over the comfort of your freesias – use star-staking approximately 12" above the soil (see pages 232-235). Your other choice is to paint chicken wire green and secure it to bamboo sticks approximately 12" high, and then let your freesias grow through it. I've used chicken wire with 2" holes and it worked perfectly.

It seems like you have to wait forever before the first bloom stems make their appearance. After 7-8 weeks at 60-65°F, they will peak through a seam in the leaves and grow quickly (see figure 7.5).

In fact, once every bloom stem has emerged and grown twelve inches, you'll find that you're no longer growing plants, but slithering snakes.

As with other bulbs, I turn my potted freesias one-quarter turn per day for uniform growth. But, what happens is that each phototropic* bloom stem tilts and bends like a cobra swaying to the rhythmic beats of a snake charmer (see figure 7.6). You'll still get blossoms, but unless you do star staking or have the stems go through some other support system, what you'll get will have all the uniformity of a large plate of spaghetti.

Ranunculus

These tuberous roots have flowers that are the most doubled of any bulb I've grown. They grow as semi-double flowers, or are available as hybrids that have layer…upon layer…upon layer of flower petals. Picture the most doubled rose in the universe and you'll get the picture. (But if you don't, see the pictures in figures 7.11 and 7.13.)

I must warn you that these bulbs are just a bit finicky, but worth the trouble.

Before you plant your first *Ranunculus* bulbs, you should know that they hate warmth so much that they'll barely sprout at temperatures above 70°F degrees. These bulbs like temperatures at 45-55°F at night and only a bit warmer during the day. **But those are the *ideal* conditions, not the *mandatory* conditions, so don't give up!**

---

* Botanically speaking, "phototropism" means bending and/or growing towards light.

This bulb is different from most of the others I describe in this book. You can stuff a pot, cheek to jowl, with daffodils, tulips, grape hyacinths, as well as many other types of bulbs and achieve eye-popping results. But, if you put ten *Ranunculus* tuberous-root clumps in a large pot, you'll end up with ten plants at different stages of growth: some in bloom, some just coming to life, and some with spindly growth because they're being shaded by their nearest neighbor. This is hardly something you or your camera will appreciate. So, I find it best to grow *Ranunculus* one clump per container (see figure 7.12).

Simply plant these tuberous roots one inch deep in a 4"-8" pot, and grow them (ideally) at 55°-65°F during

Figure 7.8 Ranunculus *tuberous roots. This clump is about 2" across. Plant it about 1" below the surface of your potting mix.*

the day and 45°-60°F at night. I know your family would throw you out of an upper-story window and change the door locks if you tried to set your house thermostat at these temperatures. So, as I've mentioned before, use a vacant, unheated room or basement as a growing area.

Start by planting a tuberous-root clump (see figure 7.8) one inch deep in moist potting mix. Within 7-14 days you'll see shoots emerging, and within three weeks you'll usually get the amount of leaf growth shown in figure 7.9. From then on, these plants grow quickly. Within another 2-3 weeks, you can expect plants as large as the one in figure 7.10. And, soon after that, buds will appear, then open to reveal the most gloriously-doubled flowers you've ever seen.

It's hard to believe, but the stems are so strong, that sup-

port isn't needed – even for tall plants.

When you purchase *Ranunculus* bulbs, they'll usually be sold by cultivar "series." For example, *Ranunculus* 'Sunset' (orange shades) produced the blossom and plant shown in figures 7.11 and 3.11. As you can tell, these plants usually get at least 12" tall.

Figure 7.9 *At 21 days, three stems have developed and are growing rapidly.*

Figure 7.10 *A 4" pot with* Ranunculus *flower buds, 5-6 weeks after planting.*

Figure 7.11 Ranunculus *blossoms are every bit as gorgeous as heirloom roses. This is a 'Sunset' hybrid.*

But, not all *Ranunculus* are as lanky. In fact, of all *Ranunculus* hybrids, the Bloomingdale series is the most beautiful and rewarding. These are perfectly proportioned plants with flowers in a wide range of colors, each with the most petals imaginable (see figure 7.13).

If you have trouble finding a source of Bloomingdale bulbs (as I have), all is not lost, since seeds are readily available. Admittedly, growing Bloomingdale hybrids from seed is mainly for the seriously-smitten bulb forcer, since it takes five months to go from seed to a flowering plant.* But these plants are well worth the wait.

My seed source is Chiltern Seeds, in Great Britain, (www.chilternseeds.com [last

Figure 7.12 *This hanging* Ranunculus *'Bloomingdale' is in an 8" pot with an 18" spread of blossoms – all from one tuberous root clump. Unlike other* Ranunculus, *this cultivar produces perfectly-proportioned plants.*

Figure 7.13 *Have a spare week or month? It might take you that long to count every petal of this* Ranunculus *'Bloomingdale' flower. This was grown in a 6" pot that produced ten blossoms.*

---

* In fact, growing potted *Ranunculus* from seed is the preferred method used by professionals who grow massive numbers of these plants.

accessed on 7/3/2011]), but you can use the Internet to find other companies that sell them.

You should be able to save *Ranunculus* roots for the following fall and winter. Simply let the pot become bone dry in late spring. I usually keep these pots outdoors under a shaded, rain-free location. I barely moisten the soil once a month to keep the roots from shriveling to the point of impossible resuscitation. Although summer temperatures outside my home in southern New Jersey can get as high as 100°F, my *Ranunculus* bulbs survive – as should yours.

At the first sign of cooler fall weather, carefully remove the clump from last-year's pots and start the process again.

Anemone coronaria

I quite simply adore this plant.

Everything above ground is lovely: it has self-arranging, parsley-like serrated foliage and blooms that are sheer elegance – I'm talking Princess Diana/Dionne Warwick*/Jacqueline Kennedy elegance.

Of course, that's what you get above ground.

What you put *into* the ground is not only not elegant, it's often baffling. Usually the bulb's bowl-like appendages go bowl-side up (as in figure 7.14). But more often than not, this tuber doesn't have anything resembling a bowl anywhere at anytime in any bag of bulbs. So, as I mentioned in Chapter 3 (see pages 27-28), if you have any doubt whatever about up from down, just plant this amorphous, bewildering bulb sideways. It will grow just fine and blossom.

But before you run to your bulb catalogs and order *Anemone coronaria*, **do yourself a favor and buy precooled bulbs.** Although anemones don't require low temperatures to break dormancy and begin flower-stem extension (see Chapters 9 through 11), cold treatment "pre-sprouts" these bulbs, which means they're ready to begin vegetative growth immediately after planting.

---

* Alas, I'm showing my age. For those born after 1975, Dionne Warwick was simply the best singer of popular songs in the 1960s and 1970s. She looked elegant and sang elegantly. Even the youngest among you have probably heard her timeless renditions of such Burt Bacharach songs as, "Do You Know the Way to San Jose," "I Say a Little Prayer (for You)," "That's What Friends Are For," and "(They Long to Be) Close to You."

Figure 7.14 *Which side of the* Anemone *bulb goes up? The up-turned bowls (as they are here) are on top. If you have any doubt, plant this tuber sideways.*

Figure 7.15 *When* Anemone coronaria *begins its life above ground, it's hardly gorgeous. To my eyes, it looks more like the hideous creature in "The Alien," as it emerges from an astronaut's abdomen. But then my far-sighted eyes have been sending my brain hallucinatory close-up images for over a decade.*

Figure 7.16 *(right) There's nothing bashful about* Anemone coronaria *'Governor'. The end result justifies all the effort along the way.*

Figure 7.17 *(over, left) I've never seen a more gorgeous bulbous-bud than* Anemone *'Mr. Fokker'. And, the blossom (**Figure 7.18**, over right) is simply divine.*

Figure 7.20 Anemone *foliage is bright green and looks like beautifully-serrated* Chrysanthemum *leaves.*

Figure 7.19 Anemone *'The Admiral' (left) is an excellent choice if you're new to forcing anemones. It blooms quickly — as much as a month before 'Mr. Fokker'.*

Non-treated bulbs will, according to *Holland Bulb Forcer's Guide*, take 3-4 months to produce any flowers. I haven't tested that time period, but I *can* tell you that pre-cooled bulbs take only two months.

Do your best to grow anemones at 55°-65°F. At warmer temperatures they will all but collapse and never fully recover.

Aside from the above commandments, I do have another tiny suggestion: ***do not grow these bulbs in water-saturated, air-deprived potting soil — especially soil mixes advertised as highly water-retentive.***

Why? Because these are the rottingest bulbs I've ever put in a flower pot. No contest. No discussion. No roots. No flowers. Lots of ***GOOOO***.

Have a gander at figure 7.22. This is what happens when anemones are grown with lots of water and virtually no air. I wish I could have afforded to include a scratch-and-sniff square next to the photo. Then you would have had the opportunity for an overwhelming, olfactory moment. Rotted anemone bulbs have a smell that can only be described as eau de maggot food.

Is there a foolproof way to get these bulbs off to a healthy, stenchless start? There is indeed: it's called moistened perlite...plain, old perlite. Keep it moist, check on the bulbs every few days, and eventually you'll see roots and shoots (see figure 7.23). When they emerge, plant the tuber 1" deep in a professional potting mix that's not soaking wet. Barely moist is better.

Figure 7.21 *(right)* Anemone coronaria *'Mount Everest' is the botanical version of a princess's wedding dress. Here, the stamens waltz adoringly above the pistil.*

60

In fact, one year I left a few tubers in pure perlite, watered with soluble fertilizer, and was rewarded with green leaves and colorful blossoms. That's how much these bulbs *love* air.

If you don't want to go through the above two-step process, plant the tubers in a soilless potting mix that's about half perlite. Most mixes don't have that much perlite, so I suggest that you purchase bagged perlite and add it to your favorite growing media. And, again, barely moisten the mix until you see shoots emerge.

I've found it's only during the early stages that these bulbs are most susceptible to rot. Once *Anemone* shoots are 2" tall, you can water these plants the same as other bulbs.

And, one more warning for those of you who plan to grow these plants on a windowsill or in a greenhouse: *Anemone coronaria roots are more susceptible to death by heat than any bulb I've ever forced.* One day you'll have white-tipped roots blithely moving through your potting mix, and the next day they'll be broiled brown (see figures 6.3 and 6.4 on pages 38-39). My advice: pots of clay save the day, because hot soil is an enemy of *Anemone*.

If you must use plastic pots, line the outside with alu-

Figure 7.23 *Using perlite is an ideal, foolproof way to start* Anemone *tubers. Note the roots and shoots. Once roots are formed, you can transplant the tubers 1" below the surface of a high-air-content potting mix.*

minum foil to reflect the sun's rays and keep the soil cool.

By the time anemones are off and running, they display the most delightful foliage imaginable (see figure 7.20). So, you get a treat for the eyes even before a single flower appears.

The flower buds are yet another surprise (see figure 7.17). They have a hint of drama, since they show you the saturated color you'll soon get when the bud opens.

And, the flowers, as you can tell from this chapter's photos, are sheer ambrosia. So, don't let this be your only glimpse of *Anemone coronaria*. Grow the genuine article and be as amazed as I am every year.

****

While bulbs like *Anemone, Ranunculus,* and *Freesia* can brighten your home during the worst winter days, they aren't the typical bulbs that temperate-zone gardeners associate with spring. For most of us, our mind's eye pictures drifts of tulips, daffodils, hyacinths, and their vernal companions.

And, it's these bulbs that we'll learn about next, starting with a special visit to an acre-sized greenhouse filled with nothing but forced bulbs.

Figure 7.22 *The most common problem with anemones is lack of air around the tuber. In water-saturated, air-deprived soil, it will rot and emit a putrid odor.*

8

A TRIP TO HOLLAND (FLORAL)

If you want to learn how to do something, it's a good idea to consult those who do it for a living. I can teach you how to force bulbs to dazzle your visitors, win blue ribbons, or produce a truckload of flowers for *Better Homes and Gardens* articles. But the pressure on me is nothing compared to what the pros have to do. After all, for them, no flowers = no income = no food on the table.

Now *that's* pressure.

So, let's take a trip to "Holland," specifically, Holland Floral* in New Jersey. It's where an acre of potted bulbs

Figure 8.1 *Holland Floral – from the outside, you'd never know that more than a million bulbs were forced to the just-before-blooming stage each year.*

Figure 8.2 *Bulbs were delivered in August and stored at 38°F.*

---

* Since my visit, Holland Floral, a successful enterprise, was sold to another company and its name has changed.

Figure 8.3 *It doesn't build a car, but this machine produces pots that contain growing mix, then sends them along an assembly line for the next step.*

was forced to the "just-before-blooming" stage each winter before being sent to supermarkets.

I first visited this company one August when they received more than one million bulbs from Holland. The bulbs were stored at 34°F and at the proper humidity (figure 8.2). In addition, there were filters (called "scrubbers") that absorb ethylene gas – a chemical that can destroy the flower buds inside bulbs, which wouldn't exactly help their profit margin. During my summertime visit, a horticulturist unveiled a computerized potting machine (figure 8.3). I was impressed, but didn't truly appreciate its usefulness until I came back in early

Figure 8.4 *(left) The soil mix used at Holland Floral had a high concentration of perlite, ensuring high air content.*

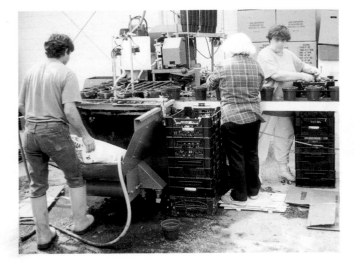

Figure 8.5 *Moist soil is fed in one end (note the hose next to the hopper), pots come down from the top, and...*

Figure 8.7 *...assembly-line bulb planters, who put six tulip bulbs in every 6" pot. Then...*

October, when I saw a bulb-potting assembly line in action.

Figures 8.5 through 8.8 show the entire warp-speed process. Potting mix, a combination of moistened sphagnum peat moss and abundant perlite (figure 8.4), was fed into one end (figure 8.5), pots were positioned at the top, and soil filled each pot at a predetermined depth. In addition, the depth of the planting hole at the top of the pot was pre-set.

The pots scurried out of the machine onto an assembly line (figure 8.6). Then staff worked as fast as possible to plant *fifteen hundred* pots per day (figure 8.7).

Trust me: if I worked on that assembly line, I would hate bulbs within thirty minutes, and swear off bulb forcing forever. It was exactly like Lucille Ball (in the TV show *I Love Lucy*) at the chocolate factory. Put me on the

"line" and bulbs would be in my pockets, in my shirt and pants, and in my mouth.

After bulb planting, pots were put in trays and given a final watering (figure 8.8). Then they were moved to a twenty-foot-tall refrigeration room set at 48°F (figure 8.9). In these conditions, two essential things happen: the bulbs root quickly and eventually begin flower-stem extension – the aforementioned **vernalization** process (see Chapter 3, pages 31-32).

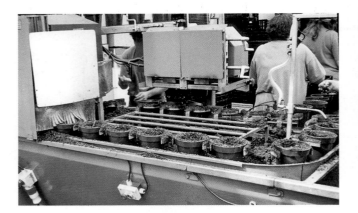

Figure 8.6 *...move along a conveyer belt to...*

Figure 8.8 *...more soil is added to the top of each pot, the pots are placed into trays, then they get one more dose of water.*

CHAPTER EIGHT

Figure 8.9 *Next, it's time for storage in a huge, twenty-foot-tall refrigeration room set at 48°F.*

Information about the contents of each tray and when the bulbs were planted was kept in a computer (figure 8.10). In addition, the computer stored information about each supermarket's order and expected date of arrival.

Once the bulbs were rooted and ready for forcing, the chief horticulturist decided when each tray should be removed, so that pots could be delivered to their final destination at the proper stage.

Figure 8.11 shows trays after they've been removed from the refrigeration room and put on pallets. Then fork lifts placed the pallets on platforms within the 60°-64°F greenhouse.

Figure 8.10 *The computer stores information about which bulbs are planted in each tray, the date the tray went into the refrigeration room, and when it should be removed.*

Figure 8.11 *After many weeks in the refrigeration room, trays of potted bulbs are put on pallets.*

In the foreground of figure 8.12, there are pots that were taken out that day. There were also pots that had been in the greenhouse at least 1-2 weeks (back right) and three or more weeks (back and left).

Usually Holland Floral sent pots to each supermarket a few days before the buds showed color. They also sent

Figure 8.12 *Then the pallets are placed in the greenhouse. The deeper green the foliage, the longer the bulbs have been out of the refrigeration room.*

directions, so the retail staff would know how to get the maximum number of days for sale.

Not surprisingly, I had to search the entire greenhouse to find the only flower bud showing color (see figure 8.13).

The most important information you can glean from my visit to Holland Floral is –

1. If you're not going to pot bulbs shortly after delivery, keep them in a cool, dry place where there's no ethylene gas. In your household, this means keeping them away from fruit or vegetables, because they emit the flower-bud-destroying gas.

Figure 8.13 *Bulb forcing is nature writ small: no bud opens before its time. These pots are usually shipped just before flower buds show any color. This was the only colorful blossom in the entire one-acre greenhouse.*

2. Use a potting mix with high air content. At Holland Floral, they did this by using large quantities of perlite in their mix.

3. If you want to produce a display for a given day, keep records of how long it takes you to force each type of bulb into bloom.

4. Allow sufficient time for rooting and flower-stem extension. This varies from eight weeks for the earliest bulbs (e.g., *Crocus* and *Iris*) to thirteen weeks for late tulips and daffodils.

5. To have a continuous display, don't force all your pots at the same time. If you force a small number of pots per week, you'll have flowers on your windowsill from January through March.

6. Lighten up! You're not forcing bulbs for a living. When you have a few failures – and everyone has them – it's not a life-altering calamity. If you're a gardener, some of your plants will die. So use it as an opportunity to learn what might have gone wrong.

****

Now that you've learned how the professionals force bulbs, it's time you got your hands on spring-blooming bulbs and learned how you can force them in your home.

That's the subject of Chapter 9, so let's head there next.

9
PLAYING IT ~~COOL~~ COLD

Snow and ice are everywhere, and you're about to cross over to your psychotic *Are-You-Looking-at-Me?!* Dark Side. You scan the landscape, and the bones of your garden, meaning the evergreen and deciduous trees and shrubs, are about as inviting as leftover bones after a barbecue.

Where are the mood-altering daffodils, crocuses, tulips, hyacinths, lilies, and the other bulbs of spring?

Well, with a bit of fall planning, you can avoid this descent into the netherworld of winter despair. Imagine looking at your windows and seeing something besides frozen earth or white snow. Instead, picture windowsills filled with red tulips, pink daffodils, purple crocuses, and the rest of their springtime bedmates.

No Prozac needed, just bring on the bulbs.

Once again, I must say that you *are* capable of doing this. These bulbs are exactly like paper whites, but need just one more step: a fall and early winter chill.

Figure 9.2 *Gardener's alert! It's time for mood-altering forced bulbs.*

> **WARNING: If you equate reading about intra-bulb flower formation with torture on a rack, please go directly to "Step 1: Potting Bulbs," on page 68.**

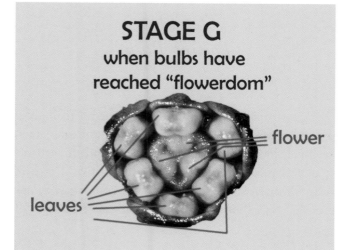

Figure 9.1 *Tulips at "Stage G," when flower buds are initiated. For bulb companies, this typically occurs when bulbs are out of the ground, before they're shipped. Photo courtesy of Applied Plant Research (PPO) Lisse, The Netherlands. (Magnification is approximately 10X.)*

Step Zero: When Bulbs Make Flowers

Now that I've eliminated 99% of my readers, let's stagger ahead.

I'm sure when you first picked up this book you thought you'd learn how *you* can make flowers.

But, as you discovered on page 25, you were wrong, because with almost all spring-blooming bulbs – the ones that need cold conditions to form roots and begin flower-stem extension – the flower is already in the bulb when you get your hands on them in late summer or early fall.*

But, here's what's incredibly, amazingly, even earth-shatteringly unbelievable: these bulbs never go dormant. (Well, that's not quite true. If you kill them, they'll go irreversibly dormant.)

---

* An exception is the lily, which forms buds after the bulb has been planted in the fall.

When bulb growers in the northern hemisphere unearth these botanical beauties in early- to mid-July, they have not formed flowers yet.* But by the time you get them, they *have*. You don't need an IQ over 130 to know what happens: these bulbs initiate flowers when they're out of the ground, sitting around, seemingly doing nothing. Yet, they're doing everything you want them to do: they form immature flowers, so that when you plant them, ***you have to work very hard to be a bulb-forcing failure.***

The formation of an intra-bulb flower is called stage G (see figure 9.1). The "G" may not stand for a botanical "G spot," but, fittingly, it *does* stand for the **gynoecium** (pronounced jeh-**nee**-see-um), which is the formative, immature female parts of a flower. When bulbs reach stage G, they're basically telling growers, "I'm 'on the mark,' now you're responsible for 'get set,' and 'go.'"

The six outer segments in figure 9.1 are leaves, and the Y-shaped, uterus-like object in the middle is the beginnings of a flower.

These tissues can be seen with a 10X lens in tulip bulbs, and are located just above the basal plate (see figure 3.3, page 25). By the time you get tulip bulbs in the fall, it's probably been many weeks since your bulbs reached stage G, meaning the flower buds have matured.†

Nearly all spring-blooming bulbs must reach stage G before they're potted. So, it's no surprise that bulbs forced before they've reached stage G produce lovely leaves and wonderful flower stems without flowers. In the bulb-growing world, this is called "blindness." (See also "bud blast" on page 212.)

Some professional bulb growers – meaning the people who pot upwards of a million bulbs a year – actually per-

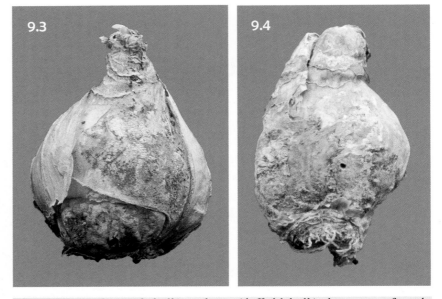

Figures 9.3 *(hyacinth bulb) and* **9.4** *(daffodil bulb) show severe fungal infection. Inspect your bulbs as soon as they arrive. If this much of their surface is diseased, throw them away immediately. If more than 10% of your bulbs have to be tossed, ask for a refund.*

form surgery to be certain their bulbs are at stage G. If their dissected samples are still immature (i.e., "G-less"), the rest of their batch-mates stay in refrigeration rooms at cold temperatures. Once they're certain their bulbs have finished the arduous road to "G," growers can begin a temperature regime to produce blooming bulbs as early as Christmas.*

Step One: Potting Bulbs

I get virtually all my bulbs from reputable mail order sources or specialty nurseries, since they provide larger, healthier, and a wider selection of bulbs than are available at typical garden centers.† When they arrive, I inspect them for disease. The three most common disease symptoms are either softness in the round, outer portions of

---

* Daffodils reach Stage G even sooner. They form internal flowers when they're still in the ground.

† Stage G occurs on different dates in different bulbs (e.g., tulips and daffodils) and different cultivars of the same type of bulb (e.g., *Tulipa* 'Angelique' and *T.* 'Apricot Beauty'). It even varies with the *same* cultivar from year to year because of differences in bulb physiology, soil fertility and composition, local weather, and other variables.

---

* For more on this scintillating and titillating topic, see *Holland Bulb Forcer's Guide*. (The citation is in the Bibliography.)

† Alas, most garden centers are no longer garden centers, but season centers…as in Halloween centers, Christmas centers, fancy glazed pottery centers, gas-grill centers, patio table centers, trinket centers, rock salt/ice melt centers, and, on occasion, garden centers.

the bulb, rot on the bottom (basal end) of the bulb, or fungus on more than one-third of the surface. Never plant these bulbs, since they can spread disease. Some bulb forcers dip their healthy bulbs in fungicide before planting them, but I never have. I've found that if I'm careful to exclude any "Typhoid Mary" bulbs at the beginning, I won't have problems later (see figures 9.3 and 9.4).

As mentioned before, whenever I grow a plant, I try to reproduce the same conditions that it encounters in nature, where it successfully competes against other plants for soil and light. And, as you now know, these spring-blooming bulbs bask in stony, granular soil where air content is high.

To simulate these conditions I do two things:

First, I almost always use clay containers. This assures that excess water within the pot is absorbed by the clay and conducted outside. Clay pots also keep roots from getting too hot (see page 38). And, they keep air content high and reduce the possibility of fungal disease.

Second, I use Fafard 1-PV potting mix (see figure 2.1, page 21). It has moderate water retention as well as high air content – the perfect combination for spring-blooming bulbs.* You usually can obtain it or a similar sphagnum peat moss-perlite mix at your garden center.

Use a pot that you've cleaned thoroughly (see sidebar, page 37). If you're using a new clay pot, let is soak in water for ten minutes before proceeding. This prevents the pot from absorbing the moisture in your potting mix during and immediately after bulb planting.

Cover the bottom drainage hole with a piece of broken clay pot, which helps keep roots inside your container. If you've been gardening for more than ten minutes, you'll have a ready supply of broken crocking.

Put pre-moistened (not saturated) potting mix approximately three-quarters of the way up for minor bulbs. For larger bulbs, like tulips or daffodils, make it two-thirds. The pot is obviously wider as you get closer to the top. And, the further up you go, the more bulbs you'll get into the pot – which is essential if you want an instant-envy-from-visitors pot.

Pay attention to the "three-quarters" and "two-thirds" mentioned, above. You'll create a mess if you plant bulbs as high as the rim, since vigorous roots can force bulbs

---

* But, as mentioned in Chapter 3, if you have your own soil recipe that works well, keep using it!

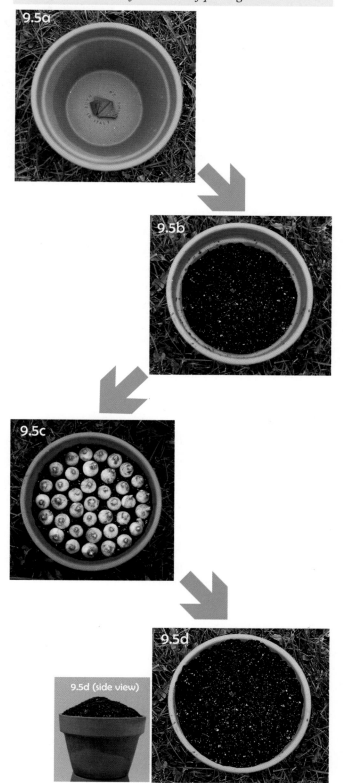

Figures 9.5a-d *Bulb-planting sequence. 9.5a: Cover the bottom hole of a clay pot with crocking. 9.5b: Fill the pot two-thirds with growing mix. 9.5c: Plant as many bulbs as possible in a single layer. YES, they can touch. 9.5d: Cover with a firm dome of potting mix.*

9.5a

9.5b

9.5c

9.5d

9.5d (side view)

out of the pot. This makes the forcing process difficult and the flowering stage so hideous that it looks like a horticultural monstrosity that belongs in a Ripley's Believe It or Not Museum.

Level the soil and begin planting bulbs in the pot. Pack your bulbs (obviously, – I hope! – bottom side down, top side up) as tightly as you like.

Some bulb books and magazine articles will tell you not to let potted bulbs touch one another.* Let me tell you what will happen if you disobey them: . Please note that there's no content between the colon and period…as in nothing…as in, if your bulbs touch, neither you nor your bulbs will be hit by lightning or afflicted with boils or blight. Instead, you'll have more flowers per pot, and isn't that why you bought or were given this book?

Remember: *more bulbs=more flowers=winter jubilation.*

After bulb planting, cover them with a dome of potting mix (see figure 9.5d, side view). Then, to keep bulbs from pushing themselves above the rim, firm the soil with your hand, pressing down with the same force you might use to spread pizza dough.† How vigorous is the rooting process? Take a look at figures 9.6a-9.6b to see what can happen within four weeks of bulb planting.

Finally, use a permanent marker to write the name of the bulb and the date on a plastic label, then insert half the label into potting mix next to the side of the pot (see Chapter 10, figure 10.1).

Figure 9.6a *Just four weeks after planting crocuses in an 8" pot…*

Figure 9.6b *…there's vigorous root growth. In three more weeks the entire soil ball will be covered with roots. (Photos by Bernard Wolk)*

---

* And, if they touch the side of the pot, they won't shrivel and dry up like a water-doused Wicked Witch of the West.

† In other words, neither use the amount of energy a woman might use to strike a man who's just asked her if she's pregnant, when she isn't, nor the energy the man would use to flee from his non-pregnant assailant.

In Pursuit of Excellence and Envy

Whether your holy grail is a blue ribbon or simply a perfect, evanescent pot of blooming bulbs for your home, you should know that the three most important things in your quest are flowers, flowers, and flowers. That may be simplistic, but not by much. If you ever get a chance to hear flower show judges "do their thing," you'll learn that there's nothing that wows them quite as much as a pot bursting with flowers. So, since flowers come from bulbs, all you have to do is get more bulbs into the pot. But how can you find more space? You already have the bulbs planted cheek-to-jowl. What's a grower to do?

The simple answer is to put a second layer of bulbs on top of the first.

It works like this (see figures 9.7-9.10):

1. Plant the first layer of bulbs a bit deeper than described in Step One – about halfway down an azalea pot (see figure 9.8).
2. Cover the first layer with potting mix, but so that you can still see the tops of the underlying bulbs.
3. Carefully plant the second layer of bulbs without blocking the shoots of the underlying bulbs (i.e., leave room for foliage and flower shoots to fit between upper-layer bulbs). The upper layer should be planted below the top of the pot. From here on, follow the same steps described above for single-layered pots (see Step One, page 68).

Double layering works for almost all the minor bulbs discussed in Chapter 14. It also works well for daffodils and some tulips (see Chapters 16 and 17, respectively.)

Figure 9.12 especially illustrates the uniform height of

Figure 9.7 *The results you can expect with a **single** layer of 'Tete-a-Tete' daffodils. Compare with figure 9.11.*

Figure 9.8 *To double layer bulbs (in this case, Scilla mischtschenkoana), begin the first layer deeper – about 1/2 to 1/3 of the way below the top, depending on the size of the bulb. Pack them as close as possible, but leave enough space for second-layer bulbs to fit between the tops of the bottom-layer bulbs.*

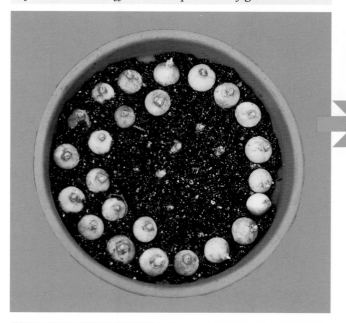

Figure 9.9 *Add potting mix, but make sure you can still see the tops of the underlying bulbs.*

Figure 9.10 *Finish adding as many bulbs as possible to the top layer, but don't block the tops of any underlying bulbs. Finally, add a dome of soil and press firmly. I strongly suggest not adding a third layer, which would ultimately sit well above your container's rim after chilling.*

Figure 9.11 *The results that can be achieved with double-layered bulbs. My wife Arlene won a rosette and praise from the judges for her pot of 'Tete-a-Tete' daffodils at the Philadelphia Flower Show.*

double-layered daffodils after they're chilled (see "Step Two," below). Can you see that the upper- and lower-level shoots are at almost the same height? This uniformity is what makes it possible to have a pot of 'Tete-a-Tete' daffodils as stunning as the one shown in figure 9.11.

I just have one warning about double layering: if you use a high-perlite mix like Sunshine #4, the upper-layer bulbs might be forced almost completely out of the pot. In fact, when I used Sunshine #4 for a pot of double-layered 'Tete-a-Tete' daffodils, one top-layer bulb was completely turned upside down! So, for double layering use a mix that's a bit heavier (i.e., one with less perlite). I suggest Fafard 1-PV.

Step Two:

*Cold Bulbs, Cold Roots, Cold Soil "Oh, Wouldn't It Be Loverly?"**

Although you'll sometimes see the leaves of spring-blooming bulbs emerge in the fall,[†] you'll never see blossoms. If you remember from page 32, there are two reasons: First, these types of bulbs need cold soil conditions to produce a good network of roots. And second, this cold period – also called **vernalization** – is needed for bulbs to begin flower stem-extension. (See Chapter 10 for easy vernalization techniques.)

So, what happens if they don't get the required number of weeks of cold temperatures? A lot of disappointment, that's what happens. Flowers will either not emerge from bulbs, or they'll be so close to the soil surface that they'll look like botanical periscopes (see figure 9.13). Most of you have already seen this at your supermarket.

---

* Disgracefully adapted from the show, *My Fair Lady*, whose ingénue, Eliza Doolittle, sings, "Warm face, warm hands, warm feet – oh, wouldn't it be loverly."
† This is especially true for *Muscari* (grape hyacinths), which have functional roots all year.

Some of the pots have tulips, daffodils, or hyacinths that bloom too close to the soil. Can you guess what the problem is? Now you know: the growers gave these bulbs too short a cold period. And, remember, by "cold period" I mean how long potted bulbs are kept at temperatures of 40°-50°F, with 48°F being ideal.*

I've found that many of the early-blooming minor bulbs, like *Crocus*, *Iris reticulata*, and *Scilla* (see Chapter 14, "Forcing the Major Minors") can bloom with as little as eight weeks at these temperatures. But larger, later-blooming bulbs need more vernalization, usually at least eleven weeks, but 13 weeks or more for very late tulips (like 'Angelique') and daffodils (like 'Actaea'). Of course, the longer spring-blooming bulbs are exposed to these temperatures, the more root growth they'll have, and the better the display will be. More than any other variable in bulb forcing, root growth is the most important. It's essential if you want a uniform pot of blossoms. As long as you pot bulbs in October or early November, you'll provide a long enough cold period to have an exuberant winter display.†‡

Figure 9.12 *After the chilling process, daffodil shoots from the upper and lower layers are at a uniform height, making it possible to produce the kind of display shown in figures 9.11, 16.6, and 16.15.*

Figure 9.13 *(left) Short-stemmed hyacinths due to improper chilling.*

I don't pretend to believe that you won't read other books on bulb forcing and compare their information with

* I've read and confirmed that hyacinths will form roots and have normal-sized stems and blooms at warmer rooting temperatures – as warm as 55°F.

† The best timetable depends on the USDA Zone in which you garden. (See www.usna.usda.gov/Hardzone/ushzmap.html, last accessed 6/21/2011.) For Zones 6a and lower (i.e. colder), plant by mid-October. Of course, this suggestion has its limitations: I'm excluding arctic gardeners whose height of March euphoria occurs not when wildflowers finally emerge, but when the *sun* finally emerges.

‡ For hardiness zones outside the U.S.A., see www.pacificbulbsociety.org/pbswiki/index.php/HardinessZoneMaps (last accessed 6/21/2011).

"Okay...let's make it
Brandywine tomatoes on the left cheek
and Angelique tulips on the right!"

mine. In fact, I encourage you to do so. That's why I listed some excellent books in the Bibliography. But, there are also some books on the subject that give ridiculously long, *mandatory* time periods for rooting. In many cases, it's more than a month longer than I've found necessary.

I think one of two things is taking place:

1. The author read or heard about these time periods and followed the directions explicitly, and (of course) obtained good results. Or-
2. The author found the information in another book on bulbs, paraphrased it, and published the information as gospel.

In the end, you can choose to use my time periods or theirs. If you chill your pots an extra month, you'll still produce pots of blooming bulbs. And, if you keep them at cold temps even longer, you'll eventually reach the point where your potted bulbs will bloom *the same time* as bulbs planted in your outdoor garden.

And, that's fine.

In fact, rooting potted bulbs for at least sixteen weeks

will give you the chance of placing your blooming pots on the soil, next to your outdoor blooming bulbs.

Just think what a lovely (and unique) photo that would make!

On the other hand, if you point your peepers at the front cover, you'll notice the words "Bulb Forcing," meaning the production of indoor flowers *ahead* of outdoor flowers.

So, starting with the next chapter, I'll focus on how to get bulbs to bloom as early as possible indoors, well ahead of those buried in the frigid ground outdoors.

It's something that's especially desirable when you're headed toward fourth-stage cabin syndrome,* whose symptoms include:

1. Having fertility rites when you see the first bee in spring pollinating a flower;
2. Strangling your significant other when he or she dares to move one of your ninety houseplants off the dining room table;
3. Papering your walls and ceilings with poster-sized pictures of screaming-yellow daffodils;
4. Replacing your curtains with kudzu;
5. Stealing potted bamboo plants from every local Chinese restaurant;
6. Rushing the growing season by using a jackhammer to break through frozen soil in your backyard;
7. Blindfolding Punxsutawney Phil to make sure he doesn't see his shadow on Groundhog Day;
8. Having a "pre-Thanksgiving" Thanksgiving when the first crocus appears;
9. Digging up the 18th green of your local golf course to turn it into your living room carpet; and
10. Getting heirloom tomato and tulip tattoos on your derrière.

*Cabin syndrome is far worse than cabin fever. A syndrome, according to the *Merriam-Webster Third International Dictionary*, is "a group of symptoms or signs typical of a disease." A fever is a fever, but a syndrome is symptom 1, symptom 2, symptom 3, etc.

10
GIVING BULBS THE COLD, WET SHOULDER

So, how do you provide the required temperatures for your bulbs? It's not as hard as you might imagine. In fact, the first technique is as simple as…

Figure 10.1 *Burying pots 15"-18" below the surface of the soil is the most common, but also the most strenuous, way to give potted bulbs the chill they need before indoor forcing. Note the stick that's used to help locate your pots in early winter.*

A Hole in the Ground

This is the most obvious place to put potted bulbs targeted for forcing. After all, don't you put bulbs in the ground in your garden? And, when you put them there, don't they bloom? So, why shouldn't this work for bulbs in pots?

It should and does.

Although this technique sounds unsophisticated, it's fine, especially for beginners. In fact, I won some of my first blue ribbons at the Philadelphia Flower Show using this method.

But, alas, there are possible problems for the gardener, namely:

1. You've got to get the pots low enough so critters won't reach them; and
2. You might have an extremely senior moment, as in *forgetting where you buried them.*

With number 2, you tramp to your garden and three things can happen: you dig, and dig, and dig, and all you get is an education in backyard soil strata. And, that's fine if you're young and planning to major in geology at a university, but not so fine if you have a barely-functional, middle-aged back that suddenly becomes a seriously out-of-kilter, way-past-middle-aged back.

Unfortunately, there's an even worse possibility: you dig, and dig, and hit something solid, as in your pot, as in your pot that you've just cut in half, as in the necessity of an immediate call to your suicide-intervention hotline.

And, finally, there's the last possibility (about 1,000,000,000,000,000 to one): that you dig, don't destroy a pot, but find an uninjured pot that you buried three months previously.

So, now that I've told you everything that can go *wrong,* I'll tell you how to go *right:*

Figure 10.2 *After burying your pots, cover with soil and create a dome so water drains away from the area.*

Figure 10.3 *Cover the soil with a two-foot pile of leaves. In an area exposed to heavy wind, cover the leaves with chicken wire and secure with a weight on each side.*

1. Pick a site where water doesn't collect, then dig down about 15"-18".
2. Place your pots next to one another in the bottom. Then make a map of where each pot is located – meaning the type of bulb and cultivar in each pot.
3. Place a tall stick in the bottom of the hole, mark its location on your map, then completely fill the hole with soil. Be sure that the stick protrudes about three feet above the soil.
4. To be certain that water drains away from this location, create a crown of soil over the entire area.
5. Pile about 24" of leaves over the soil, which will keep the ground from freezing hard in the winter. If necessary, cover the leaves with chicken wire held down with rocks, bricks, pegs, or anything else that works.
6. *Don't* lose the map. I'm so bad at filing (because I

consider it only one step above getting my teeth drilled) that I take a photo of my map and download it to my computer. So far, I haven't misfiled my computer.

7. At the appropriate time (somewhere between 8-13 weeks, depending on which bulbs you've potted), use the map and find and remove your potted bulbs. I strongly advise that you dig to the side of your pots, and then use your fingers to carefully remove them.

The next method was prompted by an interesting phenomenon at a garden club bulb workshop. During my lecture at this particular "garden club," I told members to chill their bulbs by using the above hole-in-the-ground method. In retrospect, I should have known I was in trouble when women came dressed in suits and

Figure 10.4 *The need for the stick is obvious, unless you enjoy spending an hour searching for underground pots in frigid conditions.*

shiny shoes to pot bulbs.

Still, they enthusiastically planted their bulbs and seemed happy. Then the program chairperson told me that many of the members were, "very angry with [me], because they didn't know they'd have to *dig* in their gardens!"

I stood agog. Wordless. Speechless. Senseless.

When my grey cells started firing again, I began to realize that some garden clubs are really social clubs masquerading as garden clubs.

So, for members of such groups as well as gardeners who *aren't* finicky, but don't have the resources or the back muscles to use the hole-in-the-ground technique, I developed…

The Pot in the Box

If you have an unheated garage, this method is worth a try.

It's also worth considering if you have a heated garage. Simply turn the heat off and pray that this doesn't precipitate a major fracas with family members. Before turning off the heat, I advise that you ask yourself if this is a ditch you're ready to die in.*

Here's how to use the pot-in-the-box method:

1. Get a cardboard box at least 8" wider and higher than your pot of bulbs.
2. Put 4"-6" of dry leaves or pine needles at the bottom of the box.
3. Place the pot on the mulch inside the box.

Figure 10.5 *The Procrastinator's Special: the pot in the box. Put mulch, shredded paper, or any other non-toxic, insulating material under…*

Figure 10.6 *…around, and over the pot, then…*

---

* Anytime I foresee the possibility of a fight with a formidable foe, I always ask myself, "Art, is this a ditch you're ready to die in?" Half the time…no…wait, a lot more than half the time, the answer is no.

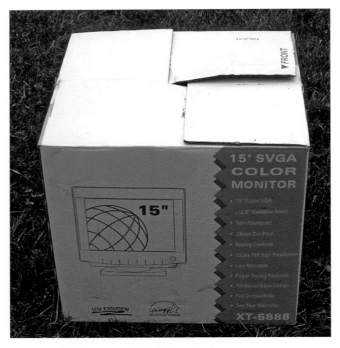

Figure 10.7 *...close the box and place it in an area where it will get an average temperature of 33°-50°F for at least ten weeks. In most areas, an unheated garage is ideal.*

4. Put more mulch around and over the pot. Be sure to fill the entire box with mulch.

5. Close the box and put it in yo--ur unheated garage by November 10th in USDA Zone 6, and earlier in colder zones. (See map at www.usna.usda.gov/Hardzone/ushzmap.html [last accessed on 6/21/2011].)

6. Take out your pot after the amount of time appropriate for the bulbs you're growing.

The Refrigerator

If you have a spare refrigerator, you can use it to chill potted bulbs, but make sure there's no fruit or vegetables of any kind inside. As you already know, they emit ethylene gas that destroys flower buds (see pages 64, 66 as well as Chapter 24).

Here are the steps to follow:

1. Set the temperature at 48°F in the refrigerator. If necessary, use a thermometer to check your thermostat setting.

2. After potting your bulbs, place the pot(s) inside.

3. Close the refrigerator and chill the pots for the appropriate number of weeks.

4. If, after vernalization, you want to extend the time your pots are in the refrigerator, hold them back by lowering the temperature to approximately 35°F.

Refrigeration is good for temperature control during vernalization. But since the inside of a refrigerator doesn't have the intensity of light that bulbs experience outdoors, their stems will eventually stretch like taffy in a candy shop. In the end, bulb forcers can have a display of stems that are so long, they look unnatural.

BUT, two extremely talented exhibitors, Charles Heiser and Walt Fisher (a.k.a. "The Botticelli of Bulbs"),

Figure 10.8 *A refrigerator is another choice for bulb vernalization. Even with a...*

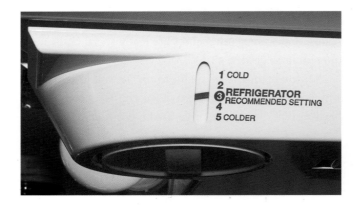

Figure 10.9 *...crude refrigerator thermostat, you'll be able to set the temperature to 45°-48°F. I use a...*

use refrigerators and produce pots of tulips that approach perfection. Fisher controls height by using stem-shortening chemicals. He also lowers the temperature from 48°F to 41°F after 4-5 weeks, then down to 34°F when leaves emerge (usually after another 4-5 weeks).* This keeps the bulbs semi-dormant until they're ready to be forced.

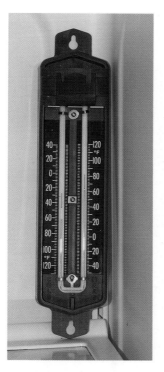

Figure 10.10 *(left)*
…min-max thermometer to help me set the thermostat. They're inexpensive and readily found online or at your local hardware store. BUT, before you put a single pot in your refrigerator, make sure it doesn't…

Figure 10.11 *…contain any fruit, because fruit emits ethylene gas, which is toxic to flower buds.*

* See *Beautiful Madness: One Man's Journey through Other People's Gardens*, James Dodson, Dutton Adult, 2005, New York. p. 23-42.

The Cold Frame

If ever there was a misnamed garden structure it's the cold frame.

Think about it: an ice box has ice in it and, logically, the purpose of an ice box is to keep things icy. Likewise, a steam room is steamy, and a hothouse is hot.

And, then there's the cold frame, which is used to keep plants warm. Well, warmer than the Arctic blasts blowing through your backyard.

But enough semantics about misnamed garden structures. What's more important is that a cold frame is warm enough, but also cold enough, to provide 40-50°F temperatures, meaning a convenient place to put potted bulbs for root formation.

There are cold frames for sale, or you could build your own. But before you flee in full panic to the next chapter, let me say that there's an effective and tremendously easy cold frame – called a window-well frame – that you can put together in less than a minute.

The Window-well Cold Frame

This is the flat-out easiest cold frame to make.

Simply buy two plastic window-well covers (available at hardware stores or online), then bind them together using clamps or strong glue. (see figures 10.12-10.14). Then you'll have a cold frame that's instantly available and easily-moved.

Figure 10.12 *The world's easiest cold frame. Use two plastic window-well covers, and have them face each other,…*

Figure 10.13 *...then use four clamps to join the two covers. Voilà! Instant cold frame!*

Figure 10.14 *A sun trap area near your house or fence is a great place for a cold frame. Make sure the soil level inside the cold frame is higher than it is outside, otherwise it can become flooded during a rainstorm.*

The Wooden Cold Frame

I mainly use wooden 4' by 8' cold frames because they're stronger and more permanent than the other frames described in this chapter. Even more important,

Figure 10.15 *This is one of my 4' X 8' cold frames. I position R5 urethane insulation on the inside walls, then...*

Figure 10.16 *...use mulch under around and...*

Figure 10.17 *...over my potted bulbs. Next, I...*

it's easier to control the intra-frame temperature using insulation, mulch, and windows that can be raised and lowered.

In the cold frame shown in figures 10.15-10.18, I employed R5 urethane insulation around the sides of the cold frame. Soil was used against the insulation to hold it in place. Then dry-leaf or pine-needle mulch was used under around and over the pots.

But before the pots are covered, I make a map of the exact locations of each pot and the bulbs it contains. It certainly makes retrieval of chilled pots less torturous in the winter, when cold rain is streaming down the back my neck.

If you'd like detailed plans for this cold frame, visit www.artwolk.com.

The Straw/Hay Cold Frame

The second-easiest cold frame to build is the hay frame, and it might be the cheapest outdoor, above-ground method of chilling bulbs – especially for U.S. gardeners.

Why? Because of the way Americans decorate their homes in the fall.

Many homeowners think the ultimate suburban art-forms are hay or straw bales and dead corn stalks decoratively placed near the front walk. Then, about two minutes after Halloween ends, the hay and straw bales are thrown away.

Which is fine.

When your neighbors throw their bales away, you can do what I do: surreptitiously nab them to create a hay frame. (I say surreptitiously, because neighbors who take "refuse" from the curb are forevermore treated with the same respect given The Village Idiot during the Renaissance.)

Figure 10.18 *...close the cold frame. Almost all of my frames are put in a location that gets maximum sunshine. If there's a warm spell (over 45°F) in the winter, I open the windows about 6"-12".*

Constructing these cold frame takes ten minutes or less. Simply arrange them as shown in figure 10.19, then add window sashes. I subtly suggest NOT using window sashes with glass, because I've already suffered the fate of broken glass shards slicing through underlying foliage. As you can tell in figure 10.19, I use translucent 4-6 mil plastic sheeting stapled to a wooden frame. I've even nabbed sashes my neighbors have tossed out, but I always get rid of the glass and staple plastic to the frame.

Incidentally, this and all the other cold frames mentioned in this chapter can be used the rest of the year to harden seedlings or extend the growing season in the fall or early spring. I've also used my wooden cold frames in the winter to grow early-blooming perennials, but that's a story for another book.

When you've chosen a site for whatever cold frame you use, be sure to get the circumference of the frame below soil level so it doesn't blow away. This is especially important for window-well cold frames. *BUT for any cold frame you make, be sure that the soil level inside the frame is higher than the soil level outside the frame, otherwise the inside will flood during rainstorms.*

Figure 10.19 *A cold frame made of hay or straw bales and window sashes is another simple structure in which you can chill potted bulbs during the fall and winter. Here, I've used six bales and three plastic-coated sashes. Create this cold frame before the bales get wet and heavy.*

There's also an ultimate, best-in-the-world cold frame for rooting and forcing bulbs. It's a story unto itself, so I'll describe it in another chapter.

As you can see from the photos in this chapter, a cold frame is like an outdoor, miniature greenhouse with windows facing south for maximum winter sunshine. But, if you have trees or another barrier blocking your southern sky, **simply put your cold frame in a place where it will get the most sun each day**. For bulb forcing, use it exactly like the box method (see pages 79-80), meaning put a layer of dry mulch under, around, and on top of your potted bulbs. Then make a map of where each species or cultivar is located within the frame.

Complete this by November 6th in USDA Zone 6, and earlier in colder zones. Of all the outdoor chilling techniques, the cold frame is the best for easy pot retrieval after chilling.

Regardless of the technique you use to chill your bulbs, once you're finished placing your pots in your chosen location, you can let winter do its worst. While you head indoors, your bulbs will burst into rapid growth.

****

"Cold frames? Potted bulbs in refrigerators? Art, have you lost your mind? Maybe I should just close your book and toss it in the gar..."

No! Wait!

Don't give up. Above all, please don't imprison my book with the chicken bones in your trash can.

You see, there are other ways to force spring-blooming bulbs, and they don't involve displacing garden soil or vertebra, or squeezing pots of wet growing mix between your milk and juice.

In fact, it's easy to buy or produce *dry* bulbs that are actually ready to pot, grow, and bloom without digging in your backyard or making a mess of your refrigerator.

They're the subject of the next chapter, so, before you hurl my book into the trash or use it to level your dining room table, have a gander at Chapter 11.

11
GIVING BULBS THE COLD, *DRY* SHOULDER

I've aimed this chapter at curious, open-minded gardeners – especially gardeners who live in areas with non-frigid winters.

Let's throw out much of what I've told you. Well, not throw it out, but put it aside for a moment. You see, there's one other way to force spring-blooming bulbs. In this case, the bulbs still need cold treatment before they begin flower-stem extension, **but you don't have to pot them first.**

If you're finished rubbing your eyes in disbelief, here's what's amazing: bulb researchers have found that once spring-blooming bulbs have formed internal flower buds (see pages 68-69), they can be chilled in the dry state* for vernalization. In this case, you *don't* pot your bulbs to chill them. Instead, either purchase pre-cooled bulbs (which many retail bulb companies sell) or chill them yourself for 12-13 weeks at approximately 40-45°F (with 41°F being ideal for tulips). Once you have pre-cooled bulbs, you can pot and force them at 60-64°F.

What this means is, even gardeners in places like Southern Florida or the desert Southwest can force tulips and daffodils into bloom despite the absence of a frigid winter.

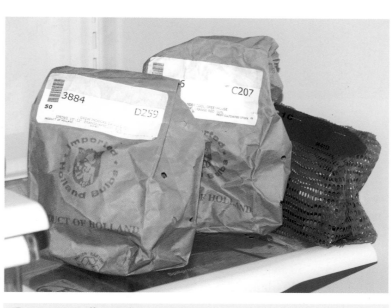

Figure 11.1 *Bulbs can be pre-cooled in a 40°-45°F, fruitless refrigerator.*

By sheer luck and accident this happened to me with a 12" pot of 'Leen Van Der Mark' tulips (see figure 11.4). I say "happened to me" because I didn't plan it at all, yet it worked exquisitely well (see "Topsy-Turvy Tulips," page 146).

Some professional bulb growers (i.e., the guys and gals who grow a massive number of potted bulbs for profit) use this technique to produce cut tulips* as early as Christmas. Indeed, the highly-regarded *Holland Bulb Forcer's Guide* emphatically says this technique is "useful only for cut-flower [tulip] production," and that "the technique is not advised for pot plant forcings"! Which means that my lucky, accidental pot should have landed me in a Dutch jail.

More important, this is a wonderful lesson for gardeners: specifically, **don't take any garden techniques as absolute, indisputable gospel.** You can follow the recipe given by garden writers like me, but you should always have a bit…no, make that a lot…of doubt. You're reading techniques that have worked for me. My methods have earned me blue ribbons and silver cups, but if I use my techniques in your conditions, I'd probably have to adjust my bulb-forcing timetables.

So, carry a notebook, record observations, and develop your own techniques. Figure out what works in your

---

* Here, I refer to neither a dry-weather U.S. State, like Arizona, nor a thoroughly dry – as in non-liquor – U.S. State, which no longer exists.

* "Cut tulips" aren't flowers that have been slashed by horticulturally-homicidal assailants. These are the flowers with cut stems (usually just above the bulb) that you've seen in florist shops or supermarkets.

Figure 11.2 *Pre-cooled, double-layered* Narcissus *'Tete-a-Tete'. Note that the top layer is in bloom, while the bottom-layer buds are just emerging. This is a wonderful, if underwhelming, display when your goal is prolonged blossoming. It's not so wonderful if you want an overwhelming display in which every bud opens at the same time (see figure 9.11 on page 72).*

Figure 11.3 *This pot contained twenty pre-cooled 'Apricot Beauty' tulip bulbs. Four weeks after planting, eleven were in bloom...at eleven different heights. The other bulbs bloomed over the next two weeks. Compare this with figure 11.5, which shows the results of in-the-pot vernalization. Remember: when you don't do wet chilling, you've got to be willing to accept uniform non-uniformity.*

home and garden and ultimately say, "To hell with Art Wolk's instructions." In other words, **start with my ideas and end with yours.**

Remember: you're the master chef of your indoor and outdoor garden, and no one orders the master chef around.

But back to the *Holland Bulb Forcer's Guide*: given their advice, don't expect perfect pots using this technique. You can try it if you have a refrigerator with a reliable thermostat. Put your bulbs in the fridge, set the temperature at approximately 41°F, wait, then pot your precooled bulbs. My experience with the sheer luck/accidental 'Leen Van Der Mark' tulips showed that these temperatures can vary somewhat (see pages 146-149). So, don't throw away your bulbs if you open the refrigerator and find the temperature at (gasp!) 44°F.

My daughter, Beth (see page 229), had to do a science experiment in middle school. I suggested that she refrigerate miniature daffodils (cultivar: 'Little Gem'), and then take twelve out each week, beginning at week one.

And, it worked, but not perfectly. After all, we had a refrigerator with fruit and vegetables in it (although we

Figure 11.4 *(right) My lucky, "pre-cooled" 'Leen Van Der Mark' tulips. Sometimes ignorance is bliss. If I had known the "rules" of dry cooling, I might have given up before I began the indoor forcing process.*

kept them in sealed plastic bags), so there had to be some ethylene exposure. In the best batch, eight of the twelve bulbs bloomed, and it was the batch potted after eight weeks of dry chilling at an average temperature of 40°F.

If I had a spare, "ethylene-less" refrigerator, I think we'd have had batches with 100% success. However, I had neither the money nor inclination to do that, because I had already worked out a near-perfect way to provide cold rooting temperatures and early growth (see Chapter 29).

For those of you who don't have access to a refrigerator for pre-cooling, there *is* something else you can try: if you have an unheated garage whose temperature averages 40-52°F from October-December, try putting a few bulbs in it to see if you can force garage-cooled bulbs.

Now that I've bent your ear about how *you* can pre-cool bulbs, please remember that some companies sell and ship pre-cooled spring-blooming bulbs – but, understandably, at a higher price.

Yes, they'll arrive through the mail, but, no, your postal employees won't continue pre-cooling your bulbs while they're en route. However, pre-cooled bulbs temporarily "remember" how long they've been cooled by your bulb dealer (or your bulb dealer's supplier), so you can pot them as soon as they arrive and immediately force them into bloom. If you can't plant them right away, try to store your bulbs at 40-50°F, but I wouldn't advise storing them for more than two weeks.

Although you can skip the wet, in-the-pot vernalization process with these bulbs, there's one drawback: double layering pre-cooled bulbs will not produce the uniformity

achieved by pot vernalization.*

As described previously, if you double layer certain spring-blooming bulbs, the shoots from the bottom and top layers will usually be at a uniform height after in-the-pot vernalization. This is what makes it possible to achieve uniform flowering.

Figure 11.5 *'Apricot Beauty' tulips that were chilled in the pot (i.e., chilled in wet potting mix). Compare the number and uniformity of blossoms with the pre-cooled pot of tulips in figure 11.3.*

To the contrary, when you double layer pre-cooled bulbs, both layers grow rapidly, meaning the top layer will bloom well ahead of the bottom layer. This is fine if your goal is to have two successive waves of flowers, but less than fine if you want an incredible pot studded with blooms. (Compare my wife's pot of *Narcissus* 'Tete-a-Tete' on page 72 with 'Tete-a-Tete' in figure 11.2).

I should also warn you that even "pre-cooled" bulbs grown in a *single* layer will not have the same degree of uniformity as bulbs chilled in pots (see figures 11.3 and 11.5). I haven't done experiments to unveil the problem, but I suspect that these bulbs are so physiologically dissimilar that there is great variation in how quickly they'll form roots and blossom.

---

* The term "pre-cooled" might cause confusion. As you may have noticed, I've used the word "cool" to mean 55°-65°F, or more specifically the best temperatures for indoor forcing of freesias, *Ranunculus*, or similar bulbs (see Chapter 7). I've used "cold" or "chilled" to mean 40°-50°F, or more specifically the ideal root-forming temperatures for spring-blooming bulbs like tulips and daffodils. But then there's the term "pre-cooled," which the bulb-forcing world at large uses for chilling dry bulbs at approximately 41°F. If the horticultural world gave me the authority, "pre-cooled" would be, forevermore, changed to "pre-chilled," but that's not likely to happen any time soon…meaning not before the moon turns purple.

CHAPTER ELEVEN

But my crotchety, obsessed-with-perfection com-plaints shouldn't dissuade you from using pre-cooled bulbs. In the end, virtually all of them will bloom, which will probably make you perfectly content.

****

This chapter has been a detour to the fringes of the bulb-forcing world. I hold no delusions that the majori-ty of you will go out and buy a bulb-dedicated refrigera-tor to pre-cool bulbs. But, perhaps a few of you, especial-ly those who live in areas that have very short winters, will purchase or produce pre-cooled bulbs to grow enchanting flowers.

But now it's time to head back to the more recogniz-able means of bulb forcing. At this point, you've learned how to pot and chill bulbs. After vernalization, it's time to retrieve your potted bulbs and get them ready for indoor forcing.

That's the topic of Chapter 12, so let's head there next.

12
PREPARATION FOR INDOOR FORCING

Use your hands to remove the excess soil and/or mulch above the pot's rim. Then you have to get rid of some of the soil from inside the top of the pot. I suggest connecting a hose and using a rapid – but not damaging – water spray to clean the top, side, and bottom. Be sure to remove enough soil from the top, so you'll have sufficient space to water your potted bulbs indoors. You want at least a one-inch lip from the top of the soil to the top of the pot.

Figure 12.1 *(left) These potted bulbs have had twelve weeks of vernalization (chilling).*

After chilling potted bulbs, you can begin your indoor flower show.

If you've used the hole-in-the-ground vernalization method, the stick you put next to your pots will be evident even if there's 30" of snow on the ground. After you remove the leaf mulch, go 12"-15" away from the stick and dig straight down until you reach the depth of your pots. Then use your fingers, not your shovel, to retrieve your potted bulbs.

Regardless of the vernalization technique you've used, remove as many pots as you like. If you want to extend the indoor display, just bring in one or two each week.

Figure 12.2 *(right) My first step toward bringing bulbs indoors is to remove mulch. Then I use...*

Figure 12.3 *(left) ...a mid-winter spray of water. It's an excellent way to prepare pots for indoor forcing.*

If you use this technique, the water spray makes it unnecessary to water your pots when you begin the forcing process. In fact, regardless of the rooting method you've used, it's unlikely that you'll have to water your pots at this point. I've used all of the techniques described in Chapter 11 and always had containers with moist soil at the end of vernalization.

****

The next important ingredient for producing flowering bulbs is light, so let's head to Chapter 13 for a short review of how and where to provide it.

Figure 12.4 *This is what a pot of miniature daffodils (in this case, 'Hawera') will look like after vernalization in a cold frame.*

Figure 12.5 *The same pot after cleaning. If you think direct sun will scorch the pale foliage you're wrong (see Chapter 13).*

13

THE ~~DARK~~ LIGHT SIDE OF THE FORCE

Before you bring your pots inside, find a location that provides either sunny conditions (at least four hours per day) or a place with artificial light of similar intensity. Three possibilities are fluorescent lights, high-pressure sodium (HPS) lamps (which are reputed to enhance bloom), and metal halide (MH) lamps (which

Figure 13.1 *The easiest and least expensive place to force bulbs is on a cool, sunny windowsill that gets at least four hours of sun per day.*

are supposed to enhance overall growth). There are also wider-spectrum versions of both MH bulbs (known as Agrosun bulbs) and HPS bulbs (known as Son Agro bulbs), which, I suppose, are the kind of lamps you'd want if you had to live the rest of your life underground. I use Son Agro bulbs...above ground...in my greenhouse (see figures 13.3 and 13.6), as an effective supplemental light source. But I also know first-class bulb forcers who get excellent results using *only* artificial light sources.

If you're thinking of doing most of your forcing indoors, away from windows, by all means investigate the great variety of light systems available to the home bulb forcer. (See especially the Hydrofarm website [www.hydrofarm.com, last accessed 6/22/2011] for information and products.)

One warning: if you decide to use artificial light,

don't use an incandescent source (i.e., typical 25-200 watt bulbs). They burn hot and will make the air too warm to force spring-blooming bulbs.

Fluorescent lights burn cool. And, although HPS or MH lamps burn warm, their light intensity is so strong that they can be used safely 24"-36" above your foliage.

Whatever location you choose, make sure the temperature range over a twenty-four hour period falls between 55-68°F. It's especially important that you choose a location where the temperature doesn't go above 70°F, even when it's sunny. If it's too warm, the flowers may not appear at all, or if they do manage to emerge, they'll last about as long as snow in Tahiti. You can check the 24-hour range of temperatures by using a min-max thermometer. Avoid a location near a radiator or directly under or over a heating vent/register. If you have to force bulbs near either of these two heat sources, turn off the radiator or close and cover the vent.

Once you've found a good indoor site for bulb forcing and cleaned your first vernalized pots, you're ready for the next step.

Figure 13.2 *Fluorescent fixtures are another good light source. They're inexpensive and burn much cooler than incandescent bulbs. Even low-temperature-loving minor bulbs like* Crocus *and* Scilla *force well under fluorescent units.*

Figure 13.3 *On cloudy days, increased light will keep your bulbs growing vigorously. I use a wide-spectrum, high-pressure sodium lamp hung 24" above the foliage. From that distance, the lamp doesn't heat the underlying plants, but illumination is close to sunlight. Don't succumb to "temperature temptation" by increasing heat to over 70°F in your growing space. You'll get leggy, unnatural-looking foliage and flowers.*

Aren't These Sun-loving Bulbs?

I'm about to step into a quagmire of quicksand by exposing an age-old commandment that belongs in every three-dimensional as well as digital recycle bin.

Many bulb publications will tell you that you should **gradually** acclimate potted, chilled spring-blooming bulbs to your light source.

Please, do yourself and your bulbs a favor and *place your pots immediately in your strongest light source.**

Since my first tentative wobbles at bulb forcing, I've forced over two thousand pots of spring-blooming bulbs and *I've always put my pots in direct sunlight.* This

* No, put back the new-business search lights that illuminate the nighttime sky and can be seen from outer space. The strongest light shouldn't be more powerful than direct, midday sun.

has never resulted in leaf scorch or distorted flowers. To the contrary, using a sunny or very bright location with cool temperatures results in dark green foliage. It also helps leaves and flower stems stay at a manageable height, reducing the need for artificial support. (See figures 15.10 and 15.11, which show unsupported hyacinths that were grown in cool, sunny conditions.)

I think the "gradual acclimation rule" has been handed down decade after decade without thorough investigation. Or, perhaps bulb-forcing vampires – for obvious reasons – have warned their fellow blood-loving gardeners against forcing bulbs in the sun.

Regardless of who (or what) started this commandment, please ignore it because using strong light with cool forcing temperatures has no ill effect.

And, isn't that completely logical? Bulbs that grow outdoors develop roots and shoots underground, where there's zero light. Then their leaves push above ground and encounter a blast of direct sun in cool conditions. And, wonder of wonders, *they don't die!*

Figures 13.4 and 13.5 *The miniature daffodil 'Hawera' was cleaned after chilling and immediately put in full sun inside my greenhouse. Wonder of wonders: two weeks later, the foliage is perfectly green.*

CHAPTER THIRTEEN

Figure 13.6 *If you have to push bulbs ahead, use additional nighttime light without increasing temperature. Even so, I never give potted bulbs more than 18 hours of light per day.*

More important, neither will the bulbs in your pots.

I followed the gradual acclimation rule the first year I forced bulbs, and, of course, got light-starved, overlong foliage and flower stems.

The following year, I tried to give bulbs the same conditions they'd get outdoors. And, amazingly, I was neither hit by baseball-sized hailstones nor a barrage of misleading bulb books. Instead, what happened was that I produced pots worthy of exhibition and photography.

By now, you're probably thinking...or screaming, "Okay, Art, enough holier-than-thou soapbox preaching. Tell us what's next?"

Fun, delight, and exhilaration, that's what's next. Given sufficient light, cool temperatures, and moisture, your potted bulbs will burst into bloom. The fastest bulbs to force are those that bloom earliest outdoors. They're the subject of Chapter 14, so let's begin with them.

****

14
FORCING THE MAJOR MINORS

It's early February and the same thought in your mind is stuck on "stuck," specifically, "Will spring never come? Will spring never come? Will spring never come?"

Blasts of winter's snow, ice, and arctic winds make you think that spring and summer gardening will be limited to caring for plants on your indoor windowsill. But in spite of all the dreariness, a few death-defying green spikes manage to poke through the frozen earth of your garden. And, if the temperature hits at least fifty degrees for a few days running, flower buds burst forth to bring color to an otherwise lifeless landscape.

These are the first bulbs of late winter, called minor bulbs, which never cease to give us hope that spring will indeed arrive.

The world at large may be content to wait for these first outdoor dabs of color. But as budding bulb forcers, you're ready to push the horticultural envelope to see, smell, and touch these flowers long before their outdoor counterparts have shown even a hint of life.

Although there are dozens of genera that are considered minor bulbs, I'll focus on four that are both well known and commonly available. I call them the "major" minors and they comprise *Crocus, Scilla,* bulbous *Iris,* and *Muscari* (also known as grape hyacinths).

Plant and chill (vernalize) these bulbs as already described in Chapters 10 and 11.

I've found that these genera will sometimes bloom with as little as eight weeks of vernalization, although ten weeks is needed to produce the kind of uniformity seen in this chapter's photos. All of them can be single or double layered, with one exception: *Scilla siberica* abhors double layering. In fact, when double-layered it will sometimes yield

Figure 14.1 *(far left) Close-up encounter of the best kind.* Muscari armeniacum *florets flare into dainty, white petticoats.*

Figure 14.2 *(left)* Crocus chrysanthus *'Blue Bird' is a wonderful cultivar that can be double layered to produce a stunning display.*

Figure 14.4 *You simply will not find a* Crocus *more heavenly than 'Blue Pearl'.*

fewer flowers than it would with one layer. To the contrary, you can double layer *Scilla mischtschenkoana* (see figure 14.5) to create one of the most glorious minor-bulb displays.

Such are the variations that can be observed within the same genus. Another example: *Muscari armeniacum* usually produces an abundance or over-abundance of foliage, but *Muscari aucheri* foliage always seems in perfect proportion to its flowers (see figures 14.10 and 14.11).

And for the Seriously Smitten...

A parameter that's important to your eye, your camera, and flower-show judges is the display as a whole (see Chapter 26). By that, I mean how everything fits together: the pot, the shoots, the foliage, and the blooms. There's nothing that leaves exhibitors more broken-hearted than when they have a pot bursting with blossoms that doesn't win a blue ribbon. Usually the reason is that the shoots are too long.

Figure 14.3 *(left)* Crocus chrysanthus *'Gipsy Girl' is an impressive and attention-grabbing minor.*

Admittedly, it does look a bit ridiculous when the pot is 4" tall and the shoots stand 9" taller. It looks more like a New York City skyline than a blue-ribbon entry or a pot you'd show off to visitors. These long shoots are usually caused by potting up bulbs too soon in the fall or by placing the pot too deeply in the ground for vernalization. For minor bulbs like *Scilla*, *Iris*, and *Crocus*, I've waited until late November or even early December for bulb planting. I put these pots in cold frames and place them near the surface, where it's colder. Similarly, if you're using the "hole-in-the-ground" method for rooting, put these pots a bit closer to the surface.

In spite of all your efforts, winters can occasionally be so mild that your pots – especially those in cold frames – start showing flower buds too early, when they're still outdoors.

If you're trying to hold back a pot for a special occasion or flower show, you might consider using my rather odd but effective technique: if you're employing an above-ground vernalization method, you could cover the pots with snow. And, if there's no snow, you can do what I used to do during my blue-silk-crazed days: use an ice crusher to produce enough artificial snow to spread on your pots.

Figure 14.5 *This pot of* Scilla mischtschenkoana *was double layered, chilled, and forced at 55°-60°F. It can be forced at warmer temperatures, but the flower stems will be taller and less uniform.*

Figure 14.7 *Chopped ice or snow work perfectly when you need to hold back minor bulbs (see also figure 25.2, page 214). This pot of* Crocus *is in a north-facing cold frame. The foliage won't fade and flowering is suspended.*

The winter of 1994-5 was so mild in New Jersey that all my pots of *Crocus* were coming into bloom in late January, five weeks before the Philadelphia Flower Show. That was the first year I resorted to ice-crusher snow to put my pots in suspenseful, suspended animation. For more than a month, I woke up a half hour early to administer this admittedly-compulsive precaution. But, it produced the desired effect: I won all three blue ribbons for *Crocus* that year, which helped me win my first Grand Sweepstakes Award.

At this point you're probably thinking, "You know, Art, you really were at the far end of the sanity bell curve that year."

But you're wrong: I was well within the *insanity* bell curve not just that year, but for many, many years.

What this means is, no matter how bitten you become by the bulb-forcing bug, you can be comforted by the fact that you'll always have my behavior to describe to your concerned family, friends, or therapist.

Your First Flowers of Winter

After chilling your pots, it's time for indoor springtime in winter.

Like most spring-blooming bulbs, *Muscari* can be forced at 60-68°F. On the other hand, *Crocus*, *Scilla*, and *Iris* all benefit from colder, but not mandatory, forcing conditions. In my glass-to-ground greenhouse, I force all

Figure 14.6 *(left)* Muscari aucheri *'White Magic' is an easy-to-force grape hyacinth with short foliage and photogenic blossoms.*

three on the floor, where the temperature is about fifty-five degrees.

These are teeth-chattering temps for all but the hardiest indoor growers. But, there are places in your home where you might find or create such conditions. For example, you could consider closing the heat source in a room to keep it cool. This may involve evicting someone, but gardeners with bad cases of cabin fever sometimes have to become non-benevolent dictators.

Place your pots in a sunny windowsill or equally bright location, and turn them one-quarter turn per day to achieve uniform flowering. Even at 55°F, *Crocus*, *Scilla*, and *Iris* will burst into bloom in just 3-7 days.

Admittedly, even with cool growing conditions, these flowers don't last more than about five days indoors.* So,

Figure 14.8 Iris reticulata *'Gordon' at the Philadelphia Flower Show. There are 90 double-layered bulbs in this 8" pot. I kept these bulbs just short of blooming with about 12" of snow. Five days before judging, I let them blossom at 55°F.*

* Mike McGrath (host of NPR's "You Bet Your Garden" and former editor of *Organic Gardening Magazine*) used to oversee the creation of superb, garden-sized exhibits each year at the Philadelphia Flower Show. One year he asked me whether minor bulbs would be a good choice as a central feature of his nine-day display. I told him, "It would be gorgeous, but you'll have to change your entire exhibit every three days." I'm glad he ditched the idea. Instead, he had a display of what a typical, current-day Native American home and garden would look like if Europeans had never shown up. It was genius.

Figure 14.10 Muscari armeniacum *is one of the easiest minor bulbs to force. It tolerates temperatures between 65°-69°F and has racemes (flower clusters) of flowers that bloom for at least two weeks.*

to extend the indoor minor-bulb season, plant more pots (or smaller pots) with fewer bulbs and bring in only one or two pots each week.

To prolong the life of your blossoms, put your pots in a location as cold as 33°F at night. I usually use my unheated garage, but monitor the temperature using a min-max thermometer (see figure 10.10 on page 79).

Another place to consider is your refrigerator. If you have to throw out a bit of food to make space for your bulbs, don't feel guilty. After all, a feast for the eyes sometimes takes precedence over a feast for the stomach.

Muscari start blooming outdoors a bit later than other minors, so it follows that they'll take longer to force. In addition, you can grow them at somewhat warmer temperatures. When I force *Muscari* on a greenhouse bench where the temperature is 60°-64°F, it takes about eighteen days until they blossom. Since the flowers are in clusters (racemes) and bloom from the bottom up, flowering lasts much longer than with other minors. That's not the only benefit in growing grape hyacinths; the other is their entrancingly sweet aroma.

When you're finished forcing minor bulbs, they can be saved for outdoor bloom (see Chapter 27).*

Figure 14.9 *(previous two pages)* Crocus tomasinianus *'Ruby Giant' is a fantastic, high-impact cultivar that looks great in a pot or in your garden.*

*Forcing usually weakens bulbs, so don't force the same batch two years in a row, unless you enjoy staring at foliage more than flowers.

Figure 14.11 Muscari aucheri *'Blue Magic' is one of the many cultivars in the Magic series. Most have two-toned racemes with the lighter color on top. In addition, the species* Muscari aucheri *has shorter foliage that's more in proportion with the floral display.*

****

Now that you've spent some time in the minor (bulb) leagues, it's time you graduated to the Big Boys and Girls. These are the bulbs that produce large, longer-lasting, and dazzling flowers – the kind you'll want to show off to anyone who comes within sniffing distance of your front door.

And, speaking of sniffing, the flowers described in the next chapter have the kind of fragrance that the slightest snivel of a sniff will easily identify. If your olfactory organ is the least bit intrigued, head to my most odiferous offering: Chapter 15.

15
"YOUR HYACINTHS ARE *KILLING* ME!"

I'm sure you're perfectly perplexed about which bulb I'm about to describe. Perhaps it's because you didn't notice the tiny chapter heading. It's also because you wisely decided not to use this bulb's stalk and flowers as a bookmark – otherwise these pages would reek and you'd be flattened by eau de *Hyacinthus*.

Yes, the topic is hyacinths – those after-shave-lotion-on-a-stem bulbs that tell everyone in your home, if not your county, that bulb-forcing season – as well as clothespin-on-your-nose season – is here.

This is the bulb that many churches have banned from their Easter services. Alas, the powers that be have put the respiration of their members ahead of the "perfumation" of the church.

During my blue-ribbon-crazed days, I used to suspend growth of my potted bulbs by employing the walk-in refrigerator of a local convenience store. Understandably, before each Philadelphia Flower Show, the manager always became my "new best friend": I gave her two tickets to the show; she gave me chilly temps.

Apparently, one year I had more that the usual number of hyacinth pots in the walk-in refrigerator. I say "apparently" because I thought everything was just dandy. Then one day, when I went to the store to check on my pots, the manager saw me streaking by. That's when she yelled, "YOUR HYACINTHS ARE *KILLING* ME."

Her customers stared at me while I stood in horror, certain they assumed I was committing a homicide. Yet, no one came to her aid. No, it was I who rescued her by removing the hyacinthoid, olfactory offenders from her store.

So, like paper whites, these bulbs are loved by half the world's gardeners and cause respiratory arrest in the other half. That's why I've aimed my directions at only 50% of those who opened this book. The rest of my readers can skip ahead to daffodils on page 113. (But, perhaps, the rest of my readers skipped away about 102 pages ago.)

For the three of you who've made it this far, let's hobble ahead.

Before you push your first hyacinth into potting mix, you'll notice something delightful about these bulbs, namely, the papery covering called a tunic. This is one of

Figure 15.1 *(above) The hyacinth 'Pink Pearl' is guaranteed to deliver a resplendent dose of spring every time it's forced.*

Figure 15.2 *(following page) A close-up of* Hyacinthus *'Sky Jacket'. Like other hyacinths, its "six-pack" scent is strong enough to attract almost any pollinating insect...meaning almost any pollinator in the Milky Way Galaxy.*

these are the ones you want.*

Sad to say, it took me far too many years to discover this. For about a geologic era, I'd have a perfectly forced pot of hyacinths that would, at best, win a yellow (third place) ribbon. I tried changing fertilizer, potting mix, water temperature, watering schedule, light intensity, and probably fifty other parameters, but my blooms were exactly the same size: too small.

I'm certain that every year my hyacinths whispered to one another, "We've been forced into bloom by a complete moron." (See figure 15.4.)

When I reached the age of 250, a very tiny light bulb shed a glow upon my not-very-functional brain cells. Finally, I thought, "Duh, maybe the number and size of the flowers has something to do with the size of the bulb."

I asked a fellow competitor if some bulb companies sold larger hyacinth bulbs and she, in a moment of saintliness, told me which company had such super-duper bulbs.†

Figure 15.3 *The tunic color says it all. This bulb produced a pink hyacinth, namely, 'Pink Pearl'.*

the few bulb genera I've grown whose outer covering is in the same color family as the flowers it produces. It means that planting a mixed color pot by mistake is very rare, even if you only have the light from a single match. I first noticed this at a garden center, and it's been the only time I've fallen in love with a bulb for the bulb itself, before even growing it. (Which is like falling in love with someone before getting to first base…while still in the batter's box…before the first pitch is thrown.)

In the Beginning…

I almost always use an 8" clay pot to force hyacinths. This is the perfect size for seven very large hyacinth bulbs. Sometimes they'll touch each other. But, as I've already slammed you over the head about this, you won't start a botanical black plague if they do.

By the way, when I say "very large" bulbs, I mean bulbs sold by companies that grade hyacinths by diameter. Big ones have a big price, but when it comes to perfect pots for home display or blue silk at flower shows,

The next year, I forced hyacinths as I had for eons, and I all but lost con- sciousness when I saw my first

Figure 15.4

---

* You should also be aware that this is not a bulb size appropriate for your garden, since their large head of blossoms can make flower stalks topple or snap during rainstorms. However, the fall *after* you've forced jumbo bulbs, you *can* plant them in your garden, because they'll be smaller.

† The company was Van Engelen (see Appendix 3, page 243).

Figure 15.5 *Eight large hyacinth bulbs fit neatly into an 8" pot. Sometimes, bulbs are so large that only seven can be squeezed into this container (see figures 15.10 and 15.11).*

hyacinth blue ribbon next to my pot.

To plant hyacinths, I put pre-moistened professional mix within four inches of the top of the pot. Why? Because the higher up you move in a pot, the wider it gets; at the bottom, an azalea pot is about 4" in diameter, at the top, 8" (see page 37).

Get it? Higher is wider, lower is narrower. Near the top you can fit more bulbs into your pots, and more bulbs mean more blossoms. Just make sure the top of the bulbs are below the top of the pot, otherwise their roots will push the bulbs above the rim.

Like other spring-blooming bulbs, hyacinths need chilly temperatures (40°-50°F) for vernalization. It's especially important that they're chilled for at least ten weeks, or you'll have blooms on extremely short stems – practically on the soil. Have a look at some hyacinths I saw at a supermarket (see page 73, figure 9.13). You don't see a flower stem, do you? And, now you know why: these bulbs were pulled out of the refrigeration room too soon. Despite this, the growers sent sad pots like these to the supermarket. Meaning that what ended up on the shelves were maxi-squat hyacinths.

And, speaking of improperly forced hyacinths, I must warn you about a technique that some gardeners espouse for growing hyacinths. I call it the "Black Tube Torture"

Figure 15.6 *'Blue Jacket' handsomely displayed with a moss mulch.*

technique.

This method is tailor-made for gardeners who 1) have a *tremendous* amount of time to waste, and 2) have decided that hyacinths growing outdoors have it all wrong, even though they were surviving outdoors long before we evolved.

Gardeners who use Black Tube Torture think they can grow hyacinths without the essential chilling period that's needed for root formation and flower-stem elongation.

So, here's the deal: if you grow hyacinths without giving them a long enough chill, the flowers will practically bloom underground…which isn't exactly your intent, is it?

However, if you put 8" black-paper tubes around the undeveloped flowers, the stem will elongate. BUT, what you end up with are pale leaves and flowers rarely at the proper height.

To the contrary, what you really want to chase away the winter blues are blooms and leaves that look natural, even though they're inside a pot.

It's exactly like great fiction: it has to seem so real that

15.7a

15.7b

Figures 15.7a and 15.7b *Black Tube Torture at its worst. If these potted hyacinths remind you of a springtime garden, it's time to come out of your cave.*

the reader "suspends disbelief." Readers are so "into the story" that they forget it's a work of fiction.

"But, Art," you might say, "how is that related to bulb forcing?"

Answer: They're related because when you look at forced bulbs, you want to and **can** feel as if you're a time traveler who's been transported from winter to spring. You're swept away by these flowers and you "suspend disbelief." Winter is gone and spring has arrived!*

Unfortunately, the tube method leaves you with hyacinths that "suspend" nothing. And, the "disbelief"

---

* This is exactly what happens year, after year, after year at the Philadelphia International Flower Show. It's what it's all about. It's not about blue ribbons, silver cups, or purchasing pussy willow branches. It's about time traveling to a splendid springtime. If you don't believe me, just ask any gardener who's been there.

will come from your visitors when you tell them they're looking at hyacinths.

So, you can either go through this wacky procedure or simply give hyacinths at least ten weeks of chilly conditions. If you want to impose botanical torture, choose the former technique. If you want to do less work, have gorgeous blossoms at the proper height along with dark green foliage, choose the latter.

I used the tube method exactly once and almost gave up forcing hyacinths altogether. Luckily, I made a U-turn away from the Dark Side of the Force.

I know I've already hit you over the head with a two-by-four about this, but I want you to look at the developing hyacinths in figures 15.13 and 15.14.

These boys got ten weeks or more of chilly temperatures. That's why there's flower-stem extension.

Figure 15.9 *Pure excitement! When hyacinths finally show signs of life above ground, you know that flowers are on the way.*

So what does this mean to you when it comes to chilling (vernalizing) your hyacinth bulbs?

It means, don't dilly-dally in the fall. It also means, don't stick your bagged bulbs in your garage and forget about them until December. Get them potted and in the ground, box, cold frame, or refrigerator so they'll get the temperatures they need for at least ten weeks.

So, what's next you might ponder? What's next is the fun part.

After vernalization and preparing your pot for forcing, it's time to produce gorgeous flowers and strong bloom stems.

The ideal temperature range for forcing is 60°-64°F.*

Admittedly, these are not the cozy temperatures most sane people are used to during the

Figure 15.8 *(previous two pages) 'Blue Jacket' hyacinths have reached their peak about four weeks after bringing them indoors.*

* But don't be discouraged. You can force hyacinths at temperatures up to 68°F and get fine results.

winter. But, if you force hyacinths at these temperatures, you'll get flower stalks that are strong, need little if any support, and are at the perfect height.

And speaking of support, I should tell you that when I first started to exhibit hyacinths at the Philadelphia Flower Show, I was agog over the advice and Herculean efforts of my kindly fellow-competitors, who told me every means of support possible:

- Some used a technique I recommend whenever you must support your hyacinths: put short floral or bamboo stakes into the soil about 2"-3" from the rim. Then use green florist string and wrap it around the stakes so that it's tucked under the lowest flowers on the bloom stem. If done properly, your support is nearly unnoticeable (see figure 15.14).

Figure 15.10 *'Carnegie' is my favorite white hyacinth for home or flower show exhibition. These hyacinths needed no support.*

Figure 15.11 *'City of Haarlem' hyacinths are a delicate, creamy yellow with a typically-indelicate scent.*

- Some used the star-staking technique described in Appendix 2, pages 232-235.
- Some used stiff metal wire pushed inside the bloom stem – and even inside the bulb – far enough so the judges wouldn't notice their bulbous abuse.
- Then I heard this doozy: some exhibitors used a needle with green thread that they "sewed" between flowers and flower stems to bolster their too-tall plants. This threading doesn't stop at one hyacinth; they circumnavigate all the hyacinths near the edge of the pot. When I first heard this technique, I felt completely inadequate. I knew I'd have to become a tailor to get it right.

In the end, I ignored these methods and used a technique no one else was employing.

I used nothing...as in zero string, wire, or thread.

I forced my pots in full sun at 60-64°F and each bloom stalk stood as erect as a miniature Washington Monument (see figures 15.10 and 15.11).

And, there's one other secret I occasionally used:

To get hyacinths to stand without artificial support, it helps to "aim" each plant toward the center of the pot. Use your palm to move leaves and flower stems toward the middle and push extra soil in between the bulb and

Figure 15.12 *Like other spring-blooming bulbs, hyacinth flower buds are pre-formed and primed for action. Failure is NOT an option!*

Figure 15.13 *The hyacinth 'Sky Jacket' beginning to show color. When all seven bulbs are this uniform, you can expect the kind of display in figure 15.14.*

111

Double-layered Hyacinths?

Because I've already explained how to use double layering to grow a splendiferous pot of blooming bulbs, I should tell you that it won't work for hyacinths. The hyacinths on the bottom layer never bloom at the same time as the bulbs in the upper layer, so there's no uniformity. You end up with a monstrous-looking abomination – namely, a pot with uprooted blooming bulbs as well as odd-angled, not-in-bloom bulbs. This combination produces a disastrous display that's ready for the compost heap. I wish I had a photo of my execrable attempt at double-layered hyacinthoid glory, but I didn't run for my camera as my bulb-forcing freak of nature evolved.*

Figure 15.14 *Stunning 'Sky Jacket' hyacinths blooming their heads off. If I could only grow one cultivar each year, it would be this one.*

****

the wall of the pot. The extra soil gives your hyacinths the support they need, but *nothing is showing*. See Appendix 2 pages 235-236, where I use this procedure for daffodils.

This produced a wonderful bonus not only in terms of gorgeous pots at home, but also blue ribbons at flower shows. Given two identical pots of hyacinths, the judges will always give the nod to the hyacinths without support.

Suddenly you've become a bulb-forcing genius, because your camera, family, guests, as well as flower-show judges will know nothing about your subterranean subterfuge (a term I can't claim as my own, because my editor, Pete Johnson, created this astute, accurate, and alliterative term).

Despite their sometimes overwhelming scent, hyacinths remain one of my favorite bulbs to force. But they aren't at the top of my list. That spot is reserved for the daffodil, a bulb that hybridizers have used to produce some of the most entrancing flowers.

They're the subject of Chapter 16, so let's head there next.

---

* I apologize for not having this photo, since it's important that I give you unending opportunities to laugh at my bulb-forcing failures.

16
DAFFODILS: KINGS OF THE UNDERWORLD

Daffodils are my favorite bulbs to force. Although they don't have the tremendous variety of color and form found with tulips, the number of choices has exploded in the past fifty years. Aside from the plain, large-nosed yellow varieties, there are some with frilled noses (coronas), pink noses, white noses, and barely noticeable noses. There are also noses that look like anything *but* noses. These include doubled daffodils as well as incredibly doubled daffodils that have so many petals they look, for all the botanical world, like long-petaled dandelions. There are also split-cup daffodils that have flattened noses, like boxers who retired twenty years too late. Both double and split-cup daffodils have their own division (see the American Daffodil Society's webpage: www.daffodilusa.org/daffodils/div.html [last accessed 6/30/2011]).

Some – the late-blooming ones, like 'Actaea' – can be extremely challenging to force. But you can force and groom to near-perfection the daffs that bloom earlier. Evolution has given us a bulb that produces so many leaves and, sometimes, multiple flowers, that you can have a pot riddled with black-tipped leaves and spent flowers, but still have

Figure 16.1 *Narcissus 'Katie Heath' is one of the easiest of the pink daffodils to force.*

enough quality foliage and blossoms left after grooming to make everyone think you're a top-notch bulb forcer.

In other words, once again, *you have to work hard to screw this up.*

For example, have a peek at the inside of the bulb of the early-blooming, miniature daffodil 'Tete-a-Tete' (see figure 16.4). Those yellow buds are actually multiple flowers on each stem. In fact, a single 'Tete-a-Tete' bulb can have six or more flowers. This means that if you cram fifteen bulbs into a six-inch pot, you could conceivably have ninety blossoms. My wife, whom I've occasionally enticed into forcing bulbs for the Philly Flower Show, once produced such a pot. It netted her a blue ribbon as well as a rosette from the Delaware Valley Daffodil Society (see figure 9.11, page 72).*

However, it's rare to get every 'Tete-a-Tete' flower to peak like this. Sometimes half the flowers look like used handkerchiefs, but you can chop them out and still have a dis-

---

* Rosettes are frilled ribbons that are awarded to the best-of-the-blues – in this case, the best of about eight blue-ribbon-winning daffodil pots.

Figures 16.2a-16.2d *When double layering large daffodil bulbs, the first layer should be close to the bottom of the pot, but with enough soil mix for root formation. The top-layer bulbs shouldn't impede the growth of underlying bulbs. When you're finished, no more than 1" of the upper-layer bulbs should be showing.*

play with forty-five blossoms. That's not bad for a six-inch pot; it still looks and smells fantastic.

I hope, by now, you're aware of my subtext: if you're looking for the best narcissi to force first, choose early-blooming daffodils, and the best cultivar for your first pot is 'Tete-a-Tete'. Next, try large, early-blooming daffs, like 'Carlton', 'Golden Harvest',* or 'Rijnveld's Early

Sensation'. Then move on to 'Dutch Master', 'Las Vegas', 'Ice Follies', or *Narcissus* 'Canaliculatus', a tazetta-type, miniature daffodil with 4-7 flowers per stem and a spicy scent (see figure 16.16). It's one of the few tazettas that are hardy to USDA Zone 6.

Also try the challenging, but stunning, 'Hawera,' which, like *N.* 'Canaliculatus', has multiple flowers per bulb. Forced, double-layered 'Hawera' can have so many blossoms that they look like a yellow cloud floating above the foliage. There aren't many things that instantly

---

* *Narcissus* 'Golden Harvest' holds a special place in my heart. It's a large-flowered, multi-blossomed bulb with which I won my first Philadelphia Flower Show rosette.

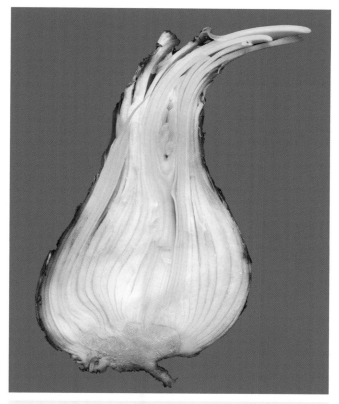

Figure 16.3 *The internal daffodil flower bud that's usually formed before August each year.*

Figure 16.4 *The buds, upon buds, upon buds inside a 'Tete-a-Tete' bulb. As many as three flowers are on each bloom stem, meaning this bulb might have nine blossoms.*

soothe my frigid winter spirit, but a pot of 'Hawera' always does (see figure 16.6). And, I suspect that if you're reading this book, they'll do the same for you.

The earliest daffs take 3-4 weeks to force into bloom; mid-season narcissi, 4-5 weeks; and the latest daffs, 6-7 weeks. (See "*Narcissus*" in the index for examples of each.)

Planting Daffodil Bulbs
and
The Secret of How You Can Produce
Out-of-This-World Daffodil Pots

You can plant daffodils in a single or double layer (see pages 68-72) and follow the same overall steps used for minor bulbs (see Chapter 14). But, before you start planting daffs, I want to offer you the secret behind incredibly bloom-studded *Narcissus* pots.

If you take a peek at Ray Rogers' amaryllis 'Pamela' on page 43, you'll see what a huge clump of offsets can produce. The offsets themselves aren't unique. In fact, every healthy amaryllis forms offsets, which are clones of the parent bulb. When first formed, they're small and need to grow fatter before a flower is formed within the bulb.

The same thing happens with daffodils. Given proper conditions, the mother bulb will also form offsets that,

Figure 16.5 *This collection has a mother bulb and attached offsets (front, center) as well as previously-separated offsets.*

115

CLASS 406   ENTRY 2

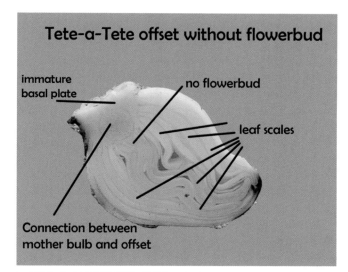

Tete-a-Tete offset without flowerbud

immature basal plate

no flowerbud

leaf scales

Connection between mother bulb and offset

Figure 16.7 *A 'Tete-a-Tete' offset, approximately 3/4" long, that contains no flower bud.*

by the end of the first or second growing season, produce a flower bud.*

Using this information, there's a way you can maximize your flower count for any pot of daffodils you grow.

As you now realize, there's a tremendous variety of daffodils, from miniatures that come from very small bulbs

Figure 16.8 *Mother bulbs and offsets of* Narcissus *'Bahama Beach' (see figure 16.11). The least massive bulb is on the left, the heaviest on the right.*

Figure 16.6 *(left)* Narcissus *'Hawera' is a prolific miniature that produces a cloud of flowers when double layered. It takes about six weeks to force after chilling.*

* The mother bulb is the largest central bulb in a clump that contains at least one offset (see figure 16.8).

(e.g., the less-than-one-inch-thick 'Baby Moon' in figure 16.14) to robust mother bulbs that form the largest flowers.

All of these daffodil bulbs form offsets, but only some of the offsets contain flower buds. If you're trying to maximize flower count, you simply have to include *only those offsets that have flower buds inside*. But how in the world can you do this without Superman's x-ray vision?

The technique is actually quite simple. Once the offsets grow enough to be easily separated from the mother bulbs, there's a good chance that they contain a flower. Of course, the odds increase as the relative mass of the offset increases.

If you want to produce a stunning pot with loads of flowers, include not only mother bulbs, but also only those offsets that have flower buds. You accomplish this by doing a bit of surgery. Here's how:

1. Carefully separate offsets from several mother bulbs by either using a gentle tug (if it's a mature offset) or a sharp, disinfected knife.*

2. Line up these offsets according to size: the smallest at one end, the largest at the other. All of them should have a piece of the basal plate (see figure 3.3

Figure 16.9 *The third smallest bulb from the left (in figure 16.8) is the first one with an internal flower bud. All bulbs included in the pot (see figure 16.11) were at least this large.*

* Some bulbs may have diseases that are easily spread by knives. I've used a variety of disinfection techniques, including ethyl alcohol, cleansers that contain bleach, and even a short stay in the flames of a stovetop burner – a method I only recommend for those (e.g., microbiologists) who have safely done this before. After disinfection, I suggest rinsing the knife in water to wash away caustic chemicals or to cool the blade.

DOUBLE-LAYERED TETE-A-TETE DAFFODILS

lower-layer bulbs

Figure 16.10 *Double-layered* Narcissus *'Tete-a-Tete'. Note the tops of the underlying bulbs. Even the smallest bulbs in this pot have internal flowers (see figures 16.8 and 16.9).*

on page 25), otherwise they won't form roots. Please note that when I say "smallest," I don't mean the shortest or skinniest offset, I mean the one with the least mass. Why should mass be more important than the bulb's dimensions? Because the heavier the bulb, the greater the nutrients stored inside. When a developing bulb has enough nutrients, it forms a flower. I don't expect you to purchase a sensitive, scientific scale to weigh each offset, but, try to see and feel which offsets seem light or heavy.

3. Cut the smallest offset in half. If it doesn't have a flower bud in the middle, cut open the second-smallest offset.

4. Continue this with larger and larger offsets until you see a flower bud in the center. You'll definitely see a difference between internal leaf shoots and flower buds (compare figures 16.7 and 16.9). The former are formless and relatively colorless, the latter are colorful, miniature versions of a flower.

5. Once you've determined the minimum size offset that contains a flower, put the two halves together and

Figure 16.11 Narcissus *'Bahama Beach' takes six weeks to force, but rewards the patient bulb forcer with dozens of flowers. Only flower-filled bulbs were used in this pot.*

Figure 16.12 *(right) Excitement time! For early-blooming, standard-sized (non-miniature) daffodils, flower buds appear when the foliage is only 3"-4" high.*

Figure 16.13 Narcissus 'Tiny Bubbles' is one of the longest lasting miniature daffodils I've ever forced.

the tops are higher than an inch above the rim – start again, with the first layer planted lower.

13. Plant as many "flowerful" offsets as possible in the remaining space of the top layer. Remember: the more bulbs you plant, the more flowers you'll get. And to make sure the pot has uniform flowering, **don't block the tops of the underlying bulbs in the first layer.** Leave enough space for the shoots to grow unimpeded to the top of the pot.

14. Cover with a dome of soil and press firmly – with your hands, not your feet.

15. Use whatever vernalization method you've chosen. As a general rule, vernalize daffs for at least ten weeks for the earliest-blooming cultivars (e.g., 'Tete-a-Tete', see figure 9.11) and 13 weeks or more for the latest (e.g., 'Actaea', see figure 16.29). (See also Appendix 5.)

place this bulb next to the pot you're planting.

6. Now, you can separate the rest of the offsets in the batch and make sure that every bulb you put in your pot is *at least as big as the minimum bulb size that contains a flower bud.* Hold your bulbs next to the dissected bulb to check that you're planting the right size.

7. I only separate and plant offsets that have a bona fide basal plate (see figure 3.3, page 25). If I'm confident that the basal plate will form enough roots for the offset to bloom, I plant it. I know you won't have a sense of this in the beginning, but you will by the second or third year you force bulbs.

8. Begin planting mother bulbs in the bottom layer. Since most daffodil bulbs are much larger than minor bulbs, you'll have to begin double layering much lower – probably two-thirds of the way down for the larger bulbs, less for smaller bulbs (see figures 16.2 and 16.10).

9. If there's space, add offsets wherever possible.

10. Add potting mix, but be certain that you can still see the tops of every bulb in the bottom layer

11. Put as many mother bulbs as possible in the second layer.

12. If you find that these bulbs sit too high – meaning

Figure 16.14 *The miniature 'Baby Moon'. At this stage, the twin-like bulbs are easily separated and can begin their life in non-conjoined solitude. Although only 3/4" wide, they both have an internal flower bud.*

119

Figure 16.16 Narcissus 'Canaliculatus' is one of the smallest and most attractive miniatures.

Some bulb forcers let the offsets remain attached to the mother bulb and plant the clump (see figure 16.5) in their pots. I don't, because it's easier to jam pack bulbs into a pot when the offsets are separated and planted vertically. And, of course, leaving all the offsets attached, means you'll be wasting space whenever a flowerless offset is included.

I repeat this surgery every year, even if I've done it many times previously for a given cultivar. The minimum size of an offset that contains a flower differs from year to year and batch to batch. Why? Because there's so much variability in growing conditions from one year to the next.

This technique is the best way to produce the maximum number of flowers per pot. Take a peek at Narcissus 'Hawera' in figure 16.6. There's no way this number of blossoms would have been possible without using this method.

So, why should you care about this surgery if you don't compete in flower shows? Because, like every other gardener in the world, your goal is eye-popping perfection, and offset surgery helps you achieve it.

When you finish this procedure, you'll have small,

Figure 16.15 (previous two pages) Narcissus 'Las Vegas' is an impressive, quick forcer (3-4 weeks) that sports huge, bicolored blossoms.

flowerless offsets leftover. I'm somewhat – but not terribly – embarrassed to say that these immature offsets wind up in my trash can. Alas, in my quest for flower-show fame as well as photos for publication, flowerless mini-bulbs are sacrificed to the Goddesses of Blue Ribbons and Bulb-Forcing Books.

But you probably aren't as impatient as I am, so you might want to plant them in your garden. It will take at least a year until they bloom, and that will only happen in the right soil, with the right sun exposure, and the right cultivar. But, it's worth the effort for experience alone. And, if you do manage to get these bulbs to bloom, you should be deservedly proud of your accomplishment.

Forcing Daffodils: The Final Steps to Paradise

Forcing Narcissus is similar to forcing Muscari (see Chapter 14) and hyacinths (see Chapter 15), but I can't stress enough the need to rotate your potted bulbs 90° (i.e., one-quarter of a turn) each day. Most daffodils have coronas (noses). For a pot to look its best, the noses should point symmetrically outward, all the way around the pot. This sounds like the sleight-of-hand employed by Houdini or Teller, but it's actually quite simple. If you turn the pot 90° per day, that's exactly what you'll get. (See Narcissus 'Tiny Bubbles' in figure 16.12.)

What I find comforting during the forcing process, is that daffodils let you know when a flower is on the way. Leaves emerge first, but before they're more than half grown, you can look between them and see a widening space. Within days, the top of a flower bud emerges, and you're approaching the Promised Land (see figure 16.17). You've done something perfectly, and the bulb is about to reward you with a flower.

If you grow impatient waiting for some sign of a flower bud, just keep watering and turning the pot each day. Unless your forcing temperatures are too high, or you've done something wrong during the chilling process, the buds will eventually appear.

As with hyacinths, if you can force daffs at 60°-64°F, you'll produce foliage and flowers that need minimal if any support. It's fine if you have to use higher tempera-

Figure 16.17 *Pulse-pounding excitement! Daffodil bulbs are excellent at telling you when a flower is on the way. Just look between the inner leaves for approaching bliss.*

tures, but not more than sixty-nine degrees unless you're forcing paper whites.* Pots forced at 65-69°F will be a bit leggier, so they'll need more support.

There are several techniques you can use to support daffodils, and they're covered in Appendix 2, pages 232-236.

A Reminder

In Chapter 11, I mentioned that pre-cooled bulbs won't produce the same degree of uniformity as in-the-pot chilling/vernalization. This is especially true for double-layered daffodils. Figure 9.7 shows double-layered, pre-cooled bulbs at their peak; figure 9.11 shows double-layered, in-the-pot vernalized bulbs at their pinnacle of perfection. Both pots look fine, but the difference is striking – so striking, in fact, that you'd have to be in a drawer, in a morgue, wearing a toe tag to miss it.

_____

* Paper whites will force at 70°-72°F, but they'll be leggy (see Chapter 6).

And Then There Are In-between Daffs

In Chapter 6 ("Easy Bulbs...") you learned that paper white narcissi can be forced without vernalization (chilling). But, aside from paper whites or pre-cooled bulbs (see Chapter 11), there are other daffodils that need little or no chilling. According to world-renowned bulb authority Brent Heath (owner of Brent and Becky's Bulbs), they include the following cultivars:

- 'Abba' (see figure 16.19),
- 'Erlicheer' (see figure 16.18),
- 'Rijnveld's Early Sensation' (see figure 16.20),
- 'Inbal', and
- 'Canaliculatus' (see figure 16.16)

Figure 16.18 Narcissus *'Erlicheer' was chilled for just 23 days, then grown for 4 weeks. This is the minimal vernalization needed for this cultivar to produce so many flowers uniformly.*

16.19a

16.19b

Figure 16.19a *Unchilled* Narcissus *'Abba' after 3 weeks of growth.* **Figure 16.19b** *The same cultivar chilled for 28 days, then grown for 3 weeks.*

I've experimented with all of them and found that, although you can get some blossoming without vernalization, it's spotty and inconsistent. However, you get uniform height and blossoming with 14 days of vernalization for 'Inbal', 16 days for 'Rijnveld's Early Sensation', 23 days for 'Erlicheer', 28 days for 'Abba', and 45 days for 'Canaliculatus' (see figures 16.18, 16.19, and 16.20).

And for Southern Growers

Before we leave this topic, it's important to note that these five *Narcissus* cultivars as well as any other spring-blooming bulbs that need just a bit of vernalization are *ideal for bulb forcers in warmer climates*, where the outdoor soil temperature gets below 50°F for less than six weeks.

Unless you're a southern grower who buys pre-cooled bulbs or you chill your bulbs in a refrigerator (see figure 10.8), you'll have to chill your spring-blooming bulbs outdoors.

But even if you live in an area with limited winter weather, there are species and cultivars of spring-blooming bulbs (especially the early outdoor bloomers) that you can force after minimal chilling. The already-described five daffodil cultivars (see above) as well as the bulbs reviewed in Chapters 6 and 7 are just a few of the many bulbs suitable for your climate. I've also found that *Muscari* 'Christmas Pearl' will bloom with *zero* chilling, but approaches horticultural perfection with just 38 days of vernalization.

So, don't give up! There's a big botanical world of bulbs to discover that are ideal for your growing area. I'll report on the results of my additional trials, but go ahead and push the horticultural envelope and do your own tests as well.

Figure 16.20 (right) *'Rijnveld's Early Sensation' is a long-nosed daff that needed only 16 days of chilling to produce these excellent results. So bulb forcers from warmer climates aren't limited to the more diminutive or tazetta (Division 7) narcissi.*

Figure 16.21 *My greenhouse in 1998. I tried new cultivars and recorded my results a year before attempting the 13-division display at the Philadelphia Flower Show.*

A Daffy Case of Triskaidekaphobia*

Sleep. It all comes down to sleep.

Doctors say we need it, that we'll go insane without it, and no matter how important the task at hand, we have to give in and let sleep overtake us.

I know it. You know it. Anyone with a bit of grey matter knows it. But for some reason we willingly deprive ourselves of it.

When I was psychotic in 1995 and entered 140 pots to win my first Philadelphia Flower Show Grand Sweepstakes, slumberland was "a long time ago in a galaxy far, far away."† I may be an extreme case, but the truth is that all bulb-forcing exhibitors have so much to accomplish in so little time that, inevitably, exhaustion takes over, and we reach the point of diminished returns. As sleep deprivation takes its toll, we do more harm than good by piling one mistake upon another. In 1999 my lack of sleep along with my otherworldly "Odd-Year Flower Show Curse,"‡ made my particular non-basketball version of "March Madness" more memorable than ever.

---

* Triskaidekaphobia is fear of the number thirteen.

† These are, of course, the first words from the first *Star Wars* film. They're only slightly metaphorical in this case.

‡ My hysterical and pitiable disasters in 1993, 1995, and 1997 are detailed in Chapters 4 and 8 of *Garden Lunacy: A Growing Concern* (AAB Book Publishing, 2005), which can be purchased at Gardenlunacy.com, Amazon.com, or BarnesandNoble.com.

That year, a group of four fellow-Philly Flower Show exhibitors and I, collectively known as The Forcers of Destiny, were trying to produce a collection of daffodils in a window display.

This would be a departure for me, since my primary goal wasn't merely to win a blue ribbon, but to educate the public about the great variety of daffodils. There were twelve divisions based on the physical features of flowers and foliage, and whether the daffodil was non-hybridized (meaning a "species"). For two years we had obsessed on how we would accomplish our goal. In 1998, I had a practice run of forcing almost all the daffodils needed for the collection. I kept careful records of every cultivar and the time needed to force them into bloom.

Finally, by November 1998, we had potted-up bulbs in enough containers to achieve horticultural glory.

Then the "Curse" hit.

I had never been superstitious about walking under ladders, breaking mirrors, or opening umbrellas in the house. Then everything changed: in late November, I

"Anybody have any tranquilizers for Wolk?"

Figure 16.22 *The dandelion-like* Narcissus *'Rip van Winkle' is a miniature double (Division 4) that's been popular since 1884. But show it to non-gardeners and they won't believe it's a daffodil.*

learned that a new thirteenth daffodil division had just been created, namely *Narcissus bulbocodium* hybrids.*

So, once again, the horticultural gods had decided to test my capabilities. It was November and the bulb dealers in my area had sold all of their daffodils in the new division. Not surprisingly, I awoke the day after learning about the new division with a neurotic fear of the number 13, otherwise known as triskaidekaphobia.

In desperation, I called Lee Raden, a member of The Forcers of Destiny. Lee was an irrepressible man straight out of a Dickens novel. He was like the characters that pop up at the end of the book to perform philanthropic miracles. Lee could get away with saying anything that would otherwise make me angry. The fact is that I loved the man and whatever he said usually put me into hysterics.

Back in the 1990s, Lee was one of the few exhibitors at the Philadelphia Flower Show with as much competitive fervor as I. We'd vie for the daffodil rosettes every year and, on the rare occasions when I managed to beat him, he wasn't reluctant to tell me what an awful daffodil cultivar I'd chosen to grow, and that it belonged in a garden, not a flower show. (And, for some reason, it was ONLY the varieties that beat him out of a rosette that he disliked the most). But his testiness was always done with humor, in the way that good friends tease one another.

He was competitive, but also quite generous. Raden once gave me very rare daffodil bulbs he'd grown from

seed. He also was a great asset when I was a fledgling exhibitor. Back then, he gave me excellent advice on ways to improve my entries, so I'd have a better chance of winning blue ribbons – many times in the very classes in which he also had an entry. So, how could I possibly have taken his irascible behavior seriously? Raden was a polished horticultural gem who was a past-president of the North American Rock Garden Society.

When I asked if he had a *Narcissus bulbocodium* hybrid, he told me that he didn't have any, but suggested that I call a friend of his in Great Britain who owned a bulb company. However, when I made the cross-Atlantic call, I again came up empty. Before I hung-up, Lee's friend suggested I call the bulb company owned by Brent and Becky Heath in Virginia.*

Figure 16.23 Narcissus *'Pipit' is a creamy yellow and white jonquilla (Division 7) that was an easy choice for the 13-division daffodil exhibit. No photo does it justice; force it once and you'll agree.*

---

* Bulbocodium daffodils are miniatures with relatively large "noses" but very thin, small outer petals.

---

* The company is known as "Brent and Becky's Bulbs" (see Appendix 3).

Figure 16.24 Narcissus *'Bridal Crown' (Division 4), one of the cultivars grown for the daffodil display, is easy to force and has flowers that resemble little roses.*

I reached Becky, who was as pleasant as possible, but said in her southern accent, "I'm sorry, honey, we just don't have any left." I told her that perhaps I should "play it dumb," and do the display as if I'd never discovered that there was a new daffodil division. Being one of the world's daffodil experts, she didn't like that idea at all, and I had to admit she was right. Flower shows are a bit like our legal system: ignorance of the rules is no excuse. She suggested I call Dr. Kathryn Andersen in Delaware, another world authority on daffs, who goes on annual trips to Europe and North Africa to see them bloom in the wild.

I had already met Andersen because she judged bulb entries at the Philadelphia Flower Show. When I asked her my question, my spirits soared when she said, "Yes! I do have bulbocodium hybrids." But they sank again when she added, "Unfortunately they're planted in my garden and I'm not sure of their location."

Then, just before I said goodbye, she interjected, "Wait a second! I'm certain that Lee Raden has a hybrid. I've seen *Narcissus romieuxii* 'Atlas Gold' [which is within the bulbocodium group] blooming in his greenhouse."

So my quest had come full-circle, navigating around the Atlantic Ocean to find a few small daffodil bulbs. I

called Lee again, told him what Andersen had said, and he responded, "Oh yeah, that's right! I do have them, and I'll force them for our exhibit."

For a while, things went smoothly – too smoothly considering it was an odd year in the 1990s and I was once again tempting fate at the Philadelphia Flower Show.

In mid-February, with the Show dead ahead and pots coming into bloom, it was up to The Forcers of Destiny to do what was necessary to make everything peak at the right time. Since I was growing about 90% of the pots needed for the 13-division display, most of the pressure was on me.

About three weeks before the Show, I started getting up an hour early every morning to water and evaluate forty pots of daffodils. Some went outside to be held back (if it was above 32°F), some were placed on the cool greenhouse floor, some went on a warm greenhouse bench, and one was put under fluorescent lights indoors to push it ahead.

Figure 16.25 *'Ice Follies' is an excellent Division 2 (large cupped) daffodil with noses that start yellow and finish creamy white. This pot needed no extraneous support because it was forced in cool (60°-64°F), sunny conditions.*

Figure 16.26 *The ethereal, creamy-yellow* Narcissus *'Cassata' (Division 11, Split Corona) has a splayed, flattened nose that's typical of this division.*

Each day I got more and more fatigued. This pattern caught up with me one week before the Show, when I had to cut out small squares of poster board that would be used to number each pot in the exhibit. I loaded a utility knife with a razor blade, and then used a power screwdriver to assemble the knife. This worked fine until the screw was tightened into place. At that point, the power screwdriver started moving the razor blade in circles and into my thumb!

Blood gushed, while I cursed and ran to the sink. Nothing I did could make the bleeding stop. So although I had a trillion things to do to get ready for the Show, my daughter had to drive me to a local hospital for stitches and bandaging.

Exhaustion, fatigue, and self-destructiveness may have been setting in, but the potted daffodils were zooming into bloom exactly on schedule. Although I had forty pots that comprised about thirty-five different cultivars, only four pots were too far behind to make it into the Show. The other thirty-six were peaking perfectly.

It looked as if this would be my best year ever for bulb forcing. I was so excited that I could barely fall asleep at night.

The daffodil display had to be set up on Saturday, March 6th. I had done enough planning for everything to fall into place, but I didn't feel complacent.

On Friday, March 5th, I cleaned pots and groomed daffodil foliage and flowers all day, then went to pick up a rented van. I had ordered one that could provide heat in the storage area. With such a van I wouldn't have to worry if I had to transport my flowers on a sub-freezing morning. But when I got to the truck rental agency, I discovered that a mistake had been made: they only had large trucks that didn't have the capability of heating the storage area. I didn't have time to argue or wait for another van to be obtained, so I rented a truck. I was heartened by the fact that it was only supposed to go down to 34°F that night.

My wife Arlene as well as my friends Bill and Mary Harkell helped me groom half the potted daffs; then a neighbor carefully loaded them onto the truck. I also added a thermometer to keep track of the temperature, since daffodil flowers can be damaged when it's colder than 32°F.

I continued grooming plants until about 2:30AM. Then I checked the truck and discovered that the temperature inside had dipped to 29°F! In desperation, I ran upstairs, got an electric heater, and used an extension cord to place it in the truck. I managed to get the temperature up to 40°F, so I went back to grooming daffodils.

I was working on pure adrenaline, and knew I only

Figure 16.27 *The 13-division daffodil display at the 1999 Philadelphia Flower Show (see legend on opposite page). Staging had to be completed by 9:00AM. We finished with plenty of time to spare, meaning about three seconds to spare. I suppose I should have planned for the possibility of a bridge fire that morning, but somehow it slipped my mind.*

had until 9:00AM to get the pots to the flower show and staged. This wasn't the time for sleep, so I forged ahead, and at 4:30AM the truck was loaded and I could relax a bit. If we left at five-fifteen, we'd be at the show by six o'clock.

Then my "Flower Show Curse" hit.

Arlene turned on the radio and heard that the bridge we always used to cross the Delaware River had experienced a power failure due to a fire. In my entire life, I had never heard of a single bridge across the Delaware River being closed because of a fire; but this was an odd year in the 1990s and I was entering a lot of plants in the Flower Show. Not even a bridge is safe if I'm planning to cross it

during Flower Show week.*

The Benjamin Franklin Bridge closure meant that we'd have to waste precious time by heading north to another bridge. After I cursed at my accursed bad luck, we went on our way. I drove the truck and Arlene and several friends followed me in their cars.

We got to the Show at 6:30AM, meaning thirty minutes later than I had wanted. By 7:00AM all the daffs had been transported from the Convention Center garage, up the freight elevator, and onto the floor in front of our

---

* A bridge supervisor later confirmed my suspicion. In his many decades of employment, it was the only time a fire had closed the Benjamin Franklin Bridge.

The Thirteen Division Display* (Figure 16.28)

1. *Narcissus* 'Thalia' - (Division 5, Triandrus)
2. *Narcissus* 'Barrett Browning' - (Division 3, Small cupped)
3. *Narcissus* 'Ice Follies' - (Division 2, Large cupped)
4. *Narcissus* 'Ceylon' - (Division 2, Large cupped)
5. *Narcissus* 'Printal' - (Division 11, Split corona)
6. *Narcissus* 'Milan' - (Division 9, Poeticus)
7. *Narcissus bulbocodium* 'Atlas Gold' (Division 10)
8. *Narcissus canaliculatus* (Division 13, *Narcissus* species)
9. *Narcissus* 'Tete-a-Tete' (Division 12, Other *Narcissus*)
10. *Narcissus* 'Hawera' (Division 5, Triandrus)
11. *Narcissus* 'W. P. Milner' (Division 1, Trumpet)
12. *Narcissus* 'Rip Van Winkle' (Division 4, Double)

13. *Narcissus bulbocodium* subsp. *bulbocodium* var. *tenuifolius* (Division 13, *Narcissus* species)
14. *Narcissus* 'Cragford' (Division 8, Tazetta)
15. *Narcissus* 'Cassata' (Division 11, Split corona)
16. *Narcissus* 'Petit Four' (Division 4, Double)
17. *Narcissus* 'Las Vegas' (Division 1, Trumpet)
18. *Narcissus* 'Jumblie' (Division 6, Cyclamineus)
19. *Narcissus* 'Avalanche' (Division 8, Tazetta)
20. *Narcissus* 'Pipit' (Division 7, Jonquilla)
21. *Narcissus* 'Jetfire' (Division 6, Cyclamineus)
22. *Narcissus* 'Actaea' (Division 9, Poeticus)
23. *Narcissus* 'Bridal Crown' (Division 4, Double)

* These are the 13 divisions as they existed in 1999. It also has the botanical nomenclature for each species and cultivar as it existed in 1999. As of the publication of this book, there are 14 divisions. The most notable change is that all miniatures are now grouped in the same division.

display window.

The other growers in The Forcers of Destiny (Arlene, Susie Ganoe, Lee Raden, Ray Rogers, and Sherry Santifer) added their potted daffodils to my collection. We let Ray, a true plantsman and a garden book writer and editor, decide which pots were good enough for the display. He selected twenty-three pots: two belonging to Lee Raden (the absolutely essential species and hybrid bulbocodiums), one that Arlene and I grew together, and the rest grown by me. Although I felt proud that Ray had picked twenty of my pots, I also felt terrible for the three growers whose daffs weren't included.

It was seven-thirty at that point, and no time could be lost. Since the pots had been jostled during the trip, they each needed a final grooming, which took until eight-thirty. With only thirty minutes to go, we set brackets and glass shelves and put pots in place. After making a few frantic changes, we called over the passers of the collection classes. It was nine o'clock and we had finished with just a few seconds to spare.

The passers checked foliage, flowers, and pots for imperfections and proper nomenclature.

Above all else, we wanted this display to be educational. Very few gardeners knew about the thirteen diverse daffodil divisions, so I had obtained permission months in advance to put the division designations on

the placard the judges would see.*

The exhibit was passed, and the approved nomenclature list was sent to typists who entered the information on poster board for the judges. We'd finished our work and were sent off the exhibit floor so judges could work in relative isolation.

I had gone thirty hours without rest, but the excitement and my overactive adrenal glands had kept me too energized to feel the need for sleep.

By 11:30AM the judging was over.

With great anticipation, we ran to see the results, only to find that we had obtained a second-place ribbon. Dr. and Mrs. Gerald Barad, (the former a past-president of the American Cactus Society) had received the blue ribbon. His collection of succulents was so rare and horticulturally perfect, that I couldn't feel upset.[†]

But then I noticed something: the typists had neglected to include the division designations on our placard. Not surprisingly, the judges' comments were, "A brilliant floricultural achievement. This display would have been more educational if daffodil division information had been included."

Figure 16.29 Narcissus *'Actaea' simply glistens and was an obvious poeticus (Division 9) choice for the 13-division display. Each blossom is its own work of art.*

---

* One example would be *Narcissus* 'Las Vegas' Division I Trumpet Daffodil. Again, for a full explanation of the divisions, see the American Daffodil Society's webpage: http://www.daffodilusa.org/daffodils/div.html (last accessed 6/30/2011).

†Dr. Barad has produced his own hybrids through cross pollination.

anywhere in the world, and he also told me that anytime I'd like to stage a similar one using minor bulbs, he'd supply me with the bulbs at no cost!

His words were worth twenty blue ribbons to me. And, on the spot, my case of triskaidekaphobia ended.

The next day, Anna Marie Amey, the chair of the Flower Show's competitive classes, heard about the nomenclature problem and had the daffodil division information added to our display. She also had the judges comments retyped…without the negative second sentence.

And, the awards weren't over. On Monday, our display also earned a rosette for being the best groomed and maintained collection, and all four entries in the class received a judges' commendation ribbon because of the distinction of the class as a whole.

I also learned that the judges had gone back and forth, over and over, trying to decide between our display and Dr. Barad's. That certainly eased the pain. It also didn't hurt that during the rest of the week I had enough pots left over to enter them individually in the Horticourt competition, where I earned ten blue ribbons and a rosette for best daffodil entry (see figure 16.6).

Looking back, I have no reason to feel disappointed about the second place ribbon for our collection. That year was a "personal best." Simply put, I could not have done a better job of forcing bulbs.

Figure 16.30 *The pristine* Narcissus *'Thalia' is a triandrus daffodil. This division is known for multiple blossoms on each stem and flowers that hang like bells.*

I was livid! I felt that all my hard work and planning had been in vain. But there was nothing I could do; the decision of the judges was final. In frustration, I walked over and had another look at Dr. Barad's display, and calmed down when I realized what an absolute jewel it was. So, perhaps placing second to this display wasn't so bad after all.

Then something incredible happened: Brent Heath, who with his wife Becky wrote the book *Daffodils for American Gardens*, saw our display and was extremely impressed. He told me that it was the best potted-daffodil displays of the thirteen divisions he'd ever seen

Figure 16.31 *(right) The cyclamineus (Division 6)* Narcissus *'Wisley' is one of the longest lasting forced daffodils. Don't be surprised if it lasts three weeks at temperatures below 67°F.*

Figure 16.32 *'Amadeus Mozart' is a double that deserves a first, second, and tenth look. It's hard to believe that any daffodil could be this beautiful; but in person, it's even more gorgeous.*

After twenty years of Philadelphia Flower Show exhibiting, I was finally starting to take a broader view. I had won many awards that gave me feelings of accomplishment, but I realized there was something else just as important taking place at the show. While everyone else is enduring winter's wrath, we bulb forcers surround ourselves with the most gorgeous flowers of spring. All the beauty and aroma, exploding at us in an ever-increasing sensual display, is too much for one person to hoard. So exhibitors bring their flowers to the Philly Show so we can share our stolen spring with you.

Just a few words of warning: when you visit competitive flower shows like the one in Philadelphia, be sure to keep your distance from exhibitors like me moving around like hummingbirds with potted bulbs under our wings. And, if it *is* me you spot, please move away. You don't want to be a victim of one of my odd-year, horrific-horticultural disasters.

Just stand back and laugh from afar.

****

Although the daffodil is my favorite spring-blooming bulb, I am in a minority. After all, when most of you think of springtime flowers, the first one that usually comes to mind is the tulip.

There's no other springtime flower that sports such diversity in flower shape, color, and even scent. And the tulip, like other bulbs, can be easily forced into bloom during the dreariest of winters.

Exactly how you do that is the topic of the next chapter. So, let's proceed there now.

Figure 16.33 *(above) Even small daffodil noses can be stunning. Narcissus 'Actaea' (see also figure 16.29) sports a red-rimmed cup with pollen-laden anthers.*

Figure 16.34 *(right) Narcissus 'Ice King' is an easy-to force double that glows when backlit. It's usually in bloom within four weeks when grown at 65°F.*

17
TULIPS: QUEENS OF THE UNDERWORLD

If daffodils are "Kings of the Underworld," then tulips are their seductive throne-mates. With their dazzling variety of color, size, shape, and scent, they're a

Figure 17.1 *No flowers brighten a winter day more than tulips. Their form and color seem infinite.*

sensual extravaganza. To me they're feminine botanical splendor at its best.

Some tulips are a bit finicky to grow; others will bloom even if you break sacrosanct bulb-forcing rules (see *Topsy-Turvy Tulips* on pages 145).

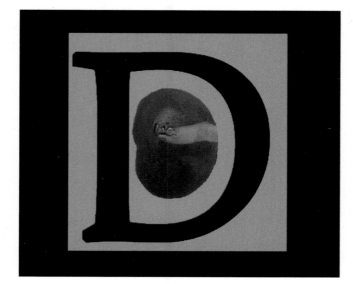

Figure 17.2 *(far left)* '*Mona Lisa*' *is a dose of sunshine even on –* **especially on** *– horrible winter days.*

Figure 17.3 *(left) Can you guess which letter a tulip bulb resembles?*

Figure 17.4 *(over) The elegant tulip 'Purple Prince' is easy to force and quite photogenic.*

Figure 17.5 *Begin by planting every bulb so the flat side faces the inside rim. Typically, an 8" pot will hold 15-20 mature bulbs.*

After more than twenty-five years of growing tulips, I've had enough trials and errors (actually, lots of trials and plenty of errors), to tell you what works.

You already know what pot I'd like you to use (i.e., a clay pot) and what growing mix to use (basically, any potting mix that's airy, and isn't bone try or sopping wet). What you may not know is how to plant tulip bulbs to have an amaze-your-visitors-or-flower-show-judges pot of blooming beauties.

And, it starts with a lesson in tulip bulb anatomy. But, it's a simple one. Put a tulip bulb, bottom-side down, on the floor or on a table and peer down. Isn't it odd? Here we have a bulb with a flat side and a round side (see figure 17.3). And, if the round side is on the right, it looks like a capital letter "D," doesn't it?

"But, Art," you might wonder, "why should I care about 'D'-shaped bulbs?"

Figure 17.7 *'Lucky Strike' forces quickly, usually within four weeks. Note how the largest, outermost leaves make it look as though the flowers are exploding out of the center, producing the Fountain Effect. See also 'Pieter de Leur' in figure 17.17.*

Figure 17.6 *After planting tulip bulbs as shown in figure 17.5, cover with potting mix, then chill (vernalize) your potted bulbs. You'll get this type of symmetrical leaf growth within two weeks of indoor forcing.*

Figure 17.9 *'Ile de France' is one of the most vivid red tulips to force.*

Figure 17.10 *The rose-like 'Calgary' is simply stunning.*

Figure 17.11 *Like boys encircling the prom queen, pollen-laden stamens surround the pistil inside every tulip.*

Because the largest (and first) leaf a tulip bulb sends above ground is always parallel to the flat side of the bulb. This makes it possible to have beautiful, concentric leaves around the outside of the pot.

But, don't limit this to the bulbs against the side of the pot. Have every bulb's flat side face the rim, regardless of its location (see figure 17.5). This makes all the largest leaves face outward, and produces what I call the "Fountain Effect." The leaves and flowers seem to be exploding outward from the center.

Have a look at 'Lucky Strike' (see figure 17.7). This is a quick forcer packed with color that lets you say, "Who gives a damn about icy roads and sidewalks, I've got tulips." Note the leaves gracefully spilling over the top of the pot, but also notice the Fountain Effect. Don't you get the sense that foliage and flowers are flowing fluidly from a central focus? It gives the blooming bulbs a sense of movement, drama,

Figure 17.8 *(previous two pages) Parrot tulips always produce huge, dramatic flowers, and* Tulipa *'Professor Rontgen' is no exception.*

Figure 17.12 *(right) The tulip 'Gavota' is a popular bicolor that's striking in a flower pot or flower border.*

142

Figure 17.13 *No other backlit flower looks as exquisite as tulips. This is 'Banja Luka', one of the largest tulips you'll ever force.*

Figure 17.14 *(below) The tulip bed at the Philadelphia International Flower Show after ribbons have been awarded. The wooden slat (bottom right) is used to separate different competitive classes.*

and excitement.

Now, I want you to especially note the snow outside the window. I'll bet you didn't notice it until I brought it to your attention.

This is what bulb forcing is all about. Perhaps I've made you think my focus is elsewhere, but, in my heart-of-hearts, bulb forcing is not about blue ribbons, it's not about impressing your family and friends, and it's not about photographs.

It's about the smile it puts on your mug despite the detestable weather on the other side of the window.

The chilling period for tulips mirrors the time of year they bloom, with the earliest needing 10-11 weeks and the latest 13 weeks or more.

The rest of my forcing instructions are basically the same as for minor bulbs and daffodils, but I strongly suggest starting your bulb forcing career with tulips that flower early (see Index under "*Tulipa* cultivars"). Leave the late bloomers, like 'Angelique' (see

page 150) or 'Professor Rontgen'(see figure 17.8), for the second year or later. You see, the later the bulb blooms, the longer it takes to force. And the longer it has to be forced, the greater the chance of the bulb (or you) not doing what's expected.

Force tulips just a bit too warm, and you can end up with wonderful leaves, but misshapen flowers or *no flowers at all* – a condition called "blasting" (see page 212).*

One other warning: when you start forcing tulips, you'll think *all* your bulbs will be blasted, because the flower buds don't reveal themselves until your forced bulbs are racing down the home stretch. I know it's useless to tell anyone – especially compulsive gardeners – not to panic. We've all panicked over the perceived imminent death of our plants.

It's just who we are.

So let me be the only authoritarian garden writer (or authoritative anything) to say, go right ahead and panic. *Have yourself one hell of a full-scale panic attack!* But as with most panic attacks, the imagined trigger for your neurosis will be unfounded, because your tulips will almost always bloom.

---

* According to the fifth edition of *Holland Bulb Forcer's Guide*, blasting (also called flower abortion) is "the failure of a bulb to produce a marketable flower after all the floral organs have been completely formed."

You should also know that most tulips will not abide double layering. The top-layer bulbs protest stridently against such a narrow rooting zone. Still, there are exceptions. My favorite four are 'Leen Van Der Mark' (see figure 17.16), 'Golden Melody,' 'Kees Nelis' and 'Cheerleader'. But be forewarned: double layering demands double the bulbs, meaning double the cash. If you're a gardener who barely glances at the price of plants (regardless of your bank balance), then go for the perfect/blue-ribbon pot. If not, you can still grow a great looking pot that's single layered.

Topsy-Turvy Tulips

Now that I've told you the correct way to force tulips, let me also say that you can grow them all "wrong," but in the end wonder, "Where did I go right?"*

Case in point: *Tulipa* 'Leen Van Der Mark'.†

In 1996, I grew a 12" pot of them for the Philadelphia Flower Show. That year I potted my bulbs too late, and all they did in my cold frame was, well, *nothing*. It was a very cold winter, they were potted too late to root properly, so it was time for desperation. I figured that if I put them in my

Figure 17.15 *(following two pages) 'Antoinette' is a kaleidoscopic, tulip with multiple flowers per bulb. Every day a new color seems to appear: it starts as a pale yellow that darkens, then adds rose-red and orange.*

---

* Fellow-lovers of the movie *The Producers* will recognize this most quotable of all quotes. The scheme: sell 10,000% of a show, and then produce a flop so backers won't expect a return on their money. The show ("Springtime for Hitler") has the wrong writer, wrong director, and wrong actors, but is a hit, making producer Max Bialystock (Zero Mostel) wonder, "Where did we go right?"
† *Tulipa* is the genus name for all tulips.

"Just look at how happy my tulips are!"

Figure 17.16 *This is the lucky/miraculous pot of double-layered 'Leen Van Der Mark' tulips that won two blues and one red ribbon despite my mistakes.*

perfection. They rooted, began producing leaves, and came into bloom the day before the Philadelphia Flower Show.

That year, the Show moved from the Philadelphia Civic Center to the new Philadelphia Convention Center. At the Civic Center, the temperatures were always on the warm side for spring-blooming bulbs: close to seventy degrees or higher. At such temperatures, a bulb exhibitor was lucky to get the same pot to do well in two of the three judging days, which are Saturday, Tuesday, and Friday of Flower Show week.

However, the first year at the Convention Center, the temperature was closer to 62°F, which was perfect for bulbs, but chilly for visitors. They obviously had their priorities properly in place: the paying visitors be damned, let's keep the place cool for Art Wolk's bulbs.

So, here's what happened: luck was heaped upon luck upon more luck for someone who showed the planning of Napoleon during his winter retreat in Russia. My pot of tulips got a red (second place) ribbon the first day of judging, a blue three days later, and another blue on the third day of judging. I defy any of my fellow competitors to name a single pot of their tulips that did any better.

And, here I do not claim a nanobit of horticultural superiority. Instead, I claim that I was ridiculously lucky. Many exhibitors had undisguised envy and asked me how I pulled it off, but I just shrugged my shoulders. Some were obviously disgruntled, and must have thought I was being secretive and unsharing, and *every one of them was wrong.*

sixty-degree greenhouse two weeks earlier than usual, they just might root and bloom.

This was a case of luck saving someone displaying zero horticultural aptitude.

Yes, as you might have guessed, they *did* begin rooting at 60°F. When I first took the bulbs into the greenhouse, you could wobble each one, because none were rooted. So I watered and waited.

Then, despite my lack of planning, the tulips grew to

Figure 17.17 *This pot of the lily-shaped tulip 'Pieter de Leur' is a perfect example of the fountain effect: the flowers and leaves are exploding out of the center. 'Pieter de Leur' forces easily after vernalization, usually within four weeks.*

I was the dumbfounded doofus who said nothing, until now, about my lack of horticultural planning or expertise. Sorry guys and gals, I had no business winning those ribbons. I had no pride in winning them. I simply thought to myself, "How the @$%# did you pull that off?"* (And, yes, I thought the same word you're thinking of now.)

****

Now that you've learned about one of the most recognizable and beautiful flowers to force, we're going to take a step in another direction. In fact, I used to consider these flowers about a million steps from "beautiful."

---

* This wasn't magic, but science...completely unplanned science. See Chapter 11: "Giving Bulbs the Cold, *Dry* Shoulder."

But I was wrong.

The truth is that forcing these bulbs is something you really should experience. The genus name is *Arisaema*, which includes the common jack-in-the-pulpit. But, as you're about to learn, these particular bulbs and flowers are not in any way common. At first glance, they'll seem merely interesting, but after a second look, you'll find them absolutely charming.

They're the subject of Chapter 18, so let's go there next.

Figure 17.18 *(below) What's not to love? 'Angelique' always rewards the patient grower with unmatched beauty.*

Figure 17.19 *(right) The fringed tulip 'Cummins' is a long-lasting, late-blooming attention grabber. Try it the second year you force tulips.*

18
ARISAEMA - AN ACQUIRED TASTE

My fellow Philly Flower Show exhibitors would be shocked to see this tuber listed as one of my favorite bulbs to force. Why? Because back in 1993 I thought it was as beautiful as The Wicked Witch of the East…after Dorothy's house fell on her…after her feet curled and shrunk from view…without the Ruby Slippers.

I was used to tantalizing tulips, dazzling daffodils, and curvaceous crocuses.

Then I saw the club-like flower (spadix) and hooded non-flower (spathe) of *Arisaema sikokianum*. It looked like my pharmacist father's pestle covered with a bad excuse for an umbrella. Not surprisingly, Ray Rogers was the competitor who had pushed the horticultural envelope by entering this plant that I had never seen at the Philadelphia Flower Show. It was in peak condition, it was rare, and (of course) it was a blue-ribbon winner all three judging days of Flower Show week.

I had three double-layered, eight-inch pots of *Scilla mischtschenkoana* (previously known as *S. tubergeniana*) that were perfect (see figure 14.5). There were so many uniform flowers that you couldn't see the underlying foliage. And, of course, they won red or yellow ribbons.

Did my blue-ribbonless pots of *Scilla* cause my anti-*Arisaema* bias? Of course they did. I was acting like a petulant child who was missing more than a few marbles from his sack…and his head. I even went so far as to tell Rogers that the plant was ugly. He smiled and said, "Well, I'll still bring them to the Show every year." He didn't have to say the second sentence, which would have been, "If you want to have a

Figure 18.1 *(left) If, at first glance, you think* Arisaema serratum *is repulsive, let me welcome you to the "Art Wolk Lack of Botanical Appreciation Club."*

Figure 18.2 Arisaema sikokianum *is an easy-to-force, absolutely gorgeous plant. When I first saw it in bloom, I thought it was hideous, meaning my brain had been taken over by an extra-terrestrial body snatcher.*

chance to win the 'Other Hardy Bulbs' blue ribbon,* you'd better re-evaluate your entries."

It took four long years of hard headedness for me to appreciate the graceful beauty of arisaemas. When I finally began growing them, I was entranced.

Before beginning the forcing process, slow down and have a squint at the bulbs themselves, (figures 18.5 and 18.6) which are unlike any you're likely to force in your lifetime. One looks a bit like a turban, another like a small, potent pepper. It's *almost* a shame that you have to tuck them underground. Alas, bulb forcing usually demands bulb burying. When I'm finally finished obsessing on *Arisaema* bulbs, I plant them so that the top of the bulb is 1½"-2" below the surface.

After chilling for at least two months, you can force this bulb as you would early or mid-season daffodils or

Figure 18.3 *(previous two pages)* Arisaema kishidae *is like a horticultural peacock spreading its feathers. The final stage is shown in figure 18.4 (right).*

* There are approximately two dozen competitive bulb classes on each of the three judging days at the Philadelphia Flower Show. (Again, the judging days are Saturday, Tuesday, and Friday of flower show week.) Most of the classes are limited to a genus (e.g., any *Crocus*), genus category (e.g., any miniature *Narcissus*), or genus cultivar (e.g., *Tulipa* 'Leen Van Der Mark'). There are also broad categories like "Other Hardy Bulbs," which includes any bulbs that are hardy in the Philadelphia area (USDA Zone 6).

tulips, meaning at least 3-6 weeks at 60-68°F.

A. sikokianum will take 5-6 weeks to reach its peak, but it's well worth the wait. The form of this Aphrodite of arisaemas is exquisite – so exquisite, in fact, that you may find yourself staring at it for a good ten minutes when it first blossoms. There's so much to discover and

Figure 18.4 Arisaema kishidae: *the spathe screams for well-deserved attention.*

appreciate, which is why it deserves to be at the top of your shopping list.

Other early-blooming arisaemas that I've forced include *A. serratum*, *A. kishidae*, and *A. yamatense*.

The fastest growing is *A. serratum*. I doubt if you've

Figure 18.5 Arisaema sikokianum *tuber: a dead ringer for a chili pepper wearing a dunce cap.*

Figure 18.6 *An* Arisaema serratum *tuber reminds me of a turban or perhaps a honeycomb wearing a shark fin – in other words, it's unlike any bulb I've ever seen.*

Figure 18.7 Arisaema serratum *– the fastest growing bulb in my universe. At some point in the distant past (way before genetic counseling), an ancestor of this bulb must have had casual sex with rainforest bamboo.*

ever grown a potted bulb that goes from a barely discernable pip to a 36" specimen so quickly. Unlike their *Homo sapiens* counterparts who need a medication so they'll be "ready when the moment is right," *A. serratum* appears – at least in profile – to be *always* ready, and *never* to have a wrong moment. Don't be surprised to see it grow 2" taller in a single evening. After vernalization, it

should be in bloom on your cool, sunny windowsill within 21-25 days.

A. kishidae is the next-fastest bloomer and the most striking of the group. The leaves have black speckles near the edges that echo the black streaks on the 2"-wide spathe. It takes about 25-28 days to flower.

And, then there's *A. yamatense*, which takes 5-6 weeks to force and defies comparison to anything but a modern raptor – a very hungry raptor – with wings (upper leaves) spread apart as it readies it's talons (lower leaves) and piercing beak (spathe) for a dispatching lunge at its prey. It's only a bit shorter than *A. serratum*, but has twice the menace – and, obviously, thrice the charm – of its taller cousin.

****

Growing bulbs is a dichotomy: gardeners venture into the land of seeming make believe, then travel back to the well-trodden land of the familiar.

Some species, like *Arisaema yamatense*, seem otherworldly, while familiar flowers, like the lily, take us back to our comfort zone.

And yet, even the common lily can be uncommon, with cultivars that can lock your senses on their extravaganza of color, size, and scent. Lilies take a bit longer to force than most spring-blooming bulbs, but their beauty makes the wait worthwhile.

They're the subject of Chapter 19, so let's head there next.

Figure 18.8 Arisaema yamatense – *a dead ringer for a modern-day raptor on the attack. Approach with care!*

19

LILIES: ELEGANCE ON THE WINDOWSILL

This is cause for celebration – as in parades and cheerleaders forming a fifty-foot-high pyramid.

I'm thankful that at least one of you made it past the first word of this chapter's title. And, there are only three possible reasons you did:

1. You haven't heard the bilge about the utter impossibility of home gardeners forcing lilies into bloom.
2. You've heard the cow-puck palaver about the need for a PhD in horticulture to force lilies at home, but you have open ears that are ready to listen to refuting evidence.
3. You've successfully forced lilies at home and want to read about other techniques.

Figure 19.1 *(above) Close-up of the lily 'Fangio', a hybrid between early-blooming Asiatics and sweet-scented Longiflorums.*

The first non-problem with lilies is that they're different from their already-described, spring-blooming pot-mates. You now know that tulips, daffodils, and hyacinths have flower buds tucked inside their "insides" when you plant them and that as long as you don't screw things up, they'll delight your ever-awaiting eyeballs.

But lilies don't come with pre-packaged flowers.

All the other flesh and bones are part of the bulb. But lilies don't form flower buds until you provide the same cold conditions that other spring-blooming bulbs need to form roots and begin flower-stem extension.

Lilies need the same conditions for roots and flower-stem shoots, but they also need them to form flower buds. That doesn't mean they're a coddled genus that

Figure 19.2 *(left) Count the growth buds, not the bulbs. This 12" pot will produce five stems. For the best display, I usually plant three, five, or more stems per pot, never just two.*

Figure 19.3
Here are the five 'Fangio' stems from figure 19.2 (there are two stems on the right). The height is uniform enough to produce a...

only exists in botanical gardens. To the contrary, they frolic in their native locales where there's airy soil and sunny days, without any help from *Homo sapiens.* And, there's no reason they shouldn't. If a type of bulb flowers in May, what difference does it make when they produce internal flower buds? They're simply late bloomers that are also late flower-formers.

The three most popular kinds of lilies to force are –

- **Asiatics**, which have no scent but make up for it with an array of colors unmatched by...
- **Orientals**, which make up for their relative lack of color choices by making the hills come alive with the scent of flowers. And, then there are...
- **Longiflorums**, which are also highly scented and have flowers that look like long trumpets. These are the lilies available by the zillions on Easter, at which time they come in a bedazzling selection of either white or...white.*

The Longiflorums are mainly forced by professional growers and are not widely available to the home gardener in the fall. Orientals *are* widely available, but take

much longer to force than Asiatics. But what's more important is that hybridizers have created many new varieties of Longiflorum-Asiatics (LA) and Oriental-Asiatics (OA). These new cultivars are moderately scented, bloom sooner than Longiflorums and Orientals, and have nearly the wide color choices of Asiatics.

Even so, the LA and OA hybrids can take 2-4 weeks longer to force than Asiatics.

If you're new to lily forcing, do yourself a favor and force Asiatic lilies first. They'll give you the best chance of having a positive, forcer-affirming experience. Then, if

Figure 19.4 *...uniform display of blossoms. Once you see and smell the flowers, you won't mind how tall 'Fangio' gets before it blooms.*

---

* I always pick the former because it reminds me so much of the latter.

CHAPTER NINETEEN

Figure 19.5 *The Asiatic lily 'Tiny Hope' looks hopelessly unbalanced at this stage, but the 'Tiny' series always seems to find a way…*

you're wild for scented lilies, try them the second year.

I always pick Asiatic cultivars that normally would bloom in May outdoors. (Retail lily dealers have the typical bloom date for each variety listed in their catalogs and online websites.) My favorite cultivars are the "Tiny" series offered by B&D Lilies. They always look well proportioned in 10" or 12" azalea pots and the color palette is exquisite.

When you're ready to grow scented varieties, pick those that bloom early, meaning cultivars that normally bloom outdoors before July.

My favorite scented variety to force is 'Fangio', which is a Longiflorum-Asiatic hybrid. Yes, it grows tall (see figure 19.4), but the color and scent make it well worth the effort and space.

Here are easy directions you can follow to have an eye-dazzling display:

1. Plant lily bulbs so that the tops are about two inches below the surface of your potting mix.

Figure 19.7 *(right) The lily 'Tiny Bee' has long-lasting, black-speckled flowers that are perfect for a 10" pot filled with five bulbs.*

Figure 19.6 *(above) …to become uniform. The flowers are long lasting and the 'Tiny' hybrids are prolific flower bud producers.*

Figure 19.9 *A 10" pot of 'Tiny Todd', viewed from above, has so many blossoms that the foliage and pot disappear.*

provide at least ten weeks at 40°-50°F, your bud count will be low. Remember: lilies form buds during vernalization. That's why **lilies are the first bulbs I pot in the fall, usually by October 15th in my Zone 6 garden**.

6. After chilling, force these bulbs at 64°-70°F.

7. Be patient! Asiatic lilies will take 7-8 weeks to force, and the "early-blooming," scented hybrids even longer.

8. As with other bulbs, turn the pot 90° per day for a uniform display.

9. Use ¼-diluted, balanced liquid fertilizer (e.g., 20-20-20) at each watering. I use this same solution for all my bulbs during forcing. Although most of them have enough food storage to blossom, I'm sure it helps those bulbs that need a boost for ideal foliage and flowers.

10. This is the only type of spring-blooming bulb in my greenhouse that occasionally gets aphids. I spray insecticidal soap on the foliage to banish them from my lilies.

11. When they bloom, run for your camera. The Asiatics are excellent subjects for horticultural photography.

An Easier Way to Force Lilies

And now, for those of you who love lilies, but refuse to go through the above process, please note that…

You can buy more expensive, but *pre-cooled bulbs* from some mail-order bulb companies. (See Chapter 11 for more information about pre-cooled bulbs.) These will already have flower buds inside, *so you should pot them and immediately force them at 64-70°F.*

If you can't pot your bulbs immediately upon their arrival, store them at 40-50°F, but not for more than two weeks.

I have one warning: companies that sell these bulbs in small lots to the public do so on an inconsistent basis, but keep searching and you'll probably find them through

2. Unlike other spring-blooming bulbs, it's best not to plant these bulbs cheek-to-jowl. If lily bulbs aren't given sufficient space, their foliage and flowers are far smaller and less robust. Even though there are fewer bulbs per pot, there are enough flower buds to give you a sumptuous display. I recommend five bulbs per 10" pot and 5-7 bulbs per 12" pot.

3. For uniform results, plant bulbs that are nearly the same size. Unlike most other spring-blooming bulbs, you won't get uniformity (i.e., all the blooms at nearly the same height) unless you plant similar-sized bulbs. The smaller ones rarely grow as tall as the larger bulbs.

4. Bulbs that arrive with roots attached (see figure 19.2) will bloom well ahead of those that don't. So, when I want a balanced display in a large pot, I tend to only plant bulbs with pre-formed roots. I plant the rootless bulbs in separate 6" pots.

5. Use the same chilling technique you use for other bulbs. This is *the* most important step. If you don't

Figure 19.8 *(previous two pages) 'Tiny Athlete' is a gorgeous, blush-pink lily that's easy to force.*

Figure 19.10 *(right) Sheer elegance. It doesn't get much better than this: six 'Tiny Snowflake' bulbs in a 12" pot reach their peak simultaneously.*

the Internet.*

This is one procedure that's been done successfully by professional growers for at least half a century: just think of all the potted lilies available for Easter, and virtually *every single forced flower* they produce comes from pre-cooled bulbs.

And, please, don't think there's anything magical about how the professionals force their lilies. They use the same techniques I've already described, so there's no reason why you couldn't produce your own fantastic pots on your windowsill.†

****

In Chapter 14, I grouped together many of my favorite minor bulbs. Because of their diminutive size and relatively early bloom season, it made sense to conjoin them in the same section.

Which is exactly what I've done again in Chapter 20. But in this case, the only thing these bulbs have in common is that I simply adore them.

For many of you, this will be your first introduction to these botanical beauties, and I envy you. There's nothing as wonderful as your first experience with new, breathtaking flowers.

Don't think twice about it: go ahead and buy these bulbs and force them into bloom this coming winter.

Exactly how you do that is the subject of Chapter 20, so turn the page and have a squint at my best-of-the-rest bulbs.

---

* To find companies with pre-cooled bulbs, you can enter "pre-cooled lily" (including the hyphen and quotation marks) using the search engine Google.com.

† Although I have more than twenty-five years of experience in forcing lily bulbs into bloom, I always used in-the-pot chilling. So, I'm not breaking Promise #1 from the Introduction, when I admit that I haven't yet forced pre-cooled lily bulbs. But, as you know from Chapter 11, I *have* done this successfully with many other spring-blooming bulbs. The next edition of this book will include the results of my forcing pre-cooled lily bulbs into bloom.

Figure 19.11 *(right) Isn't this exquisite? 'Pink Giant' takes more patience and space (each plant is approximately 3' tall) than the 'Tiny' series, but the flowers are magnificent — and a learning experience. Each black spot isn't merely an alternate petal color; it's three-dimensional. Look in the throat and you'll see that each spot is cone shaped, as if an artist added more than one hundred globs of black paint to each flower. This lily takes about 12 weeks to force at 64°-70°F, so plant and chill these bulbs as soon as they arrive in late September or early October.*

20
AND THEN THERE ARE...

Let me acquaint you with an inescapable fact: your life isn't a dress rehearsal, meaning you aren't forcing bulbs now so you can do it better once you're in your box with memorial flowers six feet above your feet.

There may be a very few of you who think you'll be reincarnated with all your memories of bulb forcing intact. I, on the other hand, think I'll be reincarnated as worm castings – a fate that might make it difficult for me to recall all my bulb-related adventures.

The moral? Force new bulbs every year.

And, I don't just mean different cultivars of a species you've forced a billion times. I mean different genera and species.

So, when you next look at a bulb catalog, don't say to yourself, "That looks gorgeous, but it might be hard to force," or, "That's a bit more than I want to spend for 'iffy' bulbs this year."

Instead, say to yourself, "This just might be the last chance I'll have to do this."

You might as well give it a go now, before you ebb off into Never Never Land or whatever euphemism you use for the hereafter.

Here are a few atypical bulbs you should force next winter:

Ipheion

For many of you, this is your first introduction to this diminutive, but attention-grabbing bulb.

Such was the case when I first forced *Ipheion uniflorum* 'Rolf Fiedler' in 2009.

Here's what I learned:
1. It's in the same family as garlic (Alliaceae) and has leaves that smell just like it.
2. It forms a lovely cushion of foliage.
3. The flowers are simply adorable.

Figure 20.1 *(left) Every part of an* Ipheion uniflorum *'Rolf Fiedler' flower is worth a second or one-hundredth look.*

Figure 20.2 Ipheion uniflorum *'Wisley Blue' puts on a charming, long-lasting show. Unlike most bulbs,* I. uniflorum *cultivars are content to spend their entire lives in containers. The above results were obtained after two years in the same pot.*

4. Unlike most forced bulbs, *Ipheion uniflorum* cultivars are perfectly happy to spend their entire lives in a container. In fact, they only get better each year.

Plant these bulbs in one layer and vernalize for at least ten weeks. Because of their diminutive foliage and short flower stems, I suggest using a 6" bulb pan. If you force them in sunny, cool conditions – meaning at 60°-64°F – the foliage and flowers will look exactly like they would in your outdoor garden.

When they're finished blooming, snip off the dead blossoms, give the foliage full sun, and water with liquid fertilizer. That's how, in future years, you produce the kind of lollapalooza display shown in figure 20.3.

Figure 20.3 *(over) The first year I forced* Ipheion uniflorum *'Rolf Fiedler' in this container I obtain a dozen blossoms. This photo is of the same pot when the bulbs were forced for the third year. This extravaganza of flowers lasted 4-5 weeks!*

Figure 20.4 Anemone blanda *'Charmer' simply sparkles. Buds hide under the leaves, then emerge and open in less than a day.*

Anemone blanda

You're probably thinking, "Hello, are you there, Art? Didn't you notice that you already have a section on anemones? And, if you did, why did you stick this one here?"

Same genus, different growth requirements, that's why.

Did you notice that Chapter 16 is about daffodils, but way back in Chapter 6 you learned about paper whites (*Narcissus tazetta* cultivars)? Again, same genus, different growth requirements.

Anemone coronaria doesn't need vernalization to blossom, but *Anemone blanda* does. Ten weeks of cold temperatures are sufficient.

However, like *A. coronaria*, these bulbs will rot if they're grown in an air-deprived, sopping wet potting mix, which is why I add extra perlite or Turface (see page 239) to my typical potting mix (one part perlite or Turface to two parts potting mix).

After vernalization, the only thing tricky about forcing this bulb is that it needs chilly conditions to bloom. You'll get sparse or no flowers at 65°F or above, but many more at 55°-64°F, and the cooler the better. In addition, surround the outer pot – even clay pots – with aluminum foil to keep the soil as cool as possible.

Figure 20.5 *I use aluminum foil on all my* Anemone blanda *containers to keep the soil temperature low.*

A. blanda cultivars vary considerably: 'Charmer' and 'Pink Star' hide their flower buds below the foliage for 3-4 weeks before blossoming. But 'White Splendor', which I urge you to grow first, has leaves and buds that emerge together. And, the flowers are much larger; so it's easier to pull off a walloping display (see figures 20.10 and 20.11).

Once in bloom, treat *A. blanda* like its coronarian cousin (see pages 56-62). In other words, don't let temperatures get above 70°F. In warm conditions, the flowers won't last and the foliage sags, sputters, goes into reverse gear, and it's all but impossible to get it back into drive.

Although *A. blanda* doesn't give you the same flower count per bulb that you get with *A. coronaria*, many more of these diminutive bulbs can be planted per pot.

Figure 20.6 *The closer you get, the better* Allium *'Gladiator' looks.*

That's why there are so many flowers in figure 20.11.

Since this plant doesn't get much taller than a few inches, use 6"-8" bulb pans for the best display.

Allium (a.k.a. onions)

Here's food for thought…and for forcing.

The first time I grew onions in my vegetable garden, I let one flower and was delighted by the huge ball of blossoms with flower stems (pedicles) all seemingly glued together at one point on the stalk (see figure 20.6). Botanists call this cluster an umbel.* And, even if you haven't grown flowering alliums, you've probably seen umbel-like structures before. Just picture the common dandelion seed head before a gentle zephyr spreads the seeds everywhere in the universe.

More germane to the agenda at hand: ornamental *Allium* umbels are knock-you-on-your-rear gorgeous.

You can get them to bloom in late winter, but you'll need to plant and chill them as soon as possible.

They don't need longer vernalization than many other bulbs – 11-12 weeks is plenty – but they take about ten

Figure 20.7 *There's nothing diminutive about ornamental onions (Allium species and cultivars). In spite of their huge bulbs, they're suitable for forcing in containers.*

Figure 20.9 *Photogenic* Allium *'Globemaster' with two bloom heads open at once.*

Figure 20.8
The explosive
Allium
'Globemaster'.
When the
flower sheath
finally
emerges from
the center, it
isn't long
before the flo-
rets burst
open to create
a huge ball of
blossoms.

---

* If you have trouble remembering the word "umbel," just think of the scheming Uriah Heep from Charles Dickens' *David Copperfield*, who tells everyone how "very *umble*" he is.

173

more weeks before they flower.

This means that if you pot them the first week in October and chill them until Christmas, you'll get blossoms in early March. But, they're well worth the wait.

The first time you grow *Allium*, especially the large hybrids like 'Globemaster' or 'Gladiator', you'll see large, deep green leaves that reach maximum size a month before the flower cluster reaches its peak.

You can water these pots exactly like most spring-blooming bulbs with one exception: since the bloom spike (known as a scape) comes out of a "tube" between the leaves, water can collect in the tube and rot the immature flower cluster before a single blossom emerges.

Just be careful not to let water go into the tube. Check after each watering, and if there's water in the tube, spill it our.

Once the anything-but-humble umbel opens, dozens upon dozens of flowers will appear and you'll be nothing less than wowed.

Tecophilaea cyanocrocus

How many times have you encountered a catalog or garden book that tells you a species' or cultivar's flowers are blue when they're actually purple? If you've gardened for more than a year, this literary malfeasance has become

irksome. Face it: there simply aren't many truly blue flowers in your horticultural world.

And yet, without reservation, I can say that the species *Tecophilaea cyanocrocus* and the variety *Tecophilaea cyanocrocus* var. Leichtlinii have glorious, even breathtaking, blue flowers. (I also grow *T. cyanocrocus* 'Violacea', but, of course, its flowers are violet colored.)

These corms hail from the Chilean Andes and were thought to be extinct in the wild because of overzealous and overabundant collectors. To reintroduce them, botanists trekked to an ideal location in the Andes. And, wonder of wonders, they found that it was still thriving, albeit in a small (20 by 50 meter) area.

Before you open a catalog or scan a website that sells these bulbs, it's important that you take a deep breath.

Now that you've exhaled, I want you to think about how easy it is to spend $18 on tomato, eggplant, and pepper plants each year. You don't even think about such a small purchase. Right?

So, when I tell you that *T. cyanocrocus* and *T. cyanocrocus* var. Leichtlinii bulbs cost as much as $18, please don't have a stroke. Although these bulbs won't put a salad on the table, they *will* give you the ultimate food for the soul. And, given the right growing conditions, they will thrive and multiply. So, for a lifetime of blue flowers, you'll only pay for a *T. cyanocrocus* bulb once.

If I've convinced you to spend your capital on a single bulb, let me also suggest that you don't tell your

Figure 20.12 *A single* Tecophilaea cyanocrocus *corm produced two stems. Ten days after this photo, a second flower graced my growing bench.*

Figure 20.10 and 20.11 *(previous two pages) 'White Splendor' is the easiest and showiest Anemone blanda cultivar to force. Unlike other varieties, the buds emerge along with the foliage (left-hand photo). Once the foliage has spread out and the majority of buds have opened (right-hand photo), take pictures. It produces a truly stunning, photogenic display.*

Figure 20.13 *(right)* Tecophilaea cyanocrocus *sports stunning, cobalt-blue flowers.* **No photograph does it justice.** *So don't wait for a sugar daddy to give you this bulb; buy it while you're still alive and digging.*

non-gardening significant other about your purchase for at least one year.

Or, better still, make that 101 years.

Given the price of this botanical beauty, I gathered more than the usual amount of data before potting my geophytic gem. I got information from research reports, books, and websites, but especially took note of the location where *Tecophilaea* was rediscovered. (See www.scielo.cl/scielo.php?script=sci_arttext&pid=S0717-66432002000200004&lng=es&nrm=iso&tlng=es [last accessed 6/30/2011]. And for a less-than-stellar but passable English translation, try using www.translate.google.com to copy and paste the article.)

If you read the above research article, you'll notice that *T. cyanocrocus* is growing in a rocky/stony area. In addition, this location is 6,000-7,000 feet above sea level where there's winter snow cover and dry summers.

Taking a hint from nature, I used a 50:50 growing mix of Turface and Sunshine #4. When you water this potting soil, moisture passes quickly through the container and out the drainage hole, which is perfect – not because drainage is important (see Chapter 1, pages 18-19), but because there's high air content in the growing medium.

I suggest growing one bulb per 4" clay pot. Plant the bulb 1-2" below the surface and keep it moist from fall until late winter. To simulate their natural habitat, I suggest a minimum of six weeks of temperatures between 33°-48°F. Living in New Jersey usually allows me to put snow on my pots every few days during the winter. If you live in an area without snow, I suggest placing chipped ice on your pots. After this cold period, grow them cool, ideally between 50°-59°F, but absolutely below 65°F, and water using dilute, ¼-strength fertilizer.

If you follow this regime, you'll be rewarded with the dazzling flowers shown in this section's photos.

After the flowers are spent, slowly reduce how often you water, and by mid-spring keep the pot dry until the following fall.

Zantedeschia species and cultivars

Of all the rhizomes you can force, I think the most beautiful is the calla lily – especially the white

Figure 20.15 *Perhaps there's something about calla flowers that isn't gorgeous, but I haven't found it yet.*

Zantedeschia aethiopica.

However, the bulb itself is as ugly as the flowers are beautiful. And, when this rhizome is yet to form obvious buds and roots, it's worse than ugly. Put it on the rugs of neat, finicky, non-gardening homeowners and three things will happen:

1. Their grey cells will process the visual input and determine that dung is on the floor.
2. They'll scream, faint, or do both.

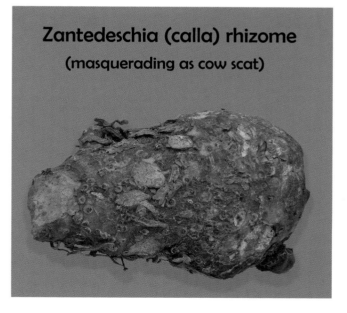

Zantedeschia (calla) rhizome
(masquerading as cow scat)

Figure 20.16 *Some bulbs are beautiful and some, like* Zantedeschia, *are at the other end of the aesthetic spectrum.*

Figure 20.14 *(left)* Tecophilaea cyanocrocus *var.* Leichtlinii *is worth every penny. The first time you grow it, have oxygen ready – the flower will make you swoon!*

3. Once you confess that "it's mine and I couldn't help it," you'll be disbarred from ever entering their homes again.

I first forced this bulb for the Philadelphia Flower Show and found that they grew so tall and wide, a full-grown woman could have hidden behind them. Ah, but when the entrancing flowers u l t i m a t e l y appeared, the lack of space in our home was forgotten. The flowers screamed for well-deserved attention.

And, sometimes the attention is not only well-deserved, but also self-deserved, since both sexes are conjoined on the impossible-to-miss spadix (see figure 20.18).

Before you dive into my directions, have a look at figure 20.21. Did you notice that these callas aren't growing in the Mojave Desert? To the contrary (or, more appropriately, to the estuary), these bulbs are native to wet, marshy regions of South Africa. Unlike the rest of the bulbs discussed in this book, this is the one bulb that adores wet conditions. Obviously, these plants aren't finicky about soil-borne air around their roots. Just as obviously, you should never let their potting mix become bone dry.

Figure 20.17 *Four calla lily bulbs in a 12" pot produced a display 4'-5' tall and just as wide. If you kick a family member out of his or her bedroom, you'll have enough space to grow these vigorous bulbs.*

To grow white callas, follow these simple directions:

1. Pick a location where there's room for a 42" tall by 42" wide display. If you grow these bulbs near a sunny window, start the top of the pot level with the windowsill. If the top of your plants begin to grow above the sunlight, simply lower the pot.

2. The foliage and flowers of these bulbs don't want to get even close to freezing. They can be damaged at 35°-40°F. Be sure to grow them in an area that's at least 62°F.

3. Use an 8" pot to force a single rhizome or at least a 10-12" pot for 3-4 rhizomes.

4. Plant the bulbs in pre-moistened potting mix. The top of the bulb should be just below the surface.

5. When shoots emerge, water thoroughly and don't let the soil dry out. Remember: these bulbs usually cavort in wet soil. As with every other bulb I grow indoors, I give callas ¼-strength balanced, soluble fertilizer at each watering.

6. When a flower opens, grab your camera. There's absolutely zero about it that isn't gorgeous.

7. You can help these flowers last longer if you move the pot to a cool location at night, but not below 40°F.

Zantedeschia hybrids: The "summer" callas

In addition to the popular *Z. aethiopica*, there are *Zantedeschia* hybrids that broaden the palette, so you aren't limited to the white flowers that sometimes adorn the top of caskets. You can choose from yellow, pink, purple, red, and even black callas that bloom atop 18"-36" plants.

And, the flowers aren't the only attraction: the foliage isn't the plain green of white calla lilies. These callas have leaves with white-edged translucent $1/4$"-$1/2$" circles and streaks, edged in white, and sprinkled liberally on each leaf.

But first, a confession: I chose to describe *Zantedeschia* hybrids last, and not just because the genus name begins with "Z". You see, these callas normally bloom during the summer in temperate zones, which make them different from every other bulb I've described until now.

As you've already learned, the white *Z. aethiopica* will grow and bloom with temperatures in the 60s. But the summer *Zantedeschia* hybrids will do absolutely nothing at these temperatures. You could wait until our sun becomes a white dwarf, but nothing significant will happen. Your bulbs will sit beneath the soil surface in a hibernation that would make a winter-time bear look hyperactive.

These hybrids demand warmth. Unlike most of the other bulbs described in this book, they love temperatures at 72°-85°F.

That's why you'll see the cool-temperature-tolerant white calla available in fall bulb catalogs, but not the warm-temperature-loving *Zantedeschia* hybrids.

Still, they're so captivating that they're worth a try – especially for gardeners in warm-winter climates and northern gardeners who keep their thermostats at 72°F or higher all winter.

You have two choices if you want to force these bulbs in the winter: either purchase them in the spring and don't plant them until fall, or grow them in

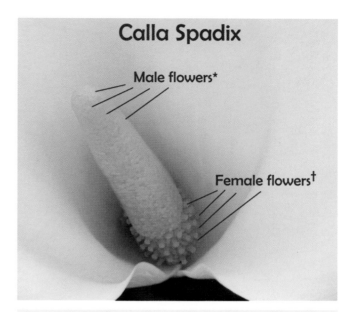

Figure 20.18 *The rather prominent calla spadix during botanical foreplay.*

the spring and summer, enjoy the blooms, then give them a rest in early fall.

I recommend the latter method, since keeping bulbs healthy during summer storage can be problematic. Besides, why not enjoy these blossoms in both the summer and winter?

Cut off the foliage in late summer or early fall, let the

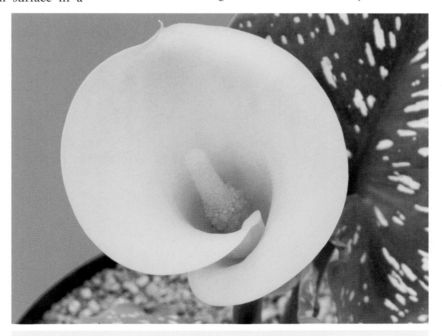

Figure 20.19 Zantedeschia *'Solar Flare' is pure sunshine.*

* a.k.a. "Outstanding Call(a) Boys"
† a.k.a. "Seldom-Standing Call(a) Girls"

soil dry completely, then give the bulb a two month rest. In the northern hemisphere, that would mean until November or early December.

And, since research has shown that cool storage increases the number of forced flowers, try to store these bulbs in a cool location (40°-60°F) during dormancy.*†

After a two month rest, carefully remove the bulb by disturbing as few roots as possible. A gentle stream of water works perfectly.

At this point, you'll have a rhizome with the appearance of an extra-terrestrial life form straight out of a 1950s horror movie. If it had teeth and could roar, you'd scream and run away from this sinister-looking, otherworldly bulb (see figure 3.13).

Figure 20.22 *Appropriately-named* Zantedeschia *'Picasso'. Every spathe is attention grabbing.*

Figure 20.21 Zantedeschia aethiopica *growing in perfect conditions at the edge of a pond. Unlike typical spring-blooming bulbs, callas love water-saturated soil.*

Figure 20.20 *(previous two pages) If you only grow one summer calla, make it* Zantedeschia *'Pink Persuasion'.*

* Goto, T., Kawajiri, K., Kageyama, Y. and Konishi, K. 2005. Flowering of *Zantedeschia rehmannii* (engl.) as affected by combination of tuber storage temperature and duration. Acta Hort. (ISHS) 673:273-277 (See www.actahort.org/books/673/673_33.htm [lasts accessed 5/2010].)

† If there's one thing I cannot tolerate in books and lectures, it's the use of the phrase "Research has shown..." without reference to the actual research. Always be skeptical of those three words when they're not followed by a reference to published research – and by published, I don't mean an Internet chat room or blog.

And yet, it's a bulb that produces gorgeous foliage and entrancing flowers.

Here's how to grow them:

1. Plant the rhizome about 1"-2" below the surface in a 6" or 8" pot.
2. Place the potted bulbs in a warm, sunny windowsill. Don't even attempt to grow these colorful callas unless you can keep the temperature above 70°F even in the evening. Remember: if the soil temperature gets below seventy degrees NOTHING will happen. (Well, actually, something will happen: you'll run out of patience and throw the soil ball out the window.)
3. Keep the soil moist. Remember: this species *loves* water. It's perfectly content at the edge of a pond with wet soil (again, see figure 20.21). *Zantedeschia* also does well with copious dilute fertilizer. At each watering, I use one-quarter or half-strength fertilizer.) Within 10-14 days you'll

Figure 20.23 Zantedeschia *'Black Star'* is probably the closest you'll ever come to growing black flowers or spathes. Note that the leaf edges mirror the spathe color. *'Black Star'* isn't as somber as you might think; in person it's curiously beautiful.

get a small nubbin of growth poking above the surface.

4. First, you'll be able to enjoy the adorable leaves. (My favorite is 'Black Star', which fittingly has green leaves with black edges [see figure 20.23]).

5. Within about ten weeks from planting, you'll see a bud emerge. After another 5-10 days, the bud will unfurl, and you'll be the proud parent of an eye-catching, beguiling, colorful spathe and central spadix.

****

Ever since Chapter 6, I've focused on how you can force bulbs in potting mix. But, as I mentioned way back in Chapter 1, many spring-blooming bulbs can be grown hydroponically (i.e., in water).

For those of you who either want to stretch your horticultural wings or who simply don't want the mess that accompanies potting mixes, hydroponic bulb growing will be an enjoyable, eye-opening – and flower bud opening – experience.

It gives you the chance to observe something you may never have seen before: watching bulb roots growing in concert with foliage and flowers.

All these wonders are revealed in the next chapter, so let's head there next.

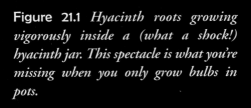

Figure 21.1 *Hyacinth roots growing vigorously inside a (what a shock!) hyacinth jar. This spectacle is what you're missing when you only grow bulbs in pots.*

21
FORCING BULBS HYDROPONICALLY

ay back on pages 18-19, I told you that air, not drainage, matters most when growing typical spring-blooming bulbs. And, I said, "If the speed with which water moves through soil is important, why is it possible to grow these plants hydroponically?"

Well, now you'll have a chance to do just that. And, trust me, if done properly this is a blast! After all, you love growing plants, but are usually limited to observing and appreciating only their foliage and flowers. With hydroponic bulb forcing, you get to see the entire botanical bundle of joy.

Here are the steps for growing hyacinths, daffodils, *Muscari* (grape hyacinths), or tulips hydroponically:

1. Put cold water in a hydroponic jar, the largest of which is also called a hyacinth jar.
2. Place the bulb in the jar so that the bottom (basal plate) is *just above the water*. The roots should

Figure 21.3 *Roots need air, so they should reach toward, not sit in, water. Swish a bit of water onto the base of the bulb each day. Within 3-7 days, hyacinth roots will emerge.*

Figure 21.2 *Jars for hydroponic bulb forcing are inexpensive and available at garden centers and on the Internet. Note that the water line is well below where the bulb will sit.*

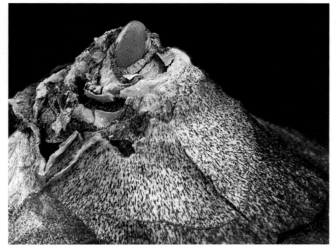

Figure 21.4 *"Let the Games begin!" Once the first bit of foliage appears, the bulb begins its Olympic dash to flowerhood.*

Figure 21.5 *This bulb developed lustrous roots during the fall in my 45-55°F garage. Then the jar was covered with aluminum foil, placed in an area at 60°-64°F, and gradually exposed to sunlight. At the above stage, the unseen cluster of flower buds has emerged.*

Figure 21.6 *About 4-6 days later, the first florets of the hyacinth 'Minos' have opened.*

have to grow through air to get a drink.

3. Swish water in the jar to moisten the bottom of the bulb. This will get daffodil, hyacinth, and *Muscari* roots to emerge, but tulips need a bit of encouragement. Simply take off the tulip's papery covering (tunic) so the white base of the bulb is exposed to moisture (see figure 21.10).

4. If you'll be forcing bulbs in sunlit locations, *surround the outside of the jar with aluminum foil*, otherwise the water temperature will become too warm.

5. Put the jar in a place where it will get temperatures of 40-50°F for 6-12 weeks. The length of time will be similar to the vernalization period for the same type of bulb grown in potting mix.

6. Change the water every 2-3 days, and be careful not to injure the roots. Hyacinth, daffodil, and *Muscari* roots are sturdy, but tulip roots are quite delicate.

7. When you dump out the old water, you don't have to break a speed record to refill the jar. Remember: roots need air. I've left hydroponic roots without water for as long as ten minutes.

8. When you have a good network of roots and the leaves and flower shoots have emerged, it's time

188

Figure 21.7 *No need for black tubes or other bulb-torture devices. The hyacinth 'Minos' flower stem stretches to the perfect height and blossoms open uniformly.*

Figure 21.8 *Hyacinths and daffodils are forced using the same technique. This bulb (Narcissus 'Carlton') had two internal flower buds which emerged and bloomed simultaneously.*

for light and warmer temperatures.

9. Unless you've given your bulbs strong light during step 4, you'll have to gradually acclimate them to sunlight over a ten-day period. ***Note that this is the only time I've given this instruction for light acclimation*** (see pages 92-93). Turn the jar 90° (either clockwise or counterclockwise) each day. This will keep flower stems and leaves from bending toward your light source.

10. When your bulbs start to bloom, you can move

them to other locations in your home where the temperature is under 70°F. To help the blossoms last as long as possible, put the jar in a cold (33°-45°F) location overnight.

Of all the bulbs you can force hydroponically, hyacinths are the most foolproof. But don't limit yourself to just one type of bulb. There are hydroponic jars made specifically for tulips, daffodils, *Muscari*, and even crocuses, but *any* glass container that holds the bulb slightly

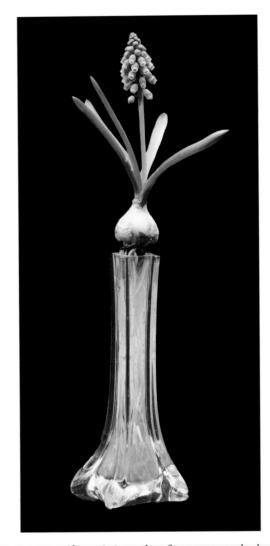

Figure 21.9 *About 2-3 weeks after roots reach the bottom,* Muscari armeniacum *began to bloom. This bulb produced a second bloom spike six days after this photo was taken.*

Figure 21.10 *The tulip 'Apricot Beauty' blooms 3-4 weeks after root formation. Handle with care! The roots are delicate. Note that the bulb's papery covering, called the tunic, has been removed to facilitate root formation.*

above the waterline will work. In fact, the "forcing jar" used for *Muscari* (figure 21.9) is actually a bud vase.

Hydroponic bulb forcing is yet another way to amaze your family and friends with your newly-acquired expertise. More important, it's also another way for bulbs to amaze *you*.

****

The reason for bulb forcing is simple: it gives you a glimpse of spring indoors when there's bleak winter weather outdoors.

So far, we've looked at many different ways to force only one type of bulb per container. But there's no reason why you can't combine many different kinds of bulbs in a large pot. In fact, you can include bulbs that bloom outdoors in late winter or early spring, as well as mid-season and late-spring bloomers.

Such pots, called bulb-garden pots, give you a preview of an entire spring season. And, if you ever decide to limit yourself to just one forced pot, you should make it this one.

How you go about planting and forcing bulb-garden pots is the subject of the next chapter, so let's go there now.

22

AND NOW FOR SOMETHING COMPLETELY DIFFERENT:
A SPRING SEASON IN A BULB-GARDEN POT

I admit it: I'm as immovable as a stubborn mule when it comes to change.

I'm probably one of the last people in America still driving a station wagon. In addition, I was undoubtedly the last garden writer to get a home Internet connection and didn't do so until editors were ready to pull out my hair. I think there's nothing ruder than call-waiting, and that it should be against the law for drivers to use cell phones – whether they're holding them or not. I also believe it would be wonderful if we returned to the practice of dressing-up to walk on a seaside promenade.*

Figure 22.1 *If you want to double layer large bulbs (in this case, daffodils), fill the pot 1/3 with potting mix, then plant the first layer. If you're only going to single layer large bulbs, fill the pot halfway.*

---

* Alas, many male visitors to New Jersey seaside towns think that showing the world their chest tattoos and body piercings is the very definition of "dressing-up."

I suppose if I had a motto it would be, "I refuse to change until the pain of staying the same is worse than the pain of change."

Having admitted this, it will come as no surprise to you that I wanted no part of the recent trend in bulb forcing, called the "bulb-garden pot," that has gardeners

Cheating Time

Gardeners anticipate spring more than any other season. It's the time of year when the world seems to go from moldering moonscape to alluring landscape. I think many gardeners facing their demise would be tempted to make a deal with the devil to have one more flower-filled spring. The orchestrated sequence of blossoms, from crocuses to daffodils to tulips, makes us feel so full of life that we put all thoughts of our impermanence aside. Perhaps that's why bulb-garden pots have become so popular: you get two springs each year...without making a pact with the Fallen Angel.

planting many different types of bulbs in the same container.

These pots are planted in the fall, chilled for three months, and forced into bloom indoors. The flower display starts with *Crocus*, *Iris reticulata*, or other minor bulbs and is followed by mid- and late-season flowers, thus simulating the bloom sequence of outdoor bulbs.

The whole idea seemed an anathema to the purist in me. I assumed that by the time the late bulbs bloomed,

Figure 22.2 *More mix is added, then the second layer of daffs is planted.*

Figure 22.3 *Next come hyacinths (center), tulips (left and right),* Muscari, Iris, *and* Crocus.

everything would look like a mess, with flowers hidden behind floppy foliage.

My horticultural prejudices started back in 1978, when I won one of my first Philadelphia Flower Show blue ribbons for a pot that contained only *Scilla mischtschenkoana.* After that, I've probably forced two thousand pots, each containing bulbs of just one species or cultivar. If a mistaken flower appeared in any pot, my anger was only soothed by ruthlessly removing the offending intruder.

Then, garden clubs started asking me to include information about bulb-garden pots during my lectures. True-to-form, I resisted as long as I could, until one club insisted that I do an entire workshop on bulb-garden pots and "made me an offer I couldn't refuse." Caught between a rock garden and a hard place, I had reached that life-altering moment when it was more painful to stay the same than to change.

So in the fall of 1997, I finally gave in and planted my first bulb-garden pot. You don't have to be a genius to know what happened: I was enchanted.

When I brought my first bulb-garden pot indoors, it looked exactly the same as an outdoor bulb garden in February, with little pips of growth venturing upward

> I didn't plant my first bulb-garden pot until a garden club "made me an offer I couldn't refuse." I had finally reached that life-altering moment when it was more painful to stay the same than to change.

like green thermometers to gauge the climate. Within a matter of days the first *Iris reticulata* bloomed, followed a few days later by *Crocus.* Ten days later, early daffodils and *Muscari* blossomed and fairly screamed, "It must be April first!" Another week passed and typical late-April tulips began to show color.

Instead of the mess I'd imagined, the foliage from the early bulbs gently and gracefully spilled over the side of the clay pot, adding to the beauty of the miniature landscape. Not surprisingly, on my first try I had become a devoted advocate of potted bulb gardens.

It isn't necessary to be a PhD horticulturist to produce your own indoor spring garden. It's truly a simple endeavor, but one that will let you flex your creative muscles with its endless possibilities of size, color, and timing. Just follow my easy directions, and you'll be able to produce a colorful bulb garden on your windowsill, when winter is doing its worst just four inches away.

Step One: Planning Before Planting

Before you buy bulbs, give some thought to the size, color, and timing of the blooms that your bulb-garden

Figure 22.4 *Another layer of minor bulbs is planted plus a few tulips. Next, a dome of potting mix is added to the top and pressed firmly (see figure 9.5d, side view). Then the pot is chilled.*

Figure 22.5 *Day 0: After chilling for 80 days, the bulb-garden pot is cleaned. Then it comes indoors for more than six weeks of flowers.*

pot will produce. I think color preference is highly individualistic, so I'd be the last person to give you hard-and-fast rules about which colors to use. I think most bulb-garden-pot growers tend to fall into two camps: those who like pastels and those who like saturated, primary colors. I tend to lean towards the latter group, but can appreciate a well-thought-out pastel bulb-garden pot.

As you plan colors, pay particular attention to the bulbs whose bloom periods overlap. It won't matter if early- and late-blooming bulbs clash, but poorly color-coordinated, identical bloom-period bulbs might give you an eye-ache.

To have a bulb garden pot that stays in bloom for 5-6 weeks, you'll need a wide variety of bulbs, including early, mid-season, and late-blooming bulbs. The early/minor bulbs are those that bloom outdoors from February through mid-March in USDA Zone 6 (see Chapter 14).

There's a tremendous variety of these diminutive bulbs, but I generally use *Crocus* and *Iris reticulata*. If you force them at 60°-66°F, they'll begin blooming within 3-7 days and last about a week, or just about the time that mid-season blossoms are beginning to show color.

The middle-season bulbs I use include daffodils, hyacinths, and *Muscari*. These typically bloom outdoors from mid-March to about April 15th in Zone 6. In your bulb-garden pot, they'll start flowering after about 16

days indoors and last about two weeks at 65°F.

My late-season bulbs are usually tulips, but there's no reason you couldn't use late daffodils as well. These generally bloom outdoors from April 15th to May 10th in Zone 6. Indoors, they blossom after 37-42 days, and the flowers last approximately two weeks.

Planting Your Bulb-Garden Pot

To stage a truly inspiring display indoors, you'll need 12"-14" pots, preferably made of clay. Standard-size pots that are 12"-14" in diameter can be unwieldy because of their weight. At the other extreme, bulb pans are lighter, but they don't have as much space for layering bulbs. Instead, I use azalea pots (see Chapter 6, page 37).

If you have your heart set on using a plastic container, which admittedly is much lighter, be careful not to over-water your bulb-garden pot.

Planting isn't very different from what you've already learned, but now you need a plot plan.

Simply look at the catalog from which you ordered your bulbs. The ultimate height of each variety is usually given in inches. With this information, you can arrange your bulb-garden pot the way a photographer arranges a group picture: namely, the tallest "subjects" go

Figure 22.6 *Day 9: The first* Iris reticulata *'Harmony' bud opened within five days, and four days later (above) they're beginning to peak.*

Figure 22.8 *Day 15: The crocuses have peaked, but a few remaining irises add to the overall display.*

Figure 22.7 *Day 11: The irises have peaked and hand the baton to* Crocus vernus *'Yellow Mammoth'.*

Figure 22.9 *Day 25: There are still more than a dozen crocuses left when 'Blue Jacket' hyacinths take center stage/center pot. In the meantime, daffodils and tulips are in the wings (rear), ready for their entrance.*

in back and the shortest in front. Consequently, minor bulbs would go up front, medium-sized plants go in the middle, and bulbs generating the tallest foliage and flowers are placed in the back.

Don't be afraid to pack the bulbs cheek-to-jowl. Remember: the more bulbs you plant now, the more flowers you'll have later. I suggest double layering *Crocus*, *Iris*, *Muscari*, and daffodils to increase the flower count and produce a glorious indoor bulb garden.

Here are a few easy-to-follow instructions:

1. Fill pots halfway with potting mix, then plant the first daffodil layer (see figure 22.1).
2. Cover these bulbs with additional mix, but so that you can still see the tops of the underlying bulbs.
3. Plant tulips, then add another layer of daffodils between the tops of the underlying bulbs (see figure 22.2).
4. Double-layering *Crocus* or *Iris* works the same way, except that you begin higher up, with the bottom layer about 4" from the top of the pot and the upper layer about 2" higher (see figures 22.3-22.4).

5. After planting your bulbs, cover with a dome of soil, and firm the potting mix with your hand.
6. Think of the bulbs that require the longest chilling time (i.e., the late bloomers) and be sure to chill your bulb-garden pot at least that long. Typically, this will be 11-13 weeks.
7. After chilling and cleaning your pot, you can get ready for an early dose of spring.
8. Put the pot in the same indoor growing site where you force other spring-blooming bulbs (see Chapter 13).

Now comes the exciting part: it's time for your first of two spring seasons.

The minor bulbs will begin blooming in 3-7 days and last for about a week, but even longer if forced in cool (60-64°F) conditions. Just when these flowers begin to shrivel, your hyacinths, *Muscari*, or early daffodils should start to show color. I let the *Crocus* leaves drape over the side of the pot and trim *Iris* foliage a bit so it doesn't hide mid-season flowers.

Before the mid-season bulbs fade, your tulips should begin to show color. At this point, your display will be at its peak, so be sure to take photos. In fact, I suggest taking photos as each group comes into flower. By the time your tulips fade, it'll be at least a month since you brought your bulb-garden pot indoors. At this point your outdoor bulb garden should show signs of life, so you'll be able to experience your *second spring season* in the same year.

In retrospect, I'm quite thankful I was forced to force bulb-garden pots. And, having accepted this new

Figure 22.11 *Day 43: Like a fireworks finale, tulips, daffodils, and grape hyacinths explode in an extravaganza of color more than six weeks after this pot was first brought indoors.*

Figure 22.10 *(previous page) Day 33: It doesn't get much better than this! After more than a month indoors, there are still crocuses in bloom. Hyacinths, 'Marieke' daffodils, and* Muscari armeniacum *dominate, while 'Apricot Beauty' tulips begin their show. Note how the foliage creates a balanced foreground and background for the blossoms.*

196

horticultural technique, I've decided to embrace change altogether. My only quandary is how accepting of change my wife will be when I come home with spiked orange hair and a nose ring.

****

Although bulb-garden pots give you a chance to see flowers bloom gradually over a six-week period, it's also possible to have a variety of bulbs in bloom at the same time, in the same pot.

This involves a different kind of forcing that I haven't described yet. The containers are different, but they're not the most important factor.

When it comes to these pots, *timing* is everything. If you're intrigued and *your* timing is right, mosey over to Chapter 23 to learn about them.

22.12a

22.12b

Figures 22.12a and b *Let your creative instincts loose when you grow a bulb-garden pot. Here, I forced an 8-inch pot that was filled with four varieties of minor bulbs. The forcing time needed for each was varied enough to produce more than six weeks of flowers. In 22.14a, Crocus chrysanthus 'Blue Pearl' and Iris reticulata 'Harmony' bloom together. Forty-one days later Scilla siberica 'Spring Beauty' and Muscari armeniacum finish the show.*

23

ARRANGING THE SELF-ARRANGING ARRANGEMENT POT

Here, we have the radiant, bulb-forcing equivalent of a typical cut-flower arrangement, but one that not only lasts much longer than its root-deprived counterpart, but produces flowers – and a new arrangement – **every day.**

An arrangement pot involves taking forced bulbs grown in miniscule containers, stuffing them, along with their root balls, into a large pot to produce a pleasing – followed by an even-more-pleasing – flower arrangement.

Once you learn how long it takes to force different

Figure 23.2 *On your mark, get set, but before you "Go!" gather all your bulbs and supplies. The plastic containers shown above have 36 cells (mini-pots), and in figure 23.3 there are 8 six-packs (48 cells) per flat. Also, see figure 23.4, which shows five planted flats.*

Figure 23.3 *Crocus 'Blue Pearl' is double layered in one cell of a 6-pack. (There are up to eight 6-packs per flat.)*

Figure 23.4 *(below) A cold frame, which provides essential vernalization, is filled with flats and pots. The flats were used to produce forced bulbs for arrangement pots.*

WARNING!

This chapter is *NOT* meant for those of you who either 1) love flower arrangements that die within a week, 2) enjoy changing vase water every two days, 3) savor the stench and green color of vase water that *isn't* changed every two days, or 4) are flat-out thrilled by throwing flowers in the garbage when they begin to look like cooked confetti.

Figure 23.1 *(left) I love this combination: orange or red amaryllis (this is 'Orange Sovereign') and yellow daffodils. If you include daffs that haven't bloomed yet, this arrangement will last two weeks or more.*

199

types of bulbs in your indoor conditions, you can aim them for the week, or even two weeks, you'll want your arrangement pot in bloom.

The first time I created an arrangement pot, it wasn't for a one- or two-week period, but for one day of judg-

Figure 23.5 *The miniature daff 'Baby Moon' is growing in 6-packs. This is about two weeks after planting.*

ing at the Philadelphia Flower Show. And, to this day, I dislike this category for exhibitors with limited space. Because everything must peak at the same moment, growers use many flats and pots and many dozens of bulbs for just one entry.

BUT, when I produced all the flats needed for the bulb-arrangement pots in this book, I learned something splendiferous: even if your arrangement looks awful in the beginning, the bulbs seem to know where to grow to make the pot gorgeous.

SO, I am now a convert. I produced numerous bulb-arrangement pots for this book and each one knocked me on my caboose. Every pot is like a small version of your garden, which, as you know, changes every day during the growing season. What I like most is that each pot improves as time goes on – as long as you don't start with bulbs on the way out. In other words, start with bulbs on the way "in"…as in, beginning to bloom.

The scope of this book stops short of explaining the basics of flower arranging. Although I've taken two flower-arranging courses, I'm the last person on Earth who should teach you how to go about it. Instead, take a class or acquire a book on the subject.

Still, let me tell you what I think are the most pleasing color combinations for such pots:

1. blue/purple and white.
2. pink and purple.
3. red/dark orange and yellow,
4. orange and purple, and
5. orange and red.

Figure 23.6 *The same cold frame seen in figure 23.4, but about eight weeks later. In a subsequent chapter, I'll reveal the secret behind this ultimate bulb-forcing cold frame.*

Figure 23.7 *This 12" pot will be filled with two 6-packs of* Crocus *'Blue Pearl' and white* Cyclamen. *Only about half the* Crocus *flower buds have opened. These 6-packs were the ones planted in figure 23.3.*

Figure 23.8 *The* Cyclamen *and* Crocus *pot after planting. This is one of my favorite color combinations: white and light purple. For the longest display, plant the arrangement pot when crocuses are just beginning to show color.*

In addition to the first color combination, white can be used in any of the other four. But be careful not to let it overwhelm the colors you want to be dominant in your arrangement.

If your pot is aimed for a special event or flower show, you'll need bulbs that are ***all in bloom on the same day.*** You should also be aware that if the earliest minor bulbs (see Chapter 14) dominate the arrangement, your display

Figure 23.9 *A flat of miniature and standard daffodils.*

will be short-lived – perhaps only a few days in a seventy-degree house. But, if your goal is either dropped jaws from your visitors or dropped blue ribbons at flower shows, go ahead and use all minors.

If, to the contrary, you want a longer-lasting flower-arrangement pot, skip the brief-blooming minors (e.g., *Crocus, Iris reticulata,* and *Scilla*) and concentrate on longer-lived flowering bulbs, especially *Muscari,* hyacinths, *Ranunculus,* tulips, and daffodils. All of these either produce or have cultivars that produce more than one flower per bulb.* And, that's what really helps arrangement pots last longer.

"But why," you might ask, "would I use a pot to arrange flowers? After all, flower arranging supplies include vases, Oasis,† wreaths, and a multitude of gorgeous containers. Aside from the fact that the arrangement lasts longer, why would you use a plain clay pot as a container to arrange flowers?"

Admittedly, I had the same questions when I first heard about these pots.

At the Philadelphia Flower Show (and almost any other flower show) the competitive areas are divided into

Figure 23.10 *It's fine to combine a variety of bulbs in the same flat. Here, there are 'Tete-a-Tete' daffs, hyacinths, and yet-to-bloom tulips.*

---

* Examples of daffodils that produce more than one flower per bulb are miniatures like 'Tete-a-Tete', 'Hawera', 'Baby Moon', 'Tiny Bubbles', and taller daffodils like 'Golden Harvest' and 'Carlton'. In addition, all triandrus and tazetta daffodils are multi-flowered. (See www.daffodilusa.org/daffodils/div.html, last accessed 7/2/2011.) My favorite multi-flowered tulip is 'Antoinette' (see figure 17.15), but there are many others that you can obtain from retail bulb companies.
† Oasis is floral foam into which you can thrust flower stems to make an arrangement. Although hard, Oasis absorbs enough water to keep cut flowers alive.

Figure 23.11 *A cornucopia of forced bulbs:* Anemone *'Governor' and a variety of daffodils.*

horticultural and artistic classes. The division is obvious: if blue ribbons go to the best grower of plants, it's a horticultural class; if blue ribbons go to the most artistically-creative competitor with striking entries, it's an artistic class.

Then, at the 1995 Philadelphia Flower Show, a new horticultural competitive class was created for bulb-arrangement pots. At the time, I questioned the decision. I thought judges would award ribbons based on artistic, not horticultural, ability. If correct, it would mean that a competitor could produce excellent blooming bulbs, but be an utter failure in the eyes of the judges. It also meant that if someone were a lousy bulb forcer but could produce enough blooming bulbs to create an eye-popping arrangement, they'd win the blue ribbon.

That year, I followed the judges and overheard them discussing the quality of entries based on artistic composition. I didn't hear a single word uttered about horticultural excellence. So, I wondered (and still wonder) why these pots aren't part of the Show's artistic classes, along with other flower arrangements.

But, that's just my disreputable, disquieting quibbling, which doesn't change the fact that if done properly, these

clay-pot arrangements can be stunning (see especially figure 23.12). And, as was the case with "bulb-garden pots" (see Chapter 22), the world had changed and I had to be dragged along with it.

In 1999 and 2000, I worked with *Better Homes and Gardens* to produce two articles on bulb forcing. By that time, this type of bulb arrangement had become popular. At the photoshoot, the *BH&G* art director sketched many of these arrangements that I put together quickly. I say "quickly" because it was one of the warmest February days on record in Southern New Jersey – about 74°F. And, as you probably know, the flowers of spring-blooming bulbs fade quickly – in hours – in this kind of heat. So, while I created the flower-arrangement pots on a porch, our photographer first took photos on the upper floors of a Victorian home without my flower-arrangement pot. Then, when she and the art director were satisfied with the set up, I literally ran upstairs to place the pot in its desired location for the photoshoot.

If the art director didn't like the set up, they moved the pot slightly and sample photos were taken. If the art

Figure 23.12 *The dynamic self-arranging arrangement pot. Three days after the photo was taken in figure 23.11, there's an explosion of 'Baby Moon' miniature daffs that find their way through the other flowers. This is what makes arrangement pots so wonderful.*

If you're tempted to produce a flower-arrangement pot, you'll need more room and more containers – perhaps a half dozen or more flats that each hold 32-48 separate cells (see figures 23.2, 23.3, and 23.4). I suggest that you not grow a flower arrangement pot the first year you force bulbs. You have to collect data from one or more years to do the following:

1. Decide which flowers you want in your arrangement pot.
2. Draw a design that indicates where you'll place each type of bulb.
3. Based on bulb type and design, decide how many bulbs you'll need, *then grow an extra 50%* to make up for variability during forcing.
4. Write down the number of days, on average, it takes you to force each type of bulb into bloom.
5. Choose the day (e.g., February 25th) when you'll want to arrange your self-arranging arrangement pot.
6. After planting and chilling your bulbs, begin forcing

Figure 23.13 *This arrangement is just getting started. It contains a variety of yellow daffs along with purple* Iris reticulata, *hyacinth, and* Chionodoxa luciliae. *The complementary color combination (yellow and purple) is striking.*

director still wasn't pleased, I ran the pot to the cooler outdoor porch while they rearranged the set-up. Finally, when the art director and photographer were happy, I was summoned to rush the flower-arrangement pot back upstairs to its final location. After a few hours of these Olympic dashes upstairs with a variety of flower-arrangement pots, my middle-aged legs told me they didn't like my "arrangement" with *BH&G* at all.

This same marathon-like scenario took place in an additional Moorestown, New Jersey, home using about two dozen different arrangement pots. The final outcome? Approximately thirteen hundred photos were snapped of which four arrangement-pot images were used in the October 2000 issue of *BH&G*. But, every photo of every arrangement pot was exquisite.

So, I became a convert.

Figure 23.14 *This is another great color combination: pink and purple. Here 'Apricot Beauty' tulips fit in with the purple* Iris *'J. S. Dijt',* Muscari armeniacum, *as well as 'Blue Jacket' and 'Pink Pearl' hyacinths. This arrangement lasted about two weeks.*

them so that they'll all be in bloom *a few days ahead of your target date*. If they start to bloom early, use some technique to hold them back (see Chapter 25).

7. Don't be married to your original design. You may not have enough of one type of bulb to produce it. If that happens, look at the flowers and colors you have, and use them in the same way you'd use cut flowers to create a flower arrangement.

8. If your pot will contain minor bulbs, plant everything a few hours before they'll be on display at home or at a flower show. If you don't include minor bulbs, you can plant your flower-arrangement pot the day before, and then keep it chilled (but above freezing).

tulips 'Yellow Purissima' and 'Flaming Purissima' in the same 8" pot and was quite pleased with the result. I had the same degree of success with 'Apeldoorn' and 'Golden Apeldoorn'.

Once you gain more experience, you can mix not just different cultivars in the same pot, but also different species. It's simply a matter of knowing which bulbs bloom simultaneously.

If you want to attempt this in a 12" pot, I suggest using any combination of –

- 'Apricot Beauty', 'Apeldoorn', 'Golden Apeldoorn', 'Yellow Purissima', or 'Flaming Purissima' tulips;
- 'Amsterdam', 'Pink Pearl', 'Jan Bos', or 'L'Innocence' hyacinths;
- the tall daffodils 'Ice Follies', 'Golden Harvest', 'Marieke', or 'Dutch Master';

The Hybrid Arrangement Pot

Here's an easier, less space-consuming way to produce a flower-arrangement pot that will give you a chance to show off your horticultural talent. In this case, you'll use a large container to grow bulbs *that all take the same amount of time to force*.

This idea (as usual) came to me when I nearly accomplished it without trying (see figure 22.10 on page 195). Note that almost every type of bulb in the pot is blooming simultaneously.

Instead of hoping for this kind of luck, you can succeed virtually every time if you plant alternate colors of the same cultivar. In figure 23.15, I used the

Figure 23.15 *You can produce a hybrid flower-arrangement pot by combining bulbs that take the same amount of time to force. Here, the tulips 'Yellow Purissima' and 'Flaming Purissima' bloom simultaneously.*

- miniature or small daffs like 'Tete-a-Tete', 'Little Beauty', or 'W.P. Milner';
- and perhaps add *Muscari armeniacum* for a purple accent.

Keep in mind the ultimate height of each bulb. You can be creative with the dispersion pattern of bulbs, but don't hide blossoms by blocking them behind taller flowers and foliage. Try to design everything on paper first. You and your camera will appreciate it later.

I have one other suggestion for combining simultaneously-blooming bulbs: open a ColorBlends* catalog or visit their website and simply purchase the combination that's most pleasing to your eye. ColorBlends generously provided two combinations for me to test. Figure 23.16 shows the result of forcing the collection they call Above and Beyond.

As you may have guessed, if bulbs bloom together outdoors, they should bloom together when forced indoors. Of the six companies from whom I usually order bulbs, only one company's website (Brent and Becky's Bulbs: www.brentandbeckysbulbs.com) groups cultivars that have similar bloom times. So, I'll be testing their combinations as well.

****

Despite how easy bulb forcing can be, there are enemies that should be kept as far from your garden and windowsill as possible. Fortunately, bulb forcers don't have an army to keep at bay. There are just a few marauders to worry about. And, the next chapter will tell you what they are and how to keep them from endangering your potted bulbs.

Let's turn to Chapter 24 to learn about them.

Figure 23.16 *The tulips in ColorBlend's combination called "Above and Beyond" forced simultaneously.*

* ColorBlends is a bulb company that has spent years testing the combinations shown in their catalog and website (www.colorblends.com), last accessed 7/2/2011).

"Voles are children of the night.
Plant bulbs of your own free will."

24

THESE ARE A FEW OF MY LEAST-FAVORITE THINGS

OR

THE DARTH VADERS OF BULB FORCING

Even if The Force is with a bulb forcer, the Darth Vaders* of the botanical world will try to thwart your attempts to produce springtime in winter. They may not dress like Vader, but they can be just as deadly. So before you give in to these marauders and escape by traveling to a time long, long ago in a botanical galaxy far, far away, I hope you'll heed my warnings.[†]

Chemicals on the Dark Side of The Force

The chemical enemies of bulb forcers are invisible, odorless, and insidious. Even so, with a few precautions, you can avoid them.

Ethylene

Ethylene is a colorless, odorless gas that is the enemy of every bulb forcer for one simple reason: you want flower buds; it kills flower buds. The most common sources of ethylene gas in your home are vegetables and fruits, especially apples. This will mainly affect forcers who plan to use a refrigerator for vernalization, but it can be a problem for all bulb forcers.

The rules to keep ethylene away are simple: 1) never put fruit or vegetables in the same refrigerator as your bulbs, 2) keep fruit and vegetables away from the room where you force bulbs, and 3) threaten bodily harm to your family if they get within twenty feet of your bulbs while chomping on fruits or vegetables.

How sensitive are bulbs to this gas? So sensitive that professional bulb forcers with acre-sized greenhouses have ethylene "scrubbers" (filters) inside their huge, bulb-packed

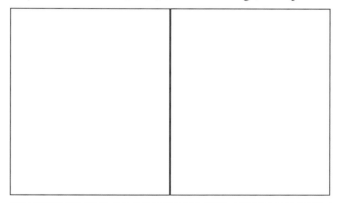

Figure 24.1 *Accurate photos of ethylene (left) and fluoride (right).*

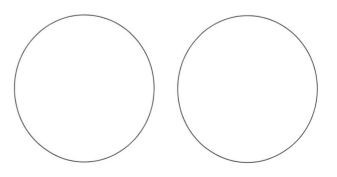

Figure 24.2 *Scratch-and-sniff area for ethylene (left) and fluoride (right).*

---

* Darth Vader is a villain in cinema's *Star Wars* series – the series I've been over-alluding to page after page. During these movies, he seems to be everywhere and related to everyone. So it's quite believable that the movies' locale is a non-Milky-Way galaxy – specifically, a galaxy with do-it-yourself cloning kits.
† See also pages 60, 62, 68-69, and 72 for other problems that can plague bulb forcers.

refrigeration rooms to sap the air of every possible ethylene molecule. (For a glimpse of such a room, see Chapter 8, figure 8.9.)

One last warning: the fungus *Fusarium* not only harms bulbs, it also damages bulbs that aren't infected because *Fusarium* emits ethylene gas. So, when you check your bulbs before planting, throw away any that are soft or have white fungus on the surface. And, if you get a noticeably lightweight bulb (compared to others in the batch) the inside may be completely consumed by the fungus. *Holland Bulb Forcer's Guide* suggests returning a batch of bulbs that is "more that 10% *Fusarium*-infected."*) NEVER plant these bulbs in your pots. Instead, throw them away or entomb them in the deep, dark, dank recesses of a hot compost pile.

Fluoride

Since my childhood, I've heard the mantra again and again that water fluoridation is beneficial because it helps prevent tooth decay.[†] On the other hand, its botanical toxicity can be similar to us getting a slightly less-than-lethal dose of carbon monoxide. You won't see it or smell it in water, but does it ever cause problems in freesias and other plants.

And, here I should tell yet another tale of learning through error, after error, after error:

Let me begin by saying that freesias are delightful corms to grow (see pages 51-53). The foliage is a deep green and the conical flowers have a spicy scent. The first year I grew them, some of the leaves had white streaks. In many other plants, this would be a symptom of viral or fungal infection. Naturally, I thought, the bulb supplier had sent a bad batch.

The following year, I bought *Freesia* bulbs from a different supplier. As the foliage emerged, I treated it with a fungicide, but to no avail: there were just as many streaks. So, "obviously" the problem was a virus.

The next year, I got freesias from a third company. I

Figure 24.3 *Fluoride toxicity in freesia leaves.*

was scrupulous in disinfecting my pots and using a new bag of sterile professional mix. Yet, I grew another batch of freesias with the same amount of streaking.

As with most of my plants in the 1990s, I tried to aim them to be at peak bloom for the Philadelphia Flower Show. But there was no way I'd ever exhibit a pot with streaked *Freesia* foliage. So, uncharacteristically, I gave up.

Well, not altogether.

Eventually, I learned that fluoride caused the streaking. So, I tried to grow freesias again, but made sure to water my pots with distilled (i.e., non-fluoridated) water.*

---

* See *Holland Bulb Forcer's Guide*, 1996 edition, pages A-116 to A-117.

† This is a trigger-finger issue with strident proponents for and enemies of water fluoridation. I'll sidestep the issue when it comes to humans. On the botanical side, the very word "fluoride" may not be uttered in my greenhouse.

* By using Google.com to search "fluoride" with "freesias," I found several websites that claimed spider plants (*Chlorophytum* species), Easter lilies (*Lilium longiflorum*), *Dracaena* species, Peace lilies (*Spathiphyllum* species), cast iron plants (*Aspidistra elatior*), parlor palms (*Chamaedorea elegans*), and prayer plants (*Maranta leuconeura*) were also susceptible to fluoride burn. From my own experience with parlor palms and spider plants, I would concur. During the summer, when I'd move these plants outdoors and use rainwater, they had no leaf-tip burn. But the foliage burned when I grew them indoors and used tap water. For many years I thought this was due to low humidity. One grows and learns.

CHAPTER TWENTY-FOUR

And, voila! I had beautiful, non-streaked foliage at last.

I do have more words of warning: I have unearthed, so to speak, further research claiming that perlite can contain fluoride. Since perlite is in virtually every professional soil mix, the solution is to use a solution – as in flushing the soil with rainwater or non-fluoridated water – before potting freesias.*

Fauna on the Dark Side of The Force

So far, this chapter has only included two chemical enemies that have wrought damage upon my bulbs. On the other hand, there are many more, perhaps thousands more, fungal, viral, and animal pests that bulb forcers have to deal with.

But there are four reasons why I've only listed voles and slugs:

First, I clean my growing benches with 10% Clorox, which acts as a disinfectant; and I use cleanser on every greenhouse window.

Second, I live in USDA Zone 6, meaning there aren't any insects walking or flying into my greenhouse during the winter. And, if there are any insect eggs on the growing benches, they're expunged by the 10% Clorox treatment.

Third, the temperature in my growing area doesn't exceed 64°F, which eliminates the chewing insects so prevalent at warmer temperatures.

And, fourth, my bulbs grow quickly and are in my greenhouse a minimal amount of time. In fact, the special technique (see Chapter 29) I've developed for vernalization reduces their visit to the greenhouse by at least 25%.

I know that most of you don't own a greenhouse, and that you probably won't make the ultimate cold frame described in Chapter 29. But, you'll still have to pay attention to ethylene and fluoride. And, if you use an outdoor vernalization technique, you'll have to stop slugs and voles (or whatever rodent haunts your neighbor-

hood) from dining on your potted bulbs.

As for disinfection, I recommend it for every growing location you use.

Voles

How fitting that Charles Dickens used the barely-masked name, "Mr. Vholes," for the unprincipled, "blood-sucking" attorney in *Bleak House*.

To bulb forcers, voles may be of less literary importance, but they can be just as blood curdling. They're often euphemistically called "field mice," but I prefer the one-word epithet. It's perfect: you have the "V" from "Vampire" and the "ol" and "es" from "Wolves."*

Figure 24.4 *My archenemy, the vole (genus* Microtus): *so cute, so fluffy, so treacherous! (Photo courtesy of Purdue University)*

---

* I've also learned that a low pH makes plants more susceptible to fluoride toxicity. If true, neutralizing the soil with lime should eliminate the problem. But since water fluoridation varies and it's difficult for home gardeners to measure the exact pH of a potting mix, I suggest using rainwater or distilled water on freesias. Given a choice, I'll always choose the zero-guesswork method.

* I apologize to vole-lovers who think I should use bulbs to feed my adorable, but ravenous grey garden gluttons. I hit on the idea of sending such vole fanciers my least favorite vermin through the mail, but when I asked my postmaster about this scheme, he gave me a look that could be translated as, "How long have you been out of restraints? And, it's a shame lithium isn't working for you."

Unless you want nightmares and daymares from these vampiric wolves of the garden, you must keep them away from your bulbs. These restive rodents love virtually every bulb on the planet except daffodils (which are poisonous to all mammals) and fritillarias (which have the

Figure 24.5 *(left) Hardware cloth is available in plain or plastic-coated metal.*

Figure 24.6 *(below) Hardware cloth is stapled to the inside wall of my cold frame and extends 12" below the bottom of the wood.*

Figure 24.7 *(left) The best way to set a mouse/vole trap: After adding bait (I use cheese smeared with peanut butter), hang the trap vertically so voles go after your bait from the proper side. If you place the trap flat on the ground, you have only a 50:50 chance of success, since the vole might go after the bait from the wrong (lever) side.*

delightful scent of eau de skunk). Aside from those two, voles have enjoyed chowing down every other type of bulb I've ever grown.

The most humane way to keep voles away from potted bulbs is a barrier. In my case, I surround the inside of my cold frames with hardware cloth that goes down 12" below the frame walls (see figures 24.5 and 24.6). Since doing so, I've never had a problem during rooting.

If you can't or won't use a barrier, your next best choice is mouse traps. You can use either a trap that captures but doesn't kill voles or a genuine, old-fashioned trap. And, there *is* a humane way to use the latter:

First, don't set them on the ground, because if the vole goes after the cheese from the lever-side of the trap, he'll simply be thrown two feet away when the trap snaps. Meaning, the vole will simply come back and dine safely on your bait.

Instead, hang the trap from string, bait-side down, three inches off the ground (see figure 24.7). This is the most humane way to use these traps, since the vole dies instantly.

Slugs

Slugs are yet another animal that I despise.*

Some grow to such gigantic proportions – and gigantic gluttony – that they could easily turn a gardener into an inveterate[†] invertebrate hunter.

Slugs are – as my friend Ellen S. would say – "sticky, icky, goo."

To be honest, I think they're misnamed. Why not leave the word "slug" for counterfeit coins and use "slimes" for these execrable creatures?

The duly-dignified *Oxford English Dictionary* (*OED*) has had thousands of volunteers try to find the first use of a word or a new meaning for a word. So, please rush off and send them this new use for the word "slime."[‡]

---

* I express my regrets to slug lovers around the world. Admittedly, I've committed slugicide quadrillions of times. Yet, in one respect, I feel your pain. Like you, I don't advocate wearing slug coats, and am empathetic with those among you who throw paint at people who do.
† *The Merriam-Webster Third International Dictionary* lists several meanings for "inveterate," but the most appropriate for this book is "deep-rooted."
‡ Although "slime" is what the OED may send me when they hear my suggestion.

Slugs can be as small as a pinhead to as large as a ruler.* There are a great variety of genera and species, and almost all of them are voracious eaters of garden plants in general, and bulb leaves in particular (see figure 24.10). Early in my bulb-forcing career I had many a pot of tulips turned into Swiss cheese by these marauders.

But, you have several things in your favor:

1. During winters in Zone 7 or colder areas, when potted bulbs are outside rooting, it's too cold for onslaughts by slugs.
2. If you root bulbs in a location with zero slugs, (for example, in your refrigerator), you eliminate the problem.
3. Slugs have soft bodies. So if you use a cold frame for vernalization, apply a stiff pine needle (not white pine needle) mulch over and around your pots (see figure 28.5). Since using this method, I've rarely had slugs in my frames. I've also heard other growers tell me they've used spiny sweet

gum balls/fruits* and even eggshells to keep slugs away. So, here's the nub: if you use a barrier with spiny, pointed ends, slugs will usually stay away.†‡
4. If you see slugs, you can pick them off and squash them against a wall or underfoot. I've found that either of these methods gives one a tremendous

Figure 24.9 *A banana slug. Although it can grow to a very scary 12" in the Pacific Northwest, it's not as damaging as the European invaders (see figures 24.8 and 24.10) that have caused the most bulb-related headaches. (Copyright © Jim Whitehead 2008; use through Creative Commons Attribution 2.0)*

Figure 24.8 *Take no prisoners when you see slugs anywhere near your potted bulbs. The most damaging slugs (like the one above) in the U.S. are descended from European invaders.*

Figure 24.10 *Who are the likely suspects in this extreme example of leaf molestation? We've got motive, opportunity, and evidence. But what's even worse than the shredded Scilla foliage is the fact that these slugs are about to mate, ensuring yet another generation of bulb gastronomes.*

---

* Thankfully, I'm not referring to England's ruler, Queen Elizabeth, but to the 12" ruler in your desk drawer. On the other hand, an expedition to the Washington State rain forest just might uncover the first queen-sized slug.

---

* I'll assume that once sweet gum fruits are completely dry, they don't release ethylene, otherwise my source wouldn't have advocated this method.
† This doesn't include sharp sand, which, after a slug exudes its slime, is ineffective.
‡ I've also heard that some growers successfully use copper strips as a barrier, but I have yet to test them.

feeling of cathartic revenge.

5. A common way to "capture" slugs is to put flat boards near a plant that has slug damage. In the morning, you'll probably find the slugs under the board. Also, check on the bottom or under the rim of flowerpots, where I've found many a slumbering slug.

Figure 24.11 *Time for a funeral dirge. With bud blast, everything looks fine until the very last stage of flower formation. Then you get anything-but-beautiful, non-flowering flower buds.*

A Physiological Malady: Bud Blast

This is a particularly disheartening disorder.

You vernalize your bulbs, remove and clean your pot, and your bulbs burst into exuberant growth. Green leaves grow vigorously and are at the perfect size and height. Then, with heightening hopes, you see flower buds.

But the buds barely grow and, within days, they take on the pallor of botanical ghosts. And, you won't have a ghost of a chance to see any flowers.

It's so demoralizing and dispiriting.

You started this process back in the fall, and three or four months later you have pots worthy of the compost heap.

The most common bulb with this disorder is the tulip. And, the most common causes are improper vernalization time, vernalization temperature, or inadequate watering when the flower bud is beginning to expand.

The good news is that bud blast (also called bud abortion) rarely occurs. Even when I was a beginning bulb forcer, I probably saw this in less than one pot in fifty. And, it was only in tulips.

To avoid this physiological disorder, make sure that the bulbs that need vernalization get at least the minimum amount of cold treatment (see Appendix 5). Even better, give them 7-10 days more than the minimum.

Also, regardless of the technique you use to provide cold temperatures, consider using a soil thermometer (see figure 6.2 on page 38) to check the potting mix temperature. During vernalization, be sure that the soil temperature is below 50°F (although hyacinths can be chilled at temperatures up to 55°F).

And, finally, the easiest way to avoid bud blast is to be certain that your pots *don't dry out completely* during indoor forcing.

I wanted a photo for this book of bud-blasted tulips. And, it happened on my first try. I simply withheld water immediately before and during flower bud expansion, and I got the most satisfying, unsatisfactory flower buds a bulb-forcing book author could ever want (see figure 24.11).

****

Occasionally, these bulb-forcing enemies can make you feel desperate. But, it's more likely that we – even more than the bulb menaces I've already described – will be the agents of horticultural despair. Some of our adventures are embarrassing, but also hilarious.

To be honest, if there were a show called "Bulb Forcing's Funniest Home Videos," I could supply enough material for a dozen episodes. But I'm not alone. In fact, some acts of desperation I've witnessed left me dumbfounded.

These hysterical exploits are the subject of the next chapter, so for more than a few chuckles, head over to Chapter 25.

25

WHEN DESPERATE BULB FORCERS DO DESPERATE THINGS

If you're forcing bulbs for a special event or flower show, it's important, as I said in Chapter 4, to "begin before the beginning." What that means is, always give yourself extra time to force potted bulbs. For example, if a pot of 'Las Vegas' daffodils normally takes four weeks to force, I'll bring it indoors *five* weeks before I want it in bloom.

Why? **Because, that's what all bulb forcers should do for every single pot that's aimed at a particular day.**

It's like this: experienced bulb forcers (which you all will soon become) can tell that their bulbs are going to reach their peak early, which is perfect. It's so much easier to hold back pots, than to push them ahead. Some of the techniques I've used to put on the bulb-forcing brakes include the following:

"Bloom dammit, bloom!"

- Placing containers in my unheated garage or outdoors, away from direct sunlight (if it's above freezing and below 50°F).
- Spreading snow or crushed ice on early-blooming bulbs like *Crocus*, *Iris*, and *Scilla* (see figure 25.2). (I also place these pots in a *cold*, north-facing cold frame that I cover with blankets or plywood.)
- Employing my food refrigerator – *after* my wife goes to work.

- Making use of the walk-in refrigerator of my local convenience store (see figure 25.1).

Then there are these creative techniques that my students and fellow-exhibitors have admitted using. They include:

- Forcing bulbs, as in *every stage of forcing*, in their *car*. If they have to push a pot ahead, they park on the sunny side of the street. If they have to hold back a pot, the car goes into an unheated garage. (Alas, the gardener who admitted this scheme is saddled with a non-gardening spouse who doesn't want any garden-related mess in their house.)
- Building a walk-in refrigerator in their *home* to chill (vernalize) and/or suspend bulb growth.*
- Doing *all* their "forcing" of minor bulbs in an outdoor, unprotected flowerbed and praying they bloom exactly when they're needed.

---

* By definition, bulb forcers who build either a walk-in refrigerator to chill their bulbs or a greenhouse (like mine) to force them have passed the point of mere horticultural dedication at least twenty years previously. If you don't believe me, just ask their spouses.

Figure 25.2 *Snow (above) or chopped ice (see figure 14.7, page 99) is ideal for holding back diminutive bulbs like* Crocus.

The last of these three is particularly futile, since forcing forced flower buds to open when they don't want to open results in ugly, dull-colored, misshapen flowers. Exhibitors usually do this at 2:30AM before a judging day – a time particularly suited for bad judgment and desperation. Naturally, I have been guilty of this nonsense. I think somewhere inside me, a Blue-Ribbon-Bedecked Body Snatcher took up residence back in 1978, when I won my first flower-show awards. The Snatcher convinced me that ugly flowers were an abomination when they're in *another* exhibitor's pots, but the height of horticultural perfection in mine.

Figure 25.1 *I bribed my convenience store manager with two Philadelphia Flower Show tickets to let me use her walk-in refrigerator. The conditions were ideal: 38°F with fluorescent lights on 24 hours a day. Note the deep green foliage of the daffs and grape hyacinths amid the milk, juice, and canned goods. Don't laugh too hard; I won 23 blue ribbons that year.*

As extreme as these methods seem, they're a zillion times easier than when you're behind schedule. That's when exhibitors do *really* wacky things...as in *scary*, wacky things, such as –

- Placing pots of *Crocus* on their stove – *which I've actually witnessed* (see illustration on page 213).
- Placing a pot of late-blooming daffodils under incandescent (as in *hot*) lights in an eighty-degree room.
- Trying to use their fingers to open unopened flower buds.

Figure 25.3 *An embarrassing photo of my frenzy for blue ribbons. Here, I'm trying to force open a daffodil bud, which is a sure sign that my neurons have stalled and misfired. (Photo by Arlene Wolk)*

CHAPTER TWENTY-FIVE

It only took twenty-two years to oust my demon. Since then, it went away to prey on other exhibitors with blue-silk lust.

****

The first time you visit a competitive flower show, you'll think the judges must be from another planet.

You look at all the entries, pick the one you think is best, and discover that it not only didn't win a blue ribbon, it didn't win anything! And, then you look at the blue-ribbon entry and think it looks like snot on a rag.

What in the world were the judges thinking?

Well, there *is* a tried-and-true method to this endeavor, and it quite resembles what your camera likes most about your non-flower-show-bound, home-grown beauties.

It's the subject of Chapter 26, so we'll head there next.

26
WHAT YOUR CAMERA AND FLOWER-SHOW JUDGES **REALLY** WANT

They cheated me!" That's what all highly-competitive flower-show exhibitors not only think, but believe in every cell of their bodies.

We look at our entry, then look at the entry that "earned" a blue ribbon, and think either favoritism or plain stupidity has come into play. Why? Because each of us sees all the good things about our entry and all the bad things in the winning entry. It's a perfect example of selective perception.

But what you have to understand is this: the judges that "mis"judge our entries don't see anyone's name. There are 4" X 6" entry cards next to each pot (see figure 26.3). On it, the exhibitor prints the class number (e.g., Class 304 "Any *Narcissus*") and the botanical (Latin) and common names of the plant, ***BUT NO HUMAN NAME!*** The exhibitor's/grower's name is printed on the other side (i.e., the unseen side) of the entry cards.

Still, since most exhibitors print the botanical information by hand, paranoid, blue-ribbon-hoarding exhibitors (like myself) think judges can identify the exhibitor's printing on

"Remember...this guy doesn't get any ribbons this year."

sight…and it *rarely if ever* crosses our minds that judges, who come from as far away as Japan, don't spend the week before the Philadelphia Flower Show memorizing each exhibitor's printing style. Some of us realize this after years upon years of exhibiting. But, once we finally comprehend that favoritism isn't involved, exhibitors like myself dementedly think that plain stupidity was the reason we weren't awarded the blue ribbon.

And, of course, this means that certain flower-show competitors have crossed over to The Dark Side and that perhaps it's time to find another aspect of our hobby – say, for example, gardening for contentment instead of insanity.

In spite of the bellyaching and petulance of exhibitors like me, we eventually step back and help others learn what it takes to be successful. Then, sooner or later, something incredible happens: *WE'RE ASKED TO BE A JUDGE!*

And, for better or worse, I was asked. And, wonder of wonders, here's what they told me to look for and how much each parameter was worth in the bulb classes:

1. Blooms – 40%
2. Rarity and/or difficulty to grow – 20%

Figure 26.1 *(left) Philadelphia International Flower Show judges in action, while an aide holds the objects of every exhibitor's desires. Although they're renowned bulb experts, only one exhibitor will agree with their blue-ribbon decision.*

217

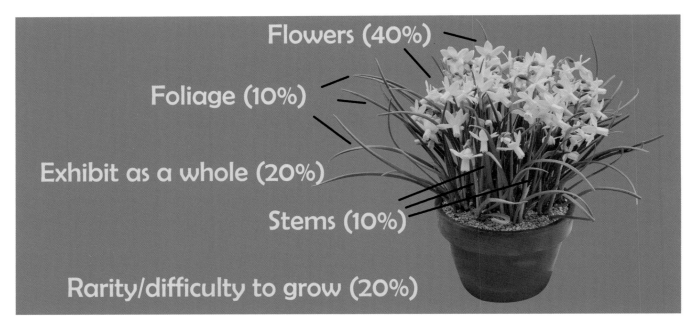

Flowers (40%)

Foliage (10%)

Exhibit as a whole (20%)

Stems (10%)

Rarity/difficulty to grow (20%)

Figure 26.2 *(above) Relative value of each parameter at many flower shows. This is* Narcissus *'Tiny Bubbles' (a new cultivar in 2008), which won two consecutive rosettes for best daffodil entry at the 2009 Philadelphia International Flower Show.*

3. Foliage – 10%
4. Stems – 10%
5. Exhibit as a whole – 20%

Notice that none of these parameters includes any of the following:

1. Favoritism as deciphered by the exhibitor's printing;
2. An IQ lower than fifty;
3. Throwing a dart in the air while blindfolded and awarding the entry closest to the dart a blue ribbon; or
4. Putting a number for each entry in a hat and having a three-year-old child pull out the "winning" numbers.

Are you catching on? Or, better still, are you a flower-show exhibitor or an aim-for-perfection home bulb-forcer that's *ready* to "catch on"? The judges at most flower shows are given a printed sheet telling them how much each factor counts when making their decisions. And, wonder of wonders, these factors have something to do with *horticulture*.

So, to win blue ribbons, bulb-forcing exhibitors have to go all the way back to the bulbs they choose to exhibit. If you choose the easiest bulbs to force, you *ain't gonna get* those twenty points (see figure 26.2, "Rarity") toward winning a blue ribbon.

That's why, back in the fall, experienced exhibitors purchase bulbs that are at least somewhat rare or difficult to grow.

All of the other parameters: blossoms, foliage, stems, and exhibit as a whole, are worth the other 80%.

Not surprisingly, pots of forced bulbs are excellent subjects for photography if growers pay special attention to parameters 1, 3, 4, and 5. (Rarity [2] probably matters far less to you than to flower show judges.) And, of these four, number 5 (exhibit as a whole) is the most important. Notice that for flower show judges this ranks above foliage and stems in value. And, for your home displays and photographs, the same holds true. If you have superb *Crocus* blossoms sitting on 12" stems emerging from a 3"-tall bulb pot you'll think it looks splendid – at first. But, then you'll take a photo and realize how ridiculous the "exhibit as a whole" looks.

Whether you force bulbs for exhibit in your home or in flower shows, parameters 1, 3, 4, and 5 (the ones worth 80% to exhibitors and 100% to non-flower-show bulb-forcing fanatics) depend on only four things: planting, chilling, growing, and grooming.

By now, you probably have enough knowledge to become an expert at planting, chilling, and growing. But, whether you're a flower-show exhibitor or strictly an in-your-home bulb forcer, there's *grooming*, which I define as "all the seemingly-unending plant buffing you do during the twenty-four hours before home display or flower-show exhibition."

If you'd like to learn about some of my grooming tidbits – and laugh at a few more of my ignominious tales – please have a squint at Appendix 2 on pages 228-241.

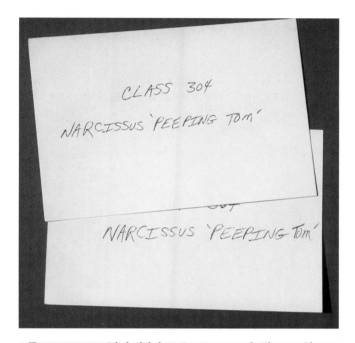

Figure 26.3 *Philadelphia International Flower Show entry cards for a single pot of* Narcissus *'Peeping Tom'. Note the absence of the exhibitor's name.*

****

Eventually, the sun sets on your indoor forcing season. Still, although your flowers are dry as dust, you still have viable bulbs and green leaves.

The inevitable question is, "Can I save anything for my outdoor garden?" For many bulb forcers, the answer is "yes" for every single bulb they've forced.

I tend to be more selective and only save bulbs that can be easily transplanted and successfully grown in my garden. Exactly how you can do that is the subject of Chapter 27, so let's head there next.

27

To Have and to Hold
or
To Have and to Trash

I have been deplorably wasteful when it comes to saving bulbs after I've forced them for the Philadelphia International Flower Show. Perhaps you'll forgive my spendthrift behavior when I tell you that by the time each show ended, I was hanging on by a cotton thread.

Please take into consideration that on the nights before the three judging days, I rarely got more than ninety minutes of sleep.

Eventually, this had dire effects. One does odd things at terrible times, like attempting to introduce yourself to someone at the Flower Show and having an embarrassing delay until you remember your name, or **much, much worse**, having an embarrassing delay until you remember your spouse's name.

To be honest, after the Philadelphia Flower Show, I shouldn't have been allowed to go up or down stairs,

Figure 27.2 *Keep the pot in the sun, then water and fertilize until the foliage turns yellow. Then snip off the leaves.*

spread butter on bread, or use a can opener. Stairs, butter knives, and can openers were lethal weapons for a sleep-deprived flower-show exhibitor like me.*

But, then there are all of you. And, the vast majority of you are not obsessively consumed with flower-show exhibiting. So, for everyone who could never be induced, at any price, to go through the idiocy I used to go through at flower shows, I've written a few directions for saving bulbs after they've been forced.

Before I list my bulb-saving instructions, I should tell you that there's an incredible diversity of bulbs that are perfectly content to spend their entire lives in pots. These

Figure 27.1 *When your flowers are ready for the compost pile, snip them off, then put the pot back in strong light.*

---

* Although I rarely exhibit in flower shows anymore, I've become a bulb-forcing-book author who's grown many bulbs purely for photographic purposes. This has prompted my wife to label me a botanical pimp – although I've never rented bulbs to anyone.

include *Hippeastrum* (amaryllis), *Tecophilaea, Anemone coronaria*, rare, diminutive *Narcissus* (e.g., *Narcissus bulbocodium* hybrids and species), *Ranunculus, Cyclamen*, and many more. (For more on this topic, see especially Rod Leeds's excellent book, *Bulbs in Containers*, the full citation of which is in the Bibliography.)

Figure 27.3 *If you procrastinate until the foliage looks like straw, it's fine.*

Potted-for-life bulbs aside, there are all the large, high-impact, over-the-top bulbs more suited to your garden. And, it's these bulbs that are the subject of this chapter.

But first, I must give you a lesson in poison, as in lethal doses of poison. You see, all daffodils are poisonous to all mammals. That single fact may not seem very important, but it's vitally (or perhaps deathly) important. Since bulb-eating rodents and other backyard mammalian pests will eat virtually every other bulb in your garden, daffodils are the bulb of choice to save after forcing.

And, that's why my directions focus on *Narcissus*. You can use the following method for any hardy spring-blooming bulbs you've forced. But your best chance for success is with daffs.

Here are directions:

1. Cut off flowers when they begin to look like shredded rags after spring cleaning.
2. Return the pot to the bright sunlit or lamp-lit area where forcing took place.
3. When watering your pot, use one-quarter strength, water-soluble fertilizer.
4. Continue fertilizing until the foliage turns yellow. And, the foliage *should* eventually turn yellow because it naturally turns yellow as summer approaches (see figure 27.2). Cut off the foliage down to the top of your bulbs. If you forget to cut off the foliage when it yellows, the leaves will eventually become as dry as straw, which is fine (see figure 27.3). Cut off the dead leaves and proceed to step five.
5. Let the pot become bone dry. This is one of the few times when it's ideal to follow your natural instincts and ignore your pampered plants. So, turn your back on them, spurn them, and forget them until winter ends and your garden soil is no longer frozen.
6. Carefully remove the bulbs. It's okay to cut into roots, but it's not okay to cut into bulbs.

Figure 27.4 *After the foliage is cut off, let the soil dry. Then you'll be able to carefully remove your bulbs.*

221

7. After you remove your bulbs, carefully separate mature offsets from mother bulbs. (They're mature if it takes very little effort to remove them.)

8. Now, it's time to put every bulb in it's final resting place, which, fortunately (or hopefully) has a different connotation for bulbs than it does for you. If you *absolutely have to* unpot forced bulbs before your outdoor soil thaws, dry your bulbs in a place with good airflow (i.e., not in the closet next to moldering shoes). *The latest you can plant these bulbs is early-to-mid fall.* Please don't be one of the unfortunate gardeners – and unfortunately there have been many, many, *very real*, unfortunate gardeners – who approach me at the end of one of my lectures to ask, "I haven't planted my dried bulbs in two years. Can I plant them now?"

Figure 27.5 *Once bulbs are out of the pot, you can divide mother bulbs from mature offsets. It's best to plant them in your garden at this stage, since these waifs are easily forgotten.*

9. Pick a site that gets at least four hours of springtime sunlight per day. If you have early-blooming bulbs, you could certainly plant them near deciduous trees that allow sun penetration in March and April.

10. Don't forget that almost all spring-blooming bulbs in temperate zone gardens *love* air around their roots. Please keep this in mind before breaking your back to plant them in hard clay.

11. If your soil needs rotted organic matter (i.e., composted anything, not fresh manure), by all means add it. Then mix it into the top ten inches of soil. If you have clayey or sandy soil, organic matter is a perfect amendment.

12. Plant your bulbs three times deeper than the diameter of the bulb. For example, if the bulb is 2" in diameter, plant it 6" deep. If your soil is sandy, you can plant a bit deeper; if it's clayey, a bit shallower.

13. Place your bulbs 6" apart for tall daffodils and 3-4" apart for miniatures.

14. In September, put bulb fertilizer over your planting area and "scratch" it into the soil.

15. Since forcing weakens bulbs, some of the bulbs will bloom the following spring and some will not. If you've followed my advice in steps 9-13, you'll probably have blooms the second spring after planting.

After their first spring outdoors, your bulbs have to recharge themselves for the following year, so allow their foliage to flop after blooming. Leaves need *maximum exposure to sunlight* to fatten the underlying bulbs enough to begin flower formation. This means that you should neither tie, nor rubber band, nor cut any green foliage. Let leaves flop and wither until they aren't green anymore, *then* you can cut them off. If you think you'll become the neighborhood pariah, and that you'll be shunned and put in stocks because you have flopping foliage in your front yard, then go ahead and cut off the green foliage. And, finally, *dig up and throw away your bulbs, since they'll only get weaker, smaller, and flowerless!*

Which is fine.

But please realize that you're now committed to treating your bulbs the same way you treat annuals…meaning, planting new bulbs every fall.

****

And now, I have a confession: although you didn't expect this how-to-garden book to be melodramatic, it is.

You see, I've placed the most exciting, pulse-pounding, eye-popping chapter at the end. At first glance, it seems out of place, since it harkens back to vernalization in a cold frame, but it's more than that. It's a technique I invented to produce potted-bulb displays that are as close to perfection as possible.

Even if you decide not to use it, it's still important to understand how and why it works so well. So, head over to Chapter 28 for the best bulb-forcing secret of all.

28

THE BEST SECRET OF ALL

For the seriously-smitten bulb forcer, I will now divulge the method I've used to win a carload of blue ribbons at the Philadelphia Flower Show. In this case, I learned not just from my mistakes, but a horticultural disaster. The two events that made the disaster possible were the winter of 1995-96 and my procrastination.

I got my bulb shipment in early October and ignored it until mid-November. During an average New Jersey winter, this wouldn't have been a problem. But that winter was one of the coldest on record.

By the time I planted my first pot, the temperatures were averaging ten degrees below normal, and it never got any better.

I potted bulbs, placed them in my cold frames, and they went into hibernation...a long hibernation.

As a result, only about one-fifth of my bulbs rooted. Not surprisingly, I had one of my least successful Flower Shows that year, and I was the only one to blame.

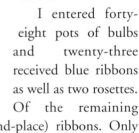

Figure 28.1 *The secret to perfect forced bulbs is controllable bottom heat, combined with bright light during the earliest stages of growth. After the heating cable is laid, 10" of soil is added.*

To be certain this would never happen again, I hatched a plan.

I wired my two cold frames with heating cables. These are preset at 70°F, which is much too warm to root spring-blooming bulbs. To overcome this problem, I bought refrigeration thermostats, placed them in my cold frames, and plugged the cables into them.

This system worked like a dream. The cables were placed about 10" underground and the pots plunged into the overlying soil, with the bottom of the pots two inches above the cable. I set the thermostats on 48°F and headed indoors. After about eight weeks, I turned the thermostats down to 41°F for up to four weeks, then at 35°F until I brought the pots into my greenhouse.* What I found was that my bulbs were at least 50% forced in these cold frames. In additions, the height of the plants was virtually identical to bulbs planted in the ground. So, basically I was simply finishing off the forcing process in my greenhouse.

When I took these pots to the Philadelphia Flower Show, I knew I was going to do well before I entered a single pot into the competition. As I brought them in, another excellent bulb forcer looked at my pots and waved me away, as if to say, "I can't win blue ribbons against those entries, so take them back home."

She was right; I succeeded as never before.

I entered forty-eight pots of bulbs and twenty-three received blue ribbons as well as two rosettes. Of the remaining pots, many received red (second-place) ribbons. Only one other exhibitor received more blue ribbons that year, but she had about thirty-times more greenhouse space than I did.

---

* This is the regime suggested in *Holland Bulb Forcer's Guide*, but I've had excellent results by keeping my pots at 48°F during the entire rooting process. I've read and been told that bulb stems are stronger if you use the varied temperature method. Yet, I've never had trouble with weak stems when I've used 48°F alone.

Figure 28.2 *(left) This refrigeration thermostat is the key that unlocks the door to perfection. Keep the temperature at 48°F. If you have to suspend growth, lower it to 35°F.*

Two years later, I used the same technique to force pots for the 13-division daffodil collection described on pages 126-134. My wife, Arlene, and I had twenty-one pots in the exhibit, and Lee Raden supplied two perfect pots of bulbocodium daffodils. It was an absolute knockout and so popular with flower show visitors that I could barely get near our display.

Aside from Brent Heath's positive reaction to the exhibit, I was particularly taken with a compliment from noted horticulturist Charles Cresson, who said that some of the daffodil cultivars looked better in the display than

Figure 28.3 *Potted bulbs are plunged into the soil and sit about 2" above the thermostatically-controlled wire. At this point, 8" of pine needle mulch is added to insulate the newly-planted pots.*

Figure 28.4 *These cold-frame windows are translucent. On cold, sunny days, dark-green foliage grows and flower stems begin to emerge. This produces more compact, natural-looking forced bulbs.*

Figure 28.5 *Pine needle mulch is ideal. I use more on the coldest days and less when leaves are growing. The pots in this photo are ready to come indoors. At this stage, they're about half forced.*

in his garden.

So, now that I've shared my biggest secret of all, please consider using it. But I have just one warning: once you start producing perfect pots of forced bulbs, you'll be so addicted to this gardening endeavor that not even a lengthy stay at the Betty Ford Center would cure you. But let's face it, there are a lot worse habits to have than beautifying your home and soothing your spirit with flowers.

As was written on Han Solo's diploma at the Star Wars School of Horticulture: "Sit coactus bulbus tecum."*

---

* May the forced bulb be with you.

APPENDIX 1
A VERY SHORT ATYPICAL HISTORY OF BULBS

If you're one of the four people who made it past the title of this appendix, I want to thank you for getting this far. To be honest, I didn't think anyone would venture into the Horticultural Realm of Forty Winks. (So, if most people find reading about botanical history similar to scratching their fingernails on a blackboard, imagine how difficult it is to write.)

Here's the problem with natural history as I see it: when a history of anything (whether alive or not) is committed to paper, the historian should make it as thorough as possible – without giving the reader a good reason to commit hara-kiri.

So, what I don't understand is why natural histories of botanical entities usually start when humans began plundering the earth. Don't the other tens of millions of years before then matter? And, isn't it remotely possible that a history that starts at the beginning is better than a history that starts beyond the middle or (depending upon whether worldwide fall outs produce nuclear fallout) the very end?*

Occasionally one finds a true natural history of a plant or group of plants that starts at their very beginning. But, they rarely appear in books for the home gardener.

Instead, what is usually foisted

Figure A1.1 *An extremely metaphorical depiction of bulbous DNA with amaryllis and Ranunculus "nucleic acids" and Anemone "sugars."*

upon you is an *unnatural* history.

As such, I'd like to give you an honest-to-Art Wolk history from the *real* beginning of bulbs. Unfortunately, I don't have an H.G. Wells or a Rocky and Bullwinkle/Mr. Peabody time machine, so I can't interview the first tulip or daffodil that came into being, so bear with me.

Plants, as biologists tell us, started their life on Earth in the sea. Like sea animals, they eventually evolved into species that could live on land. But these early terrestrial plants were sad, non-sensuous, sexless photosynthesizers. Once on the land, evolution to new species was slow, specifically because of their Barbie-doll-lack-of-evident sexual apparatuses.

When the first flowers appeared, they were so small and simple that they would have been unnoticeable to today's average gardener.

Then, 125 million years ago, an evolutionary blast occurred: a beneficial mutation* produced a plant that had recognizable flowers and seeds that contained nutrients and a protective coating. These new

---

* Don't scratch your head – or anything else – for an answer; these questions are rhetorical.

---

* The overwhelming majority of mutations are detrimental, but some are beneficial – allowing the resulting organisms to compete more successfully for food, light, and root space. This is how evolution "moves," through occasional beneficial mutations. If there were no beneficial mutations, you wouldn't be reading this…and I couldn't have written it.

plants, collectively known as angiosperms,* evolved quickly into a seemingly endless diversity of new flowering species.

How diverse are angiosperms? If you take a very thorough stroll around the Earth you'll find only 700-800 species of gymnosperms.†
But more than 42,000 angiosperm species exist today.‡

It's not hard to understand the success of angiosperms. Imagine a baby trying to develop without nourishing amniotic fluid. That's what gymnosperm seeds face. But, angiosperm moms (pistils) and dads (stamens) are caring enough during procreation to protect and feed each seed they bring forth. (Of course, seductive angiosperm flower petals and scent also help the reproductive process in plants…and have been known to be quite helpful in humans, especially when delivered by florists to enamored sweethearts.)

Once angiosperms (which includes bulbs) got started, flowers of all shapes, sizes, colors, textures, and scents appeared practically overnight (evolutionarily speaking). There was also an incredible variety of leaves, stems, branches, trunks, and, most important to this discussion, roots.

Now, think of all the turmoil that has passed in your lifetime (which isn't even as long as a finger snap in evolutionary terms). You've seen or read about floods, hurricanes, fires,

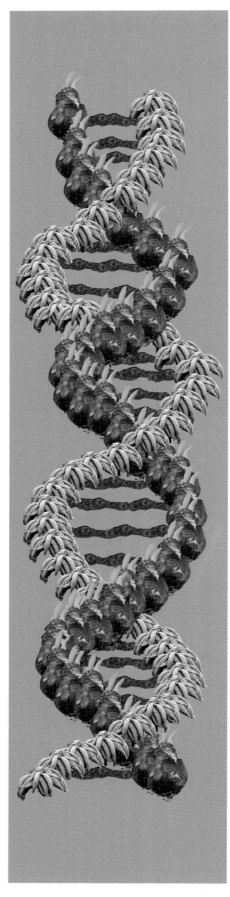

tornadoes, clouds of locusts, and, worst of all, the botanical pillage wrought by our fellow humans.*

Having cited just a few of the plagues that have occurred since the doctor smacked your bottom, imagine all of this carnage taking place over tens of millions of years. Now, you can throw in multitudinous ice ages, huge asteroids dropping from space, fires as far as the eye could see, unrelenting droughts, and volcanic explosions that threw so much dust into the air that few of the sun's photons made it to the Earth's surface.

If you think about these disasters and the plants that might survive them, the first ones that come to mind are, of course, bulbs.† These are the plants that store enough nutrients and tissue from the original plant in underground packages that allow them to reappear when these biblical plagues take a sabbatical.

And, it all started with plants that mutated into species with not just flowers, but also underground bulbs.‡ Admittedly, there were fits

---

* Angiosperm means "seed borne in a vessel."

† Gymnosperms are plants that produce "naked seeds," with virtually no food or protection. The most recognizable gymnosperms are conifers.

‡ *Plants*, Editor - Janet Marinelli, DK Publishing, 2005, New York, p. 27.

---

* You can do your own research. Just ask anyone from the southeastern United States about the kudzu (which we unwisely planted to control soil erosion) that has taken over eight million acres by literally smothering every other plant in its path.

† I'm barely exaggerating. Those who live in U.S.A.'s Tornado Alley (meaning, Oklahoma, Kansas, Nebraska, eastern Colorado, western Iowa, and parts of Texas) know that if a tornado is coming, the best place to seek shelter is underground – where bulbs have wisely decided to reside.

‡ Plants (not just bulbs) that have a significant amount of their anatomy underground – aside from roots – are called geophytes.

and starts along the evolutionary highway before plants mutated into the recognizable bulbs sold in catalogs and nurseries. Unlike humans, bulbs did not evolve from one "missing-link" bulb (i.e., the first bulb to appear on Earth). There's such a variety of bulb shapes and sizes, that a common single bulbous ancestor is unlikely.*

But the important thing is that through a series of mutations, some plants eventually made it all the way to "bulbdom," thus enabling you to run your hands through these golden beauties every fall.

I should also mention that although we've been instrumental in developing the hybrids and cultivars you see in catalogs, we had nothing to do with the evolutionary development of bulbs. The reason? We didn't show up until 150,000 years ago.

So, if I'd have started this history with human-bulb interactions, you would've only had the last two paragraphs to read. I imagine that some of you are thinking, "If only he had done that, if only he had done that, I wouldn't be nodding off to sle...." But, I'm sure at least one of you, actually, I *hope* at least one of you thinks this history was more interesting because I *ended* with humans.

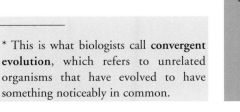

* This is what biologists call **convergent evolution**, which refers to unrelated organisms that have evolved to have something noticeably in common.

Appendix 2
Grooming

When you grow bulbs in potting mix, they form roots, foliage, stems, and flowers. But the probability of growing any bulb in potting soil without getting potting soil and other debris on the plant is ZERO. So, whether you're preparing your pot of blooming bulbs to amaze your family and friends, for photography, or for a flower show, grooming is a necessity.

I've forced more than two thousand pots of bulbs in my lifetime. Some have been barely acceptable, and some have been knockouts, but all of them needed grooming. There's no difference between grooming yourself and grooming potted bulbs: you want yourself and your blooming bulbs to look as close to perfection as possible. (But, admittedly, in my case, the primary goal is avoiding humiliation.)

My end goal has always been clean, uniform leaves and flowers. To that end, I've had woeful trials and pitiable errors. But each one helped me learn and develop a few grooming tricks and techniques I'd like to share.

Of course, your main objective is to have incredibly gorgeous flowers, so let's start with them.

Flowers

I'll begin with the most difficult procedure in the history of grooming blossoming bulbs and perhaps all containerized flower gardening. Here I refer to: ***REMOVING PERFECTLY HEALTHY, GORGEOUS FLOWERS!!!***

Now that you've recovered from the stupor caused by the above five words, let me explain. Your goal is to produce a pot with perfect foliage and perfect flowers at a uniform height. Typically, novice bulb forcers are horrified when I suggest cutting off flowers that are too tall or too short. I can read his or her mind, because, like everyone else, I was a beginner once. What the new bulb forcer is thinking is, "Are you out of your $%#&*!@ mind? I grew that flower, it's gorgeous, and gorgeous flowers shouldn't be cut. I don't care if it's on the soil or

six-feet tall, it's staying!"

And, that's fine – as long as you don't care a whit about a beautiful home display, photographs, or blue ribbons.

The key query is this: if you have a pot of daffodils with thirty perfect blossoms at exactly the same height and a thirty-first perfect blossom hovering six inches above the others, what will attract your visitor's or a judge's eyes the most? You already know the answer: the

Figure A2.1 *Every bulb forcer's hardest task: removing ungainly flowers. Here, my daughter Beth is removing a too-tall tulip that was 6" above the other blossoms.*

odd, out-of-place, "what-the-hell-was-I-thinking?" blossom.

Once I bit the botanical bullet and started to remove ungainly flowers, a wonderful thing happened: I won a lot more blue ribbons.

"But Art," you might say, "I don't care about flower shows or blue ribbons. Why should I care about uniformity?"

Because you'll undoubtedly take photos of your forced bulbs. And, once you view the photos, your eyes will react exactly like a judge's eyes. Your focus will be on the single, loose-cannon-on-the-deck blossom. To stick a dagger into the heart of "Save-the-Flower Syndrome," put the photo on your refrigerator, and stare at it every time you walk in the kitchen. Within a week, you probably won't be skittish about eliminating an offensive blossom…or the photo.

If you still find it impossible to eliminate and throw away the ungainly flower, there's a compromise: cut the flower stem and stick it in a bud vase. Trust me – it will look better in the vase than in the pot. And, while you're at it, present it to the love of your life. He or she will be absolutely delighted, give you a very romantic/enticing look, and never suspect that you had to choose between him or her and the garbage can.

When you finally remove a flower from a potted bulb, you'll usually want to get rid of that bulb's foliage, unless it produced a second or third flower that's worth keeping. If there's nothing worth saving, I usually remove the flower, foliage, and the top of the bulb, guaranteeing that no one will suspect my surgery. I do this most often for tulips, only occasionally for daffodils (because there's almost always something worth saving), very rarely for minor bulbs (for the same reason), and *never* for pots containing only one bulb (e.g., amaryllis).

The extent of my surgery depends on where the offending flower or foliage resides. If I eliminate a flower from a bulb near the edge of a pot, I usually remove the foliage as well. I only keep it if I can discretely move a blossom over to hide the non-productive bulb.

Sometimes I've removed a tulip from the middle of a pot and wanted to keep the underlying foliage. I usually cut the stem just above one of the leaves and angle the cut away from the front of the pot, to hide my surgery from a visitor's or judge's eyes.

Let's Twist Again

I'd like to share another act of desperate grooming that's worked well.

I've already told you many times that you should turn pots one-quarter turn per day during forcing to produce pots with uniform foliage and flowers. This is especially

Figure A2.2 *(right) Twisting daffodils to change direction.*

Doing "The Twist" to change daffodil direction

Figure A2.2a

Twist blossom 180° and hold for 30 seconds

Figure A2.2b

Final position has changed 90°

Figure A2.2c

Figure A2.3 *Decision time at the Grooming Table. I'm looking for spent or out-of-place blossoms, imperfect leaves, and which side of the pot should face the judges. (Photo by Arlene Wolk)*

important with daffodils, since the coronas (noses) should point symmetrically outward for a pot to look its best.

But I've also discovered that if you carefully hold the flower stem directly in back of the flower, you can twist the stem to make the flower point in the direction you want (see figures A2.2a-A2.2c). This doesn't always work, but for me it's worked about 75% of the time. Have a look at the photo of *Narcissus* 'Peeping Tom' (see figure A2.9). If ever there was a pot of daffodils with symmetrical noses, it's that one. Yet, I'm certain I twisted a few of the blossoms while grooming them the night before. And, it worked well enough to win the blue silk next to the pot.

If you decide to try flower twisting, do it only for daffodils and do it carefully. Their flower stems seem the most flexible and least sensitive to this malleable maltreatment.

Also, this works if you turn the flower to the left or right (what astronauts call "yaw"). If, on the other hand, you think a daffodil is pointed too far up or down, *do not under any circumstances* try to change the angle of the blossom (what astronauts call "pitch"). Daffodils can take a lot of punishment and still look divine. However, if you try to move a blossom up or down, you'll usually end up with a lovely bloom in your hand that's irretrievably separated from the stem.

When this happens, you'll feel the need to call a crisis intervention hotline, but don't bother. When you tell the counselor why you called, you'll be the only person he or she hangs up on that day.

Foliage

At flower shows, foliage is an important factor in determining who wins a blue ribbon, and for good reason (see figure 26.2). If your pot contains yellowish leaves, it won't matter how many gorgeous flowers it has. In fact, it probably wouldn't be allowed into the competition at the Philadelphia Flower Show. After all, would you pay more than twenty dollars for a flower show ticket, only to look at sickly foliage? And, for non-exhibitors: would you really want to put such a pot in the middle of your dining room table as a horticultural accent?

To the contrary, if you only have a few faded leaves, you can remove them. But do this in a way that hides your surgery from visitors, flower-show judges, and your camera.

This endeavor is easiest for daffodils, because each bulb usually produces at least three or more leaves. Simply remove the bad leaves, and you'll still have enough left over to produce a Class AAA pot. When you cut daffodil leaves, go all the way down to the leaf sheath (see figure A2.4).* If you're removing foliage from an interior bulb and can't remove the entire leaf, then make sure you cut as far down as possible, and slant your cut toward the middle of the pot (i.e. away from judges' or your visitors' eyes). I've done this hundreds of times and the judges never noticed: a blue-ribbon-worthy pot still won a blue ribbon.

Tulips demand a different procedure, since a few

Figure A2.4 *You can make daffodil leaf removal almost invisible if you cut leaves down to the top of the leaf sheath.*

---

* The daffodil leaf sheath is directly above the bulb and surrounds the emerging leaves.

Figure A2.5 *Tulip leaf before (above) and after (below) repair using – very carefully using! – a single edge razor blade. Sharp scissors can also be used, but they sometimes crush, instead of cut, leaves.*

brown leaf tips are the most common problem. My personal solution demands precision and care.* I use a single-edge razor blade and try to remove as little of the leaf as possible. I shape the cut so that the leaf retains its original shape. If this isn't possible – usually because of holes in the leaf – I remove the entire leaf, all the way to the stem. If done properly, the missing leaf won't be noticed.

I suggest using small, sharp scissors the first time you try this…and, perhaps, every time you try this, because single edge razor blades are for the **extremely adept, wide-awake grower** – something I learned the hard way.

Back in 1993, while grooming a pot of tulips for the Philadelphia Flower Show, I saw one tulip leaf that had

---

* …as well as good eyesight, dexterous digits, non-frayed nerves, and rapid-fire reflexes.

"Where the hell are these red spots coming from?"

holes, a brown tip, and was terribly misshapen.

It had to go.

I used a single-edged razor blade and neatly excised it. I did such a perfect job that a judge would have had to fall into the pot to notice it. I tried to quickly clean blossoms and the remaining leaves.

But, there was a problem: a red spot was on a tulip leaf. I removed it with a clean rag, then focused on other leaves. However, red spots kept reappearing over and over again. Of course, you know what the red spots were, but I didn't. I had gotten only two hours of sleep the night before, and even my overactive adrenal glands didn't keep my brain from sputtering.

After I'd cleaned a dozen red spots, my "attic light" finally switched on and I looked at my fingers. Sure enough, I'd made an efficient, well-groomed cut into one of my digits, which was dripping like a slow faucet. After a full-scale panic attack, an angelic fellow-exhibitor supplied a band-aid, and I continued grooming my pots.

I wish I could say the story ends there, but it doesn't.

As the judges were considering all the potted tulips in the class I entered, I sidled up next to them to hear their discussion. Looking over my competition, I thought my tulips would get a second- or third-place ribbon.

Oh, my stars, was I ever wrong. Really wrong.

> The clerk...teetered...tottered... twisted, and did every gyration humanly possible. Then she fell into the tulip bed and *sat on my entry!*

During their discussion, a judge's clerk slipped on the line of granite bricks used to separate the plants from the public. Her fall seemed endless. She teetered, she tottered, she leaned, she twisted, and did any other gyration humanly possible.

After what seemed like twenty minutes, she fell into the tulip bed and *sat on my entry!*

My brain flat-lined. My body flat-lined. Everything seemed to be flat-lining except my tulips. They were anything but linear, because each one had developed new mid-stem joints.

Then, in a ghastly scene, the judges did their best to straighten my unstraightenable tulips. And, the more they tried, the more horrified I became.

After another ten seconds, I fled in excruciating horror.

But that wasn't the worst part. Ten minutes later, when judging was completed, I returned to see pristine entries surrounding my zigzagging tulips that now displayed my name. My pot screamed to thousands of people, "Who in the world is Art Wolk and why was he, much less his entry, allowed through the front door?"

Now I fumed. I didn't have the authority to move my pot, which not-so-amazingly didn't win a ribbon of any color. But I found a sympathetic clerk who handed it to me.

Once I had the pot in my arms, I thought of the Winston Churchill quote, "I have nothing to offer but blood, toil, tears, and sweat." It summed up the six-month process of producing these tulips – from planting to growing to blood to almost winning a ribbon.

Fortunately, I had other entries to soothe my smitten spirit. Within twenty minutes after the tulip debacle, I saw a blue ribbon next to my pot of primroses and felt sheer bliss. At least grooming had paid off for that plant. And, I thought, it helped that my primrose was on a shelf at chest level, meaning clerks, judges, or even I could fall next to my pot without causing another disaster.

"So...whad'ya want to do with this ribbon now?"

Star Staking

As I've mentioned before, bulb forcing is like good fiction: you suspend disbelief and are pulled into the story. But the plot of the bulb-forcing story is always the same: spring has arrived at least a month early.

To suspend disbelief, you don't stare at the pot or soil in which the bulbs are growing. You stare at the foliage and flowers, take in the aroma, and touch the blossoms.

It's spring.

The object is to have your indoor bulbs look as genuine as they would in a springtime flowerbed. But that only happens with perfectly forced bulbs. Many times

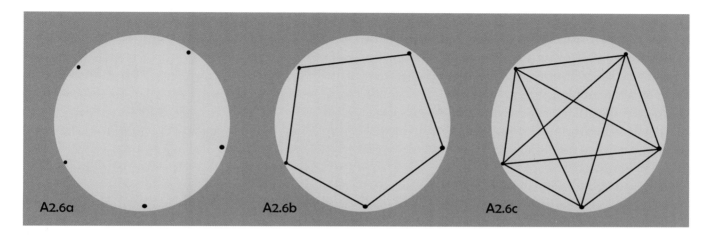

Figure A2.6a *Star staking – Step 1. Place five floral stakes equidistant around the inside edge of the pot.* **Figure A2.6b** *Step 2. Tie green floral string to one stake, then loop it around the other floral stakes until you're back where you started. Then tie a knot.* **Figure A2.6c** *Step 3. Tie the string to a different stake (i.e., not the first one used in step 2). Then loop the string around every second stake until an internal star is completed. Finally, tie the string to the last stake.*

the foliage and flower stems simply get too tall and, without support, they flop. What was vertical becomes horizontal. And, your suspended disbelief is suspended.

It's winter again.

But, there *is* a way you can help your horticultural novel by using support that's green, specifically, green floral string and green floral stakes (see figures A2.14 and A2.17). They're as close to the average green color of plants as possible. So, if you have loads of flowers, the last thing you, your visitors, or flower show judges will look

at is the minimal support you've provided.

For some pots, your best non-visible means of support is star staking.

"Star staking?" you're probably thinking. "Are you about to kidnap winners of Idol/Talent TV shows and burn them while they're bound to huge floral stakes? Or, are you perhaps referring to the best way to kill famous 'star' vampires, by thrusting floral stakes through their hearts?"

Figure A2.7 *An overhead look at the uneven spread of daffodil blossoms before star staking.*

Figure A2.8 *The same pot after star staking. Notice the symmetrical spread of blossoms.*

No, this particular "how-to" book is still about how to grow and show blooming bulbs in pots. Perhaps someday I'll write a book about the combustibility of singing stars or whether Hollywood vampires can be killed with green floral stakes, but not this time.

You see, star staking has everything to do with making potted flowering bulbs look perfectly situated for well-deserved envy from your visitors or a well-deserved blue ribbon from judges.

First, you have a decision to make. You can either star stake immediately after chilling or wait until after your flowers blossom. I tend to do the latter for several reasons, most of all because I'm not sure the bulbs will blossom uniformly.

> **For some pots, your best non-visible means of support is star staking.**

But this is all subjective: some flower show competitors stake in advance and produce marvelous pots of forced bulbs.

I suppose if Shakespeare would have had to make the same decision, he might have said, "It's a matter of confidence, dear Brutus, not in ourselves, but in our bulbs."* And, that sums up the situation.

When you're ready to star stake, do the following:

Use five floral stakes. You want the least bit of mechanics/support visible, so use the shortest sticks possible. (In some cases, I've broken off a piece from the bottom of sticks to make them shorter.) Put your sticks in potting soil, against the pot's rim and equidistant from each other (see figure A2.6). (This comes to 72° apart, since 360° divided by five is 72°, but don't run for your protractor or your family will run straight for a straight jacket.)

To star stake, tie the florist string to one stake, then loop it once around the stake closest to the first, and continue looping the string around the rest of the stakes.

Figure A2.9 *Star-staked* Narcissus *'Peeping Tom'. Notice the unnoticeable internal star and the evenly spread blossoms.*

When you're back at the first stick, tie the string next to the first knot (see figure A2.6b).

If you look down from above, you'll see a pentagon – at least I hope you'll see a pentagon. If you see some other shape, you –

1. didn't make the sticks equidistant around the inside circumference of the pot; or
2. it's time to walk carefully to your bed, slide under the covers, and take a nap, because you're hallucinating.

---

* Shamefully adapted from act I, scene ii of Shakespeare's "Julius Caesar." The actual line, by Cassius, is *The fault, dear Brutus, is not in our stars, but in ourselves…*

If necessary, remove the string, and adjust the position of the stake or stakes that are out of place. Then re-string the stakes to make a pentagon.

There's still more to star staking. After all, this *is* called *star* staking, and at this point there's nothing resembling a star anywhere in sight. (If there is, see number 2, above).

Now, start at a different stake and tie a knot around it. (I never use the same stick for every knot, since it can be unsightly.) Once you've made the knot, loop the string around *every second stake*. Move in a clockwise or counter-clockwise direction until you're back at the original stake. Make another knot close to the first one and you're finished.

When you look from above, you should have a five-point star staring at you. If you don't, something is amiss, so make sure you looped the string around every *second* stake.

If you produce a wacky-looking star, your stakes weren't equidistant from each other. Usually, just one stake is out of place and will be obvious. You can either live with the imperfection or simply re-adjust the stake and produce a new star.

This star should sit about two-thirds of the way from the top of the soil to the top of foliage. If you star stake on the first day you bring your pot inside after vernalization, you'll have to use your experience or knowledge of how high the foliage will rise.

To Stake or Not to Stake? That's Your Conundrum

And, now, I'll give what would seem to be conflicting information, specifically, if your foliage and flowers look fine without support, then don't use one-billionth of an inch of string or floral stake. You shouldn't need any support for minor bulbs (meaning *Crocus, Iris reticulata, Muscari, Scilla,* and other early-blooming, diminutive bulbs). This also holds for the shorter miniature daffodils, diminutive tulips, and other "lowly" bulbs.

Back in Chapter 15 (see page 111-112), I mentioned that I often use a type of "subterranean subterfuge" to reduce the need for any extraneous support. The technique involves slanting foliage and flowers toward the

center of the pot, and pushing potting mix between bulbs and the inner wall of the pot (see figures A2.11a, b, and c).

If done properly, no one will know that you've done anything to help support your foliage and flowers, and you pots will look fantastic.* Note the difference between figure A2.11a and A2.11c. The only thing used to bring

Figure A2.10 *Free-standing* Narcissus *'Arctic Gold'. When standard (non-miniature) daffodils are forced in cool (60°-64°F), sunny conditions, they might not need any artificial support. See also figures 16.25 and 16.29.*

the foliage and flowers to the center was extra potting mix. This same technique was used for the pots shown in figures A2.10, 16.25, and 16.29.

Obviously, this doesn't work for every display (otherwise I wouldn't have any star-staked pots). But it works for pots without flopping foliage and flowers. So, before you run off and gather string and stakes, try this technique first.

And, if you *do* have to use extraneous support, don't

---

* And, as mentioned previously for flower-show exhibitors, when judges see two virtually identical pots, the one with the least support always gets the better award.

A2.11a

A2.11b

Figure A2.11a, b, and c *Sometimes, the only additional support needed is extra growing mix pushed between bulbs and the inner wall of the pot. I started with the pot shown in figure A2.11a, used my "subterranean subterfuge" technique (figure A2.11b), and produced the pot shown in A2.11c.*

A2.11c

automatically assume you'll have to use star staking. Sometimes, all that's needed is support around the outside of the pot. In fact, I've never star staked hyacinths or tulips. Of all the bulbs I've forced for the Philadelphia Flower Show (and that's more than I'd care to admit to my wife), standard (non-miniature) daffodils were the *only* ones I've star staked.

So there's even more reason to wait until flowers bloom to do staking, including:

1. If you give potted daffodils perfect forcing conditions, (e.g., temperatures of 60°-64°F on a sunny windowsill), they sometimes need *no staking*. Such pots have a marvelous added attraction: they transport you, in your mind's eye, to glorious springtime.

2. If you accidentally put a stick into the middle of a bulb it doesn't matter, the flower will survive.

3. You can place the stakes a bit inside the foliage, where you, your visitors, or flower show judges won't see them.

4. I know where the flowers are, and I can do a bit of "flower arranging" to make the blossom spread uniformly. This is where later star staking is truly the method of choice. I've had many pots that looked like a disaster after forcing, but looked nearly perfect after grooming and star staking.

Pot Switching/Cleaning

Every part of a potted bulb display matters: the leaves, the flowers, the mulch, and the pot itself.

I almost always use clean, untarnished clay pots for display. If I grow hyacinths in an 8" azalea pot, I transfer it to a pristine 8" azalea pot within two days of judging, photography, or when I want to impress family or friends. You don't have to use a new pot to do this (see figure A2.12). I wash each pot in hot, soapy water. Then I soak the pot in a 10% bleach (Clorox) solution for ten minutes, then rinse thoroughly.

Water the soil in the original pot, then carefully nudge the soil ball out and transfer it to the pristine pot. After transfer, put vegetable oil on a clean rag and coat the second pot with a thin layer of oil. This can make a ten-year-old pot look like a ten-hour-old pot.

About Face

After decades of looking at photos of yourself, you know you have a good side and a not-so-good side. Potted plants are the same, but unlike you (unless you're an actor in a movie about demonic possession*), they can be turned 360°. So if you want to have the best side of the pot facing your visitors, your camera, or flower show judges, take the time to turn the pot slowly and pick out the best front. If your pot is going to be placed in the middle of a dining room table at a family event, it's not worth the trouble: your plant will be surrounded on all sides by your guests. But in any other case, find the best

Figure A2.12 (left) What a good cleaning can accomplish. (top) A truly filthy, salt-stained pot. (middle) After cleaning in hot, soapy water, I placed the pot in a container with 10% Clorox for ten minutes, then thoroughly rinsed it. (bottom) The same pot after I applied a thin layer of vegetable oil.

* If you have the stomach for it, see the 1973 film *The Exorcist*. In it, Linda Blair shows off her circumnavigating head. As for me, I'm glad if I can turn my head 45° in each direction without hearing my vertebra crack.

Figure A2.13 *Determine which side looks best and have it face forward. At the Philly Flower Show, we mark the back of the pot with a chalk line. Then "stagers" put the pot in its final location before judging, with the unmarked side toward the front. (Photo by Arlene Wolk)*

front and have it staring the world in the face.

At the Philadelphia Flower Show, all horticultural exhibitors pick out the best side, then put a chalk line on the exact opposite side of the pot (see figure A2.13). Then volunteers, known as "stagers," carefully position the pot on the floor (on top of mulch or sand) so that the chalk line faces away from where judges will stand. Occasionally, there's an overzealous bulb judge who marches into the bed of pots to look at each one from all sides, but it's quite rare. I've exhibited at the Philly Show for more than thirty years and only saw it happen once. Sometimes, a few committed bulb judges bend at the knee to become more intimate with the entries, but the majority remain standing.

And, there's another important factor to consider. I've seen so many exhibitors groom pots on waist-high tables, pick a best side of their pot, then, when the plant is put on the floor for judging, they don't understand why they get a lower award than they thought their plant

deserved.*

At this point in my horticultural career, I've earned more than enough blue ribbons. So, now I try to help new exhibitors by working as a passer at the Philadelphia Flower Show. Before I "pass" a pot into the competition, I insist that the exhibitor put the pot in the vertical location where it will be judged (i.e., on the floor or on a shelf). Invariably, novices look at their pot on the floor and gasp. Then they grab their pot and either perform further grooming, or simply pick a better "front."

It's the same for home display: once you think you're finished grooming, put the plant in the position where your visitor or camera will see it. If it needs more grooming to look its best in that location, by all means, do it. But, in most cases, it just needs a simple turn.

Brooms for Blooms

Here are virtually all the supplies I use for grooming:

1. **Green florist string** – This string is close enough to the color of leaves to be almost invisible when you use it to support blooming bulbs (see figure A2.14). You can purchase it in short or long spools from florist or craft supply companies.
2. **Surgeon's hemostats** – This is the same surgical instrument used by surgeons to compress blood vessels (see A2.15). They're quite handy when you need to nab something unsightly that's settled in a place unreachable by a human hand. *"Surgeon's hemostats!"* you might be saying aloud. "You've completely lost your mind." Well, of course you're right. I began losing my mind many decades ago. But surgeon's hemostats are actually quite useful during grooming. You neither have to empty your bank account to purchase them, nor fake an injury to steal them from your local hospital. They're readily acquired from hardware and sewing stores as well as Internet sources.
3. **Rags and wash cloths**– You know you'll need them, and you know where to get them. But make sure you use clean rags. I've yet to discover any use for dirty rags during grooming.

---

* Regrettably, this happens by default to virtually all flower show exhibitors (including myself) who don't win a blue ribbon – regardless of the reason.

Figure A2.14 *Green floral string is best for lending support to tall, forced bulbs. Notice in figure A2.9 how it all but disappears amid the foliage.*

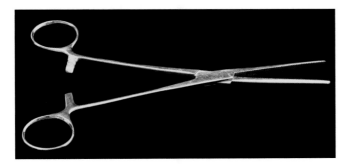

Figure A2.15 *Surgeon's hemostats are readily available and are the best tool for nabbing dirt or pebbles you can't dislodge with your hand or a water sprayer.*

4. **A large roll of paper towels** – I never think I'll need them, but always use at least a dozen sheets whether it's entry day at a flower show or photography day at home.

5. **Turface** (figure A2.16) – In my opinion, Turface (see www.turface.com) is the best material to use to top dress* your pots when they're ready for display. It's a gritty mix whose color blends well with clay pots, which is ideal. Why top dress? Because you want

Figure A2.16 *Turface*

your visitors, family members, or judges to keep their eyes on the flowers, not perlite, vermiculite, or a pot with a screaming, look-at-my-purple-pebble top dressing.

6. **Vegetable oil** – No, you won't use it to cook bulbs for breakfast. But, you *can* use the corner of a clean rag dipped in vegetable oil for a non-gastronomic purpose: specifically, to apply a coating of oil to the outer surface of a clay pot, which will hide salt stains (see figure A2.12).

7. **Spray bottle** – This has a multitude of purposes, the most important of which is to gently spray away dirt on leaves or flowers. I use it to do more than 75% of my grooming. The best bottles are equipped with a nozzle that's adjustable. This allows you to use a strong, bullet-like stream of water (rarely); an extremely diffuse, cloud-like spray; and everything in between. You'll get a feel for what spray setting you should use on leaves and blossoms. The idea is to clean without marring any part of the plant. I only use the "bullet-stream" if I see a piece of mulch clinging to a strong stem.

8. **Florist's (or floral) stakes/sticks** – These are an absolute necessity (see figure 2A.17). Sometimes your foliage and/or bloom stems will need inconspicuous support. These sticks are the same color as florist's string (see #1, above) and come in a variety of sizes. I use 12" and 18" stakes. You can get them from garden centers as well as craft or floral supply companies.

Figure A2.17 *Green floral stakes (12" and 18").*

---

* Here, "top dress" refers to what you put on top of potting mix.

9. **Scissors** – You'll need a small 3"-4" pair and another about 6"-7" long. Spend a few extra bucks and get quality scissors. I use Fiskars (pronounced *fis*-cars).

10. **Clean pots** – No matter how carefully you handle your groomed pots, you'll eventually break one just before company visits or when you're about to enter your potted bulbs into a flower show. (See "Pot Switching/Cleaning," on page 237.) So, you'll want extra pots that are the exact same size as the pots you use to force bulbs.

11. **Sponges** – Have at least two available, including a small bit of sponge glued onto the end of a stick to clean hard-to-reach places.

12. **A small, clean artist's paintbrush** – Use this to brush pollen off petals. You probably think it won't be noticed, but it will. If this doesn't work, try using a wet sponge on a stick (see #11), a wet paper towel, or a gentle stream from a water sprayer.

Figure A2.18 *Sometimes a moistened thumb is all that's needed to recurve misbehaving petals.*

13. **Saliva and a thumb** – I can see you rolling your eyes. Of course, I know you don't need to be reminded to bring these. They usually can be counted upon to go wherever you go. I've listed them so I can tell you to occasionally use a wet thumb to curve or straighten disobedient, mature petals of tulips, daffodils, and crocuses (see figure A2.18).

14. **FOR EXTREMELY CAREFUL ADULTS: Single-edged razor blades** – Use them to remove ugly blemishes on leaf tips – especially on tulip leaves – while still retaining leaf shape. (See tulip grooming on page 231.)

Especially for flower-show competitors:

1. **Two cardboard boxes with the tops cut away** – You'll want to put your supplies in boxes about 24"-36" on each side. Seal the bottoms with 3"-wide clear tape or duct tape. (The latter is what I consider the ultimate U.S.-male cure for any problem on Earth or outer space.*) The height of the boxes should be about 8". Spread out your supplies in the boxes so they're easy to see. On flower show morning, you'll be so spiked with adrenaline that you'll find it impossible to find anything not directly in front of your non-botanical irises.

2. **Pens, pencils, and permanent markers** – If you're exhibiting at a flower show there will be times when you'll have to write down information about yourself and the plant you've grown (usually, the Latin name) on entry cards. As I learned from personal experience,

Figure A2.19 *Play by the rules! After planning, planting, and growing, the last thing you want to do is break a rule or enter your plants in the wrong competitive classes. Even if I've looked at the exhibitor's guide fifty times, I still bring it to flower shows. (Photo by Arlene Wolk)*

---

* I'm not exaggerating. When our unlucky Apollo 13 astronauts had to deal with a malfunctioning space capsule, duct tape was the essential item used to make the repairs needed for them to return safely to Earth.

there's nothing more pathetic than an exhibitor running around the exhibit floor begging everyone for a pen or marker.

3. **Exhibitors guide (figure A2.19) and completed entry cards (figure 26.3)** – Even if you plan ahead and have all your cards/forms completed, something eventually goes awry. In 1995, when I first won the Philadelphia Flower Show Grand Sweepstakes Award, I left behind one hundred entry cards needed for fifty pots. Since time is limited because judging begins the same morning, I had two-and-a-half hours of sheer torture.

4. **Sleep** (meaning shut-eye the night before judging) – If you work all night preparing your entries, it's guaranteed that you'll do something idiotic, like destroying plants, cutting a finger, getting into a car accident, and on, and on, it goes. The possibilities are endless. Have a peek at Chapters 4 and 8 in *Garden Lunacy: A Growing Concern* for some of my worst screw-ups, when I put blue ribbons ahead of sleep.

APPENDIX 3
BULB SOURCES

B&D Lilies
www.bdlilies.com
contact: www.bdlilies.com/contact-us.html
phone: 360-765-4341
fax: 360-765-4074
address: B&D Lilies/Snow Creek Daylily Gardens
   PO Box 2007
   Port Townsend, WA 98368

Brent and Becky's Bulbs
www.brentandbeckysbulbs.com

email: info@brentandbeckysbulbs.com
toll-free: 877-661-2852
phone: 804-693-3966
fax: 804-693-9436
address: 7900 Daffodil Lane
   Gloucester, VA 23061

Chiltern Seeds (especially for *Ranunculus* 'Bloomingdale' seeds)
www.chilternseeds.co.uk
email: info@chilternseeds.co.uk
phone: +44 (0)1229 581137
fax: +44 (0)1229 584549
address: Chiltern Seeds
   Bortree Stile/Ulverston/Cumbria/LA12 7PB
   England

ColorBlends
www.colorblends.com
email: info@colorblends.com
phone (toll-free): 888-847-8637
local: 203-338-0776
fax: 203-338-0744
address: 747 Barnum Avenue
   Bridgeport, CT 06608

Dutch Gardens
www.dutchgardens.com
email: use www.dutchgardens.com/contact_us.asp
phone: 800-944-2250
fax: 800-451-6481
address: 4 Currency Drive/ P.O. Box 2999
   Bloomington, IL 61702-2999

McClure & Zimmerman

www.mzbulb.com

contact: www.mzbulb.com/ContactUs.asp

phone: 800-546-4053

address: 335 S. High St.
　　　Randolph, WI 53956

Old House Gardens (heirloom bulbs)

www.oldhousegardens.com

email: charlie@oldhousegardens.com

phone: 734-995-1486

fax: 734-995-1687

address: 536 Third St.

Ann Arbor, MI 48103-4957

Scheepers

www.johnscheepers.com

customerservice@johnscheepers.com

phone: 860-567-0838

fax: 860-567-5323

address: 23 Tulip Drive
　　　PO Box 638
　　　Bantam, CT 06750

Telos Rare Bulbs

www.telosrarebulbs.com

e-mail address: info@telosrarebulbs.com

phone: not listed

address: P.O. Box 1067
　　　Ferndale, CA 95536

Van Engelen

www.vanengelen.com

email: customerservice@vanengelen.com

phone: 860-567-8734

fax: 860-567-5323

address: 23 Tulip Drive
　　　PO Box 638
　　　Bantam, CT 06750

This list is not an endorsement of any company. I have obtained either quality bulbs or seeds from these establishments. But, as you probably know, businesses are bought and sold with little or no notice to the public. And, the devoted, knowledgeable personnel are not necessary retained by the new owners. Regardless of the company you choose, you should be vigilant for batches containing a high percentage of diseased bulbs. If that happens to you, insist upon replacements or credit. Any company that won't do that should not expect your business in the future.

Appendix 4
Bulb Organizations

Note: All explanatory information came directly from the websites of these organizations.

• American Daffodil Society (www.daffodilusa.org)

"The American Daffodil Society (ADS) was founded in 1954 to promote wider interest in daffodils; to encourage scientific research and education on daffodil culture, breeding, diseases, pests, exhibiting, and testing; to encourage, coordinate, and sponsor shows and exhibitions of daffodils; to record and disseminate horticultural information about daffodils and issue publications for such purpose; and to register daffodil varieties and standardize their names in cooperation with international authorities. To that end, the ADS publishes quarterly The Daffodil Journal, an 80-page magazine that covers all aspects of daffodil culture, breeding, and exhibition. The ADS cooperates with The Royal Horticultural Society (RHS) by accepting and forwarding registrations for new daffodil cultivars from American registrants. The ADS publishes several books that list and describe registered daffodil cultivars, including Daffodils to Show and Grow, which is updated approximately every four years."

• Pacific Bulb Society (www.pacificbulbsociety.org)

"The Pacific Bulb Society (PBS) was organized for the benefit of people who garden with bulbs. This includes both cold hardy and tender bulbs, and all the bulbs in between. By 'garden with' we also mean to include plants, shrubs, and even trees that we grow as companions to our bulbs. Membership in PBS is open to bulb lovers around the world. We welcome all to come forward to join us in the celebration of bulbs and in mastering the challenge of gardening with bulbs. Our emphasis will be on successfully growing bulbs in our yards and gardens and in sharing our successes, and our failures too, with our fellow members. Through that sharing, we will all learn to be better bulb gardeners. Member benefits are quarterly newsletters, a biannual membership list, online bulb and seed exchanges through the PBS list, and social events. We are pleased to sponsor an Internet discussion list, the PBS list, a list available to anyone around the world interested in learning more about bulbs (or more broadly geophytes, plants with underground storage organs). The Pacific Bulb Society List (PBS list) maintains the Pacific Bulb Society Wiki, an ever expanding educational resource. On the wiki there are pictures of bulbs, photographed by members of the list, showing plants grown by members and ones observed in habitat. In addition there is a lot of helpful information."

• International Bulb Society (www.bulbsociety.org)

"Established in 1933, the International Bulb Society is the only international, non-profit, educational and scientific organization devoted to the dissemination of information on the growing, conservation and botany of all geophytic plants (commonly referred to as "bulbs") The International Bulb Society is singular in that it serves all interest and knowledge levels from novices to professional growers and scientists, and covers bulbs—both species and hybrids—of all climates and habitat types. The International Bulb Society aims to [do the following]: disseminate information about bulbs via a variety of media; educate and encourage the general public, gardeners, horticulturists, conservationists, scientists and educational and botanical institutions to take an interest in bulbs and become actively involved in their culture, preservation, advancement and enjoyment; encourage and sponsor research on bulbs; promote the conservation of bulbs (both in habitat and in cultivation) and preservation of bulb habitats, and facilitate propagation and distribution of bulbs and their seeds to further bulb conservation and enjoyment; propagate, maintain and distribute rare bulbs for reintroduction into their native habitats; and facilitate communication between individuals interested in bulbs."

• North American Rock Garden Society (www.nargs.org)

"NARGS is for gardening enthusiasts interested in alpine, saxatile, and low-growing perennials. It encourages the study and cultivation of wildflowers that grow well among rocks, whether such plants originate above treeline or at lower elevations. Through its publications, meetings, and garden visits, NARGS provides extensive opportunities for both beginners and experts to expand their knowledge of plant cultivation and propagation, and of construction, maintenance, and design of special interest gardens. Woodland gardens, bog gardens, raised beds, planted walls, container gardens, and alpine berms are all addressed. Toward this end NARGS offers its members the Rock Garden Quarterly, an annual seedlist, local chapter meetings, and a growing web presence. Yes, membership has its advantages. NARGS, organized in 1934, currently has approximately 2,650 members in the US, Canada, and thirty other nations."

• The Daffodil Society (www.the daffodilsociety.com)

"Established in Birmingham as The Midland Daffodil Society in 1898, The Daffodil Society is the specialist society of Great Britain for all who are interested in the genus *Narcissus*, by way of exhibiting, breeding or just lovers of the true heralds of spring. The Society objectives are to advance the education of the general public into awareness of the whole of the genus *Narcissus* by its publications, shows and displays, supporting other organisations and groups in the conservation of *Narcissus* growing in their natural environment, [and by] encouraging educational plantings in public gardens and the raising and introduction of new cultivars of *Narcissus*."

• Wakefield & North of England Tulip Society (www.tulipsociety.co.uk/)

"Today only one society remains specialising in tulips, the Wakefield and North of England Tulip Society dating from 1836. The Annual Show is held in the Wakefield Area each year, and open to the public . As well as the classes for English Florists' Tulips, there is a section for Dutch Tulips. In recent years the Society has revived its Dutch Tulip show which is held at the Harrogate spring Show. The Society holds its Annual General Meeting in October with entertaining discussions and presentations following the items of business. The Society publishes a Newsletter for Members, arranges a Garden Visit Day, and sends out schedules of competition classes in advance of the shows."

• North American Lily Society (www.lilies.org)

"The North American Lily Society (NALS) was organized in 1947 to promote interest in the genus Lilium. The society has active members from almost every state and province in North America, as well as from many countries around the world. NALS members enjoy: the Quarterly Bulletins and the Annual NALS hardcover Yearbooks, covering lilium culture, lilium species, how to grow from seed, propagation, and hybridization, and much more; a Seed Exchange, offering seed from lilium species and hybrids from around the world; an annual meeting and lily show, where you can see fabulous lilies, attend educational seminars, and meet like-minded lily enthusiasts; a Lending Library for member use, funds Lilium research through its Research Trust; and an annual Lily Popularity Poll to identify lily species and varieties that perform well for members."

There are, of course, many other bulb organizations around the world. If you know of an organization that you'd like to see listed in future editions of this book, please contact me through my website, www.artwolk.com.

APPENDIX 5
CHILLING AND FORCING TIMES

Bulb genus, species, or cultivar	Minimum weeks of chilling at approximately 48°F	Minimum weeks to force at approximately 60°-65°F (except where otherwise indicated)
Allium 'Gladiator'	10	8-10
Allium 'Globemaster'	10	8-10
Anemone blanda cultivars	9-10	3-4
Anemone coronaria cultivars (pre-cooled)	not needed	7-9
Arisaema kishidae	9	5-6
Arisaema serratum	9	4-5
Arisaema sikokianum	9	5
Arisaema yamatense	9	5-6
Crocus chrysanthus cultivars	9	1-2
Crocus tomasinianus species and cultivars	9	1-2
Crocus vernus cultivars	9	1-2
Cyclamen persicum	not needed	4
Freesia cultivars	not needed	10-12
Hippeastrum (amaryllis) cultivars	not needed	6 at 72°-75 °F
Hyacinthus (hyacinth) cultivars	10-11	4
Ipheion uniflorum cultivars	9	4-5
Iris reticulata cultivars	8-10	1-2
Lilium - Asiatics	10	8-9 at 64°-70°F
Lilium – Longiflorum-Asiatic hybrids	10	9-11at 64°-70°F
Muscari armeniacum	10	3
Muscari aucheri cultivars	10	3
Narcissus – early-season cultivars *(see index)*	10-11	3-4
Narcissus – mid-season cultivars *(see index)*	11-12	4-5
Narcissus – late-season cultivars *(see index)*	13-14	6-8
Narcissus – paper whites *(see Chapter 6 and pages 123-4)*	usually not needed	3-4
Ranunculus cultivars	not needed	5-7
Scilla mischtschenkoana	9	1-2
Scilla siberica 'Spring Beauty'	9-10	2-3
Tecophilaea cyanocrocus	6	3
Tecophilaea cyanocrocus var. Leichtlinii	6	3
Tulipa – early-season cultivars *(see index)*	10	3-4
Tulipa – mid-season cultivars *(see index)*	11-12	4-5
Tulipa – late-season cultivars *(see index)*	13-14	6-7
Zantedeschia aethiopica	not needed	9-10
Zantedeschia – summer hybrids	not needed	8-9 at 72°-75°F

BIBLIOGRAPHY

Ball RedBook. Ball Publishing. 16th edition. 1998. 802p. ed. by Vic Ball. maps. photogs. index. ISBN 1-883052-15-7.

Barnes, Don. Daffodils for Home, Garden and Show. David & Charles. 1987. 176p. photogs. index. ISBN 0-7153-8853-3.

Bryan, John. Bulbs. Timber Press. 2nd edition. 2002. 524p. maps. photogs. bibliog. index. ISBN 0-88192-529-2.

Bulbs for Indoors: Year-round Windowsill Splendor. Brooklyn Botanic Garden. 111p. Ed. by Robert M. Hayes & Janet Marinelli. photogs. index. ISBN 0-945352-94-8.

Crockett, James Underwood. Bulbs. Time-Life. 1971. 160p. photogs. index. ASIN B000VZ1L2U.

Daffodil Handbook: A Special Issue of the American Horticultural Magazine. 1966. 227p. ed. by George S. Lee, Jr. photogs. index.

Daughtrey, Margery. & A. R. Chase. Ball Field Guide to Diseases of Greenhouse Ornamentals. Ball Publishing. 1992. 218p. photogs. index. ISBN 0-9626796-3-1.

De Hertogh, August. Holland Bulb Forcer's Guide. International Flower Bulb Centre & The Dutch Bulb Exporters Association. 5th ed. 1996. 5 sections. photogs. bibliog. ISBN 90-9008455-X.

Field, Xenia. Growing Bulbs in the House. St. Martin's Press. 1966. 136p. photogs. index. ASIN B0000CN3WV.

Heath, Brent & Becky Heath. Daffodils for American Gardens. Elliott & Clark. 1995. 144p. maps. photogs. index. ISBN 1-880216-33-7.

Heath, Brent & Becky Heath. Tulips for North American Gardens. Bright Sky. 2001. 144p. maps. photogs. index. ISBN 0-9704729-6-X.

Hill, Lewis & Nancy Hill. Bulbs: Four Seasons of Beautiful Blooms. 1994. Storey Press. 218p. photogs. bibliog. index. ISBN 0-88266-877-3.

James Jr., Theodore. Flowering Bulbs Indoors and Out. Macmillan. 1991. 150p. photogs. index. ISBN 0-02-558915-6.

Jefferson-Brown Michael. Narcissus. Timber Press. 1991. 224p. photogs. bibliog. index. ISBN 0-88192-195-5.

Killingback, Stanley. Tulips. Chartwell Books. 1990. 128p. photogs. bibliog. index. ISBN 1-55521-704-4.

Leeds, Rod. Bulbs in Containers. Timber Press. 2005. 224p. photogs. bibliog. index. ISBN 0-88192-735-X.

Lodewijk, Tom. The Book of Tulips. Vendome Press. 1979. 128p. photos. ISBN 0-670-18063-7.

Manual of Bulbs. Derived from The New Royal Horticultural Society Dictionary of Gardening. Timber Press. 1995. 383p. ed. by Anthony Huxley. illus. bibliog. ISBN 0-88192-339-7.

The New Royal Horticultural Society Dictionary of Gardening. Macmillan. 1999. 4 vols. ed. by Anthony Huxley. illus. bibliog. index. ISBN 0-333-770188.

Pavord, Anna. **Bulb.** Mitchell Beazley. 2009. 544. maps. photogs. bibliog. index. ISBN 978-1-84533-532-8.

Pavord, Anna. **The Tulip.** Bloomsbury Publishing. 1999. 440p. illus. bibliog. index. ISBN 1-58234-013-7.

Phillips, Roger & Martyn Rix. **The Random House Book of Bulbs**. 1989. 255p. photogs. bibliog. index. ISBN 0-679-72756-6.

Plant. DK. 2005. 512p. ed. by Janet Marinelli. maps. photogs. index. ISBN 0-7566-0589-X.

Powell, Charles, C & Richard K. Lindquist. **Ball Pest & Disease Manual**. 2nd edition. Ball Publishing. 1997 426p. photogs. index. ISBN 1-883052-13-0.

Rockwell, F. F. & Esther C. Grayson. **The Complete Book of Bulbs**. J. B. Lippincott. 2nd edition. Revised by Marjorie J. Dietz. 1977. 368p. photogs. index. ISBN 0-397-01194-6.

Taylor's Guide to Bulbs. Houghton Mifflin. 4th edition. 1986. 464p. photogs. index. ISBN 0-395-40449-5.

Van Patten, George F. **Gardening Indoors with Soil & Hydroponics**. Van Patten Publishing. 2008. 374p. photogs. index. ISBN 978-1-878823-32-8.

Wells, James S. **Modern Miniature Daffodils**. Timber Press. 1989. 170p. photogs. bibliog. index. ISBN 0-88192-118-1

Wolk, Art. **Garden Lunacy: A Growing Concern**. AAB Book Publishing. 2005. 246p. illus. ISBN 0-972-9730-3-6.

Index

Bold page numbers=photos or illustrations
Italic page numbers=footnotes